THE THIRTY BOB KID

By Dave Dutton

To Mabel and Lynn for their love, support and forbearance

The years teach much which the days never know – Ralph Waldo Emerson

PREFACE

The Thirty Bob Kid…being a true account of me, David Dutton, ~~scholar and gentleman.~~

Herein will be found…

My life changing conversion in a Victorian police cell
My dad who never appeared
My granddad who suddenly disappeared
My sister who suddenly appeared
My Mam who slowly disappeared
My grandmother who wanted to drown me but later changed her mind
My fox hunt in Coronation Street and much more
My abduction by aliens in Emmerdale
My unwitting part in advancing Gay Rights
My big bang incident with God
My time with the famous "sincere hypocrite"
My shattering revelation at primary school
My life as a 50's kid
My surreal scene with Rik Mayall in a smelly bog in Plymouth.
My meeting with a most fascinating man
My rooftop rescue by the fire brigade and other escapades
My dealings with famous people
And other stuff to titillate, amuse, edify and, hopefully, entertain.

No it's not – it's all true!

CONTENTS

Once a winker, always a winker…

NICKED

Clang!

The burly bobby pushed me roughly into the semi darkness of the clammy, cold Victorian police cell and slammed shut its rusty old door.

There was a chilling, echoing clang. He glared at me through the bars, his lips tightly drawn.

"This is where Joe Knowles the old tramp sleeps and this is where you're going to end up permanently my lad if you don't change your ways"

Wide-eyed and shaking, I hesitantly peered round at the sparse, soulless interior which contained nothing but a cracked sink with a dripping tap; a smelly old stained lavatory and a hard wooden bed attached to the wall.

No one spoke for a few minutes. It felt like forever.

I turned to him moist-eyed.

"Let me out please"

He stood unmoved.

"Please. Tell him Mam"

My Mam looked on, biting her lip.

"I'll be good from now on, I promise"

He narrowed his eyes.

"You better had or I'll make sure you end up back here before you know it. Now get out and don't let me see you here again"

Gratefully, I grabbed my Mam's hand and made my escape.

I was nine years old. It was a turning point.

The old Dickensian police station where I got my short, sharp shock.

WHY BOTHER?

You've got the wrong person

My great granddad was a tough Royal Marine; my granddad was a hardworking Lancashire miner; my dad was a soldier and bomb expert and my Mam worked in a munitions factory department they called The Suicide Squad.
Me? I juggle with words and sometimes ponce about pretending to be someone else for a living.
No comparison really.
Okay, I've done other stuff along the way: not proper jobs though like hewing coal with a pick; rounding Cape Horn in a hurricane; taking potshots with a rifle at Germans or working with lethally volatile explosives but I suppose I'm grateful I didn't have to do that anyway.
I don't think I would have been tough enough or brave enough.
To a certain extent, I have mainly avoided the dreaded 9 to 5; lived off my wits and done many jobs that suited the circumstances at the time.
There's a word for it. QUOMODOCUNQUIZING. You've probably used that a lot.
No? It means to make money in any way that you can. It's a proper word in the Oxford English Dictionary but there's only one recorded use of it. Correction – there's two now.
Anyway, turning my hand to this and that has always kept a roof over my head and provided full bellies for me and my family and for that I am truly thankful.
Knocking out an autobiography feels a bit pompous for a working class lad but I must have some sort of urge to validate my life.
It feels a bit like I'm a spawning salmon on its last swim upstream - tempting fate that nothing much else is going to happen in my life after I finish writing it.
If that is the case, thank you and goodnight but I hope for a lot more daftness and fun before I pop my clogs.
A good reason to get it all down in writing is if my mind starts to slide down the helter skelter of time into the bottomless pit of not knowing, it might remind me of who I was when I read it back.
Don't laugh: there's a lot of it about.

Towards the end of her life, my mother had dementia and forgot who I was. Often when I visited her in the care home, she asked if I had seen "*our David* ". Meaning me of course.

That's a real hard kick in the guts and one of the saddest things life can throw at you: to be forgotten by your own mother with whom you had shared so many decades and so many loving, happy memories.

It was with a heavy heart I had to see this happen and my sympathy goes out to anyone suffering the same circumstances.

It's torture for all concerned but I also feel we were all given a sense of humour to lighten the dark situations we encounter and it's a tool that has served me well so far that it's almost a reflex action now.

As Lord Byron brilliantly put it:

And if I laugh at any mortal thing,
'Tis that I may not weep

Spot on, George lad.

Comedy has played a big part in my life: I love to laugh but above all, I love to make others laugh. I suppose it's a way of attracting attention or making yourself popular.

The reason might be in my childhood. You be the judge of that as the story unfolds.

Writing an autobiography might look like an ego trip but it's also a real chance to analyse the events and situations that made you the person you are today.

It's also a nice way to leave some memories for the family which might otherwise be lost. Besides, no other bugger can do it for me.

I also hope that some people might find it helps them and encourages them to have a go at stuff they might be dithering over. We shall see.

It's also partly my mother Mabel's story. After all, she brought me into existence and almost single-handedly cared for me. Her sometimes tragic life deserves to be acknowledged and remembered.

As for me, I'm a pretty outgoing, confident and sociable sort of bloke nowadays but it wasn't always that way.

God, no.

Finding out at an early age you're somehow different to other kids makes you lose confidence and sets you apart.

That's what happened to me when I discovered my illegitimacy. It changed me.

Yet, conversely, I've done things in my life that the former shy, self conscious person with a lack of self esteem would never have thought possible.

If I had been able to tell the young me what the future held, he would've said *"Haha. No. Not me. You've got the wrong person. I could never do owt like that"*.

There was also a period in my life where I could also have taken the wrong path and become a bad 'un.

At an early age, I smoked; drank (nicked Gran's brandy); stole from shops (mainly toffees and marbles); vandalised (a greenhouse); absconded from school and generally got into scrapes which sometimes involved the police, fire brigade and ambulance service. It's not that I was totally wicked and unredeemable but I can easily see now how some kids can screw their lives up completely if they go unchecked.

I can hardly reconcile who I am today with who I was then.

Nowadays, I even think inconsiderate sods who drop litter should be hanged, drawn and quartered. Or at least have their ears nailed to a pillory.

I wish I could reach back in time to that nervous, unsure young lad and reassure him. He would be amazed.

Me on the radio and in top television shows?
Me work with famous people?
Me write poems and songs?
Me start a successful business?
Me sing and act on a stage?
Me write for a newspaper?
Me pen jokes and sketches for top comedians?
Me write lots of books?

Yes *you*, young man!

I never thought I'd do all that but my fragile confidence built up gradually over the years by doing things I was afraid of and feeling the fear.

Slowly and imperceptibly we can all change for the better and, looking back, it's a fascinating process. It's like when you have a child and you don't notice the changes in his or her appearance as much as someone who only sees the child every few weeks.

Yes: *The years teach much which the days never know.*

I want to show people CAN change and achieve what initially seems impossible.

The inner sneering demons of childhood could have easily have caused me to make a mess of my life.

If this book encourages anyone, young or old, to think twice about the way their life is headed or gives them the confidence to have a go at something just a little out of their comfort zone, then I'll be happy.

I'm quite lucky inasmuch as my life seems to have turned out okay up to now but it didn't really get off to a good start.

Oh dear me, no.

Don't worry though: this is not a book full of undiluted misery and painful introspection.

It's been a relative doddle compared with some but it's all relative and what happens to you at the time can seem soul-destroying even though, in retrospect, it might be the crucial link that forges you into the person you become and all the better for it.

The child is father of the man, as Wordsworth put it.

I reckon being banged up in that Victorian police cell by that long dead bobby did me a massive favour.

Enough of this psychobabble.

Pour yourself a glass of something to your taste put your feet up (unless you're reading this on the bus) and let's delve into my early bits...

No, it's not a crap ventriloquist act.
It's me and my Mam, Mabel.

THE THIRTY BOB KID

"You have a lovely grandson Mrs Dutton"
"Drown him in the dolly tub!"

Not many people know their worth.
I do.
£1.50p.
Give over, you say. As much as that?!
Thanks.
It's true though. That's what I cost.
Quite a bargain eh?
I can see you're a bit puzzled.
So how do I come to that evaluation?
It's what the midwife charged to deliver me.
Thirty bob in old money. Thirty shiny shillings.
Don't believe me?
I have proof.
I still have the receipt! (My Mam threw nowt away).
But surely it's free you remonstrate.
Ah no, you see this was in the year before the dear old National
Health Service was created and you had to pay for everything
concerned with health or medical matters.
Thirty bob then is probably equivalent to between £40 and £50 in
today's money, so I have definitely increased in value but not by
much when you take inflation into account.
Still, it was a fair amount of money then.
You could get a pint of beer for the equivalent of 7p and 2lb of
spuds were a mere 1p.
By those standards, you could say I cost 300 lbs of King Edwards
or two and a half gallons of best bitter.
(You can probably guess spuds and beer are two of my favourite
things).

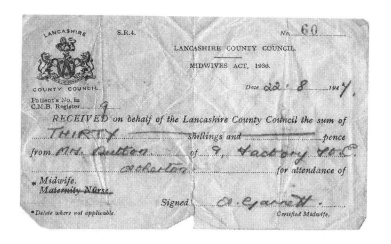

Only thirty shillings. A snip!

I assume my grandmother paid for me as the receipt was made out to a **Mrs** Dutton. My Mam was a **Miss**.

That's right. She was a single mother.

So what you say. There's lots of them.

Ah but there's a big cultural difference.

Being single and having a baby seemed to cause serious offence to a lot of people in those days. It wasn't as prevalent as it is now when it's almost as commonplace as having kids within marriage. No one thinks twice about it these days but they did then. My God, yes.

In fact if you were thinking of writing a hackneyed kitchen sink type of tale set in that era, it might begin :

He was born illegitimately to a 25 years old factory girl in the back bedroom of a Victorian two-up, two-down terraced house in a cobbled Lancashire street overshadowed by a huge cotton mill at the time of rationing just after the Second World War.

The house, rented from the mill, though kept spotlessly clean by his mother and grandmother, had no hot water, an outside lavatory down the yard and a tin bath hung on a hook outside the back door.

That's how it began for me. The Thirty Bob Kid…only we didn't call it a kitchen sink, we called it a "*slopstone*" and I was brought into this world in the middle of an L S Lowry landscape dotted with massive factory chimneys belching thick smoke that made your snot black.

As in the great man's paintings, a lot of local folk were still wearing clogs and shawls: in fact my gran's alarm clock was a clog shod mill worker who always clattered noisily on the cobbles past her bedroom window at the same time early every morning.

D (for David) Day was Tuesday, August 19th, 1947 during one of the hottest summers on record. It was so searing there was an almost Biblical plague of caterpillars in the town of my birth.

They covered front doorsteps and even invaded local cinemas, causing them to close down. I like to think it wasn't God's judgement on me being born but it might have been a sign of His displeasure. I certainly upset Him later, as you will see.

My first public appearance took place with a small supporting cast of 18 of Mam's friends and relatives gathered in the kitchen downstairs and in the back yard to await my birth in the rear bedroom of the ancestral brick-built, terraced house at 9, Factory Street (East) in the cotton mill's dark Satanic shadow in Atherton, Lancashire.

I've worked to bigger audiences since but the much appreciated little coterie was there out of love and concern for my mother, Mabel who worked as a cotton tester in that nearby factory.

At 6-55pm the crowd heard my first lusty cries and someone yelled *"What is it?"*

The midwife, one Mrs A Garnett, flung open the sash window and bellowed: "*It's not over yet. Only his head!*"

Mabel had one foot on the midwife's waist and the other on the shoulder of Mrs Trungle -a neighbour from number 3 who had popped in to lend a hand. Or rather in this case a shoulder.

I was about to choke so the midwife produced a pair of scissors and cut poor Mabel in three places, then heaved me into the world.

She bobbed out the window again and yelled "*It's a boy!*" (Cue loud applause)

Voila! There I was - no doubt to my mother's relief after suffering two weeks of excruciatingly slow labour with terrible pains every five minutes. Some might say I've been a pain ever since.

I have to qualify that with the proud information that five days after I was born, Midwife Garnett came back to the house and brought six of her friends to have a look at me.

She declared I was the most beautiful baby she had ever delivered into the world, with skin like a peach and no wrinkles, unlike most others who, she observed, resembled skinned rabbits. Mabel put it down to chomping on lots of fresh fruit her sister in law Mary had wangled from the local greengrocer. It was still a bit sparse and a banana was a rare treat.

Back to the birth. Mrs G hadn't finished wielding the scissors. I was born tongue-tied but this wasn't a problem to Mrs G. who deftly snipped the flesh underneath it to free it up. (When I read this in my Mam's diary, after I stopped wincing it suddenly hit me that I have always had a fear of sharp objects like scissors near my face -such as at the hairdresser's when I had hair- and this might be the reason.) Mam's brother, my Uncle Walter, who was always a joker had enquired if she was going to cut my tongue up the middle " *y'know, like they do with puppies...* "

"*Why do they do that?* " asked the unsuspecting midwife.

"*So they can lick their arses on both sides at the same time* " quipped Walt.

That was the first joke told in my presence. A belter as it happens. Mrs Garnett had a good laugh then went downstairs to impart the news of my birth to my 66 years old Victorian grandmother Frances who was sitting scowling alone in the front parlour.

"*You have a lovely grandson Mrs Dutton*" beamed the midwife.

My grandmother didn't even bother to look up.

"*Drown him in the dolly tub*".

*dolly tub = a galvanised metal massively oversized bucket shaped container that folk used to hand wash their clothes in. Not really intended for drowning babies.

"*You wicked woman*!" cried the shocked midwife. "*It's you who wants drowning. You should be ashamed of yourself after what that young girl has gone through*".

She might well have been because, as far as I know, that was the only bad thing my lovely Lancashire grandmother ever said about me (and don't forget she paid for me).

She even took me to bed with her that first night so Mabel might have a good sleep.

My gran helped to bring me up and looked after me when my Mam went out to work and we became very close: but it wasn't exactly the most loving remark with which to welcome a new-born grandson into the world.

I can understand how she felt. Times were very different then and there was great shame brought on a family whose daughter gave birth out of wedlock.

"*Chance child*" was the name given to one such as me in our neck of the woods. Like throwing the dice and getting a bad result. Or "*born on the wrong side of the blanket* " – whatever that's supposed to mean. Which side is the *right* side?

Mabel told me that when she asked the local C of E vicar to christen me, he refused point blank to do it because I was illegitimate. As if it was my fault! Nice man eh?

Presumably she had to wait until a more amenable clergyman came along. Talk about "*suffer the little children*".

Hadn't the hypocritical cleric read that bit of the Bible?

The animosity even reached into our family. Mam's elder brother, my Uncle Bert, took such exception when he found out about the pregnancy he drunkenly threw a bottle of Stothert's Chest and Lung Mixture at her head with such ferocity the bottle split.

She was convinced for some reason it would cause a birthmark on me but happily, it didn't.

Mam noted in her diary that my belly button had gone a bit septic and needed drops but didn't need to be fastened down with an old copper penny and a bandage. Must have been something they did in those days as a folk cure.

My willy needed attention though. I had difficulty peeing so she thought I needed to be circumcised and took me to Doctor Smythe – our family doctor who was an Irish Catholic and didn't believe in such practices.

"*Look at it. Sure it's only as big as an acorn. If you cut any more off, sure he'll have nothin' left to pee through*" he growled.

Ignoring his advice, she made an appointment at Bolton Royal Infirmary where a little bit off the top was removed under chloroform.

You know what they say: from tiny acorns grow mighty oaks…

By this time, you may have started to wonder where and who my dad was.

He was nowhere in sight. After all, he was a married man from London with a child of his own: a daughter (aged 25 and the same age as Mabel) who, incredibly, I developed a relationship with a lot later on in life as you will read.

I never met my father: Stanley Alfred Grant. He wanted us all to be together but his wife and my Mam had other ideas.

The Second World War threw Stan and Mabel together, then they threw me together, so to speak.

I probably owe my very existence to Hitler being a crap painter – because if he had been admitted to the Vienna Academy of Art, he would probably have followed that profession and the Second World War might not have taken place…

Then bombs wouldn't have been needed…so there would have been no need for the local munitions factory which played a big part in the war effort; caused a bombshell to be dropped in my Mam's world and exploded me into life.

For my first few years, I was thankfully ignorant of the stigma of being born illegitimate (what a bloody awful word). As far as I knew, I was like any other kid in the neighbourhood. But a painful incident in a school playground some years later brought it home to me like a slap in the face with a wet wellington.

Doubtless some narrow-minded people did resent my birth. I recall Mam telling me about a snidey neighbour who sneered at her predicament and talked about her disparagingly to the other locals. Mam summed her up:

"She was nowt but a ruddy hypocrite. She'd had half the Americans from the base at Burtonwood when her husband was abroad fighting in the Army. She flattened acres of grass all right".

I've just remembered that this woman was a bit of a cruel sod too. When I was about 8 or 9, she came up to me and enquired *"Have you ever seen a match burn twice?"*

Well of course I told her I hadn't.

"Would you like to see?"

Well what child wouldn't?

So she struck the match, waved it with a flourish, then blew it out. *"That's once"*

Then she pressed the still hot match head on my bare arm making me yelp in pain.

"And that's twice".

That probably constitutes assault. I mustn't have told my Mam or she would have flattened her.

I can't recall meeting any other children in our area who "d*idn't have a dad* " in the way I didn't have a dad. I mean one or two had widowed mothers but they hadn't been born on the wrong side of that ruddy proverbial blanket.

Gradually, I suppose, my gran warmed to me then warmed me even more by carrying me about under her Lancashire shawl and I was raised in a loving environment, though not without its arguments.

My Victorian Gran with her brood.
Husband Herbert was away taking a pop at Germans.

DAD'S LOT

The Vanishing Granddad

As I said, I never met my dad but meeting my paternal granddad
would have been an even bigger problem as he vanished into thin air
one day in 1903 and was never seen or heard of again – at least by
his poor mystified family.

He was born in 1860 and *his* dad was born in 1819 during the reign
of Mad King George III.

I often wonder how many people are alive who, like me, have a great
granddad who was born before even the Regency period during the
reign of old Farmer George - presuming I'm still alive when you read
this.

*(I thought this was unusual until my mate the actor and singer
Bernard Wrigley – aka the Bolton Bullfrog - who is a couple of years
younger than me, told me his dad was born in 1883 and fathered him
in his late 60's.*

*His Mam and dad were second cousins which made Bernard his own
Mam's second cousin, once removed.*

*Then when his dad died in 1960, she married his dad's brother a few
years later and thus became his auntie as well as his Mam!*

*You'll probably have to read that a couple of times to take it all
in. I'm still trying to figure it out.)*

I love the West Country, so it's good to know I have a touch of the
"*Ooo-arrs*" in my blood.

While researching my family history, I discovered to my great
delight that my great great granddad George Grant who was born in
the village of Barton St David in Somerset in 1783 was a wrong 'un
described as having a pockmarked face and ruddy complexion who
had done time in 1826 for smuggling. He was also charged with
assault and counterfeiting coins but found not guilty.

He was lucky there because at the same sessions, a man was jailed
for life for nicking two chairs and another hanged for the theft of
five sovereigns.

Earlier that year he had spent three months with hard labour in Wilton Prison for being a rogue and vagabond. That sounds quite romantic but I have no idea what qualifies you as one of those.

His son Edmund - my great granddad - who was born in the village of Chilthorne Domer in Somerset became a Royal Marine for 23 years and served on nine different ships all over the world.

Edmund's son, my paternal granddad Alfred Edmund had also served in the Navy and I suppose this genetically explains why I never get seasick despite over 30 cruises in some terrible conditions including a hurricane in the Bay of Biscay and once sank pints on a storm-tossed Isle of Man Ferry while all around were shouting for Hughie.

My granddad is a bit of a mystery man.

When he vanished in 1903, he left my gran with three children and one on the way.

No-one ever found out what happened to him.

He had gone into central London one day and arranged to meet gran with the children later under the clock at Waterloo Station. She went and waited…and waited…and waited but he failed to turn up and that was that. No more Alfred Edmund.

Granny's first name was Elizabeth. She had a twin sister Emma and was born in 1865 in Erith. She was one of seven children of Daniel Dyke, a farm labourer of Kemsing, Kent, born in 1823.

Gran died at the age of 96 and her twin predeceased her by two years.

Apparently, there was talk that the Dyke side of my family was descended from a child illegitimately fathered by the Earl of Feversham in Kent who had an affair with a servant.

Both Alfred Edmund and his dad had jobs as hammer men at the Royal Arsenal in Woolwich: an arduous occupation working with the drop forge heavy machinery that made armaments to sustain the Empire.

His son Stanley Alfred followed a similar career path there before going into management which led to his appointment as a munitions boss at the Royal Ordnance Factory at Risley near Warrington and his subsequent ill-fated wartime love affair with my mother.

Granddad Alfred Edmund had served 12 years straight from school on a number of ships and his service records show he was a bit of a lad who spent a few spells in navy jail, including a prison in Malta.

24

I'm glad my own spell behind bars was both brief and salutary.

In the 1881 census, he was serving on HMS Elk as a 20 years old able-bodied seaman and among his shipmates were the colourfully-named Jabez Blow; Harry Crup; John Tooth; Moses Snowball and Edmund Hatt who sound straight from Pirates of the Caribbean.

Perhaps as a well travelled man, he had been unable to settle down to humdrum family life and the strain of three kids and a fourth one on the way may have tipped the scales and caused him to do a runner.

He was also a gambler and there was talk he may have simply skedaddled to escape a large debt (or been murdered by those to whom he owed money) or perhaps he decided he preferred life at sea and simply hopped aboard the first ship he saw.

As he lived close to the Thames, he could easily have sailed away on it to warmer climes or even thrown himself into it. Maybe I have strolled past his trapped bones on my many walks by that great river.

It's possible he made a new life for himself under an assumed name in another country as at 43 he was still a youngish man.

In his former travels abroad, he might previously have met and fallen in love with someone in a far off land and then reignited the relationship.

Or was there a reason closer to home that caused him to vanish? Earlier that year there had been two terrible accidents at the Arsenal where he worked which killed 19 men, some of whom were blown to bits when a naval shell weighing a massive 435 lbs suddenly exploded and obliterated the building in which it was housed.

The munitions workers who filled the shells were on an absolute pittance.

For each shell they filled they received the modern equivalent of 25p - between 90 of them!

There had been other accidents at the Arsenal before but with two major ones so close together, this may have been another factor in my granddad's decision. It's possible he knew some of the men who died in the blasts who were only identified by their limbs and tattoos.

Whatever the reasons, my granddad's disappearance is a conundrum that has fascinated and absorbed me ever since I first heard about it. If anyone can help solve the mystery, I'd be very grateful. I've even had my DNA tested to see if there's a connection anywhere in the world but nothing so far is forthcoming.

The mysterious disappearance of her husband sent poor Granny into a steep decline.

Unable to prove whether he was alive or dead and with the loss of the family's breadwinner, she was forced to put three of her children, including my father, into a workhouse followed by a children's home and was only able to look after one of the girls – my aunt Jessie May who was born shortly after. She also went partly deaf with the shock.

In the 1911 census, she is described as working from home, sewing tennis balls, which sounds like a sad, arduous,mind-rotting way to earn a crust. She only had seven years old Jessie to keep her company.

From what I have been told about her, she sounds like a character. She had no teeth and smoked a cigarette at the rate of one every six months because she believed it *"cleared the tubes"*.

She, like me, thought her husband had jumped on a ship and gone to live abroad. He had been restless after he left the Navy. She described him as a man's man.

His disappearance threw her into direst poverty and she had to sell her possessions to enable her to survive: including the exotic presents granddad had brought her from the foreign countries he had visited in the Navy.

As if this wasn't bad enough, for a few years, whenever dead bodies were washed up in the Thames, she had to attend the coroner's office to view the bloated corpses in case one was her missing husband which would enable her to prove he had died so she could claim the insurance.

One can only imagine the horrible sights she must have seen and the nightmares she had.

Thankfully, her twin, Emma, who had married a wealthy banker, helped her out from time to time with food and clothes.

I find it slightly ironic that I was fatherless from the age of zero and my father was fatherless from the age of four. So that's one thing we had in common. I wonder if this thought ever went through his mind in subsequent years?

At least my upbringing was more pleasant than his, for young Stanley Alfred soon found himself in an almost Dickensian situation.

After a spell with his brother in Woolwich Workhouse, he was sent to the Goldie Leigh children's home based in Kent which was run by horrible strict religious types who starved the young inmates of affection and fed them on basic rations of weak porridge for breakfast and watery stew with one measly slice of bread for dinner. They were also not allowed to have any toys.

Imagine being so swinish you wouldn't let children have toys.

In later life, he rarely spoke to anyone about his time there, so badly was he scarred by the experience.

MAM'S LOT

*"Aren't you lucky having all these aunties and uncles?" beamed
Auntie Phyllis.*
*"Yes" I replied. "But look at all the bloody funerals I'll have to go
to".*

Not having met my father or taken his name, I regard myself as a
Dutton through and through. Well, that's my given name anyway
although I once saw an insurance document with the full David
Dutton Grant on it. I quite liked the rhythm of that.
We've heard about the Grants, so what about the ancestral Duttons, I
hear you ask.
I found out in a strange way.
Several years ago, I went into Leigh Library where I overheard a
man next to me giving someone advice on how to trace their family
tree and later on I approached him to see if I could get some tips.
He chatted amicably for a few minutes then asked what name or
names I wanted to investigate as part of my genealogical attempts.
I told him Dutton and his face registered some surprise and he
pushed an A4 sheet under my nose then enquired if I recognised
anybody on the page.
It was *my* turn to be surprised as I saw the name of my great
grandfather Sam Dutton and his wife Ellen in the massive family
tree that the man had outlined.
It turned out this man's great great grandfather and my great
grandfather Sam were brothers so he and I were some sort of cousins
several times removed.
The beauty of it was he had all my family's history going back to the
1700s: complete with birth and death certificates and census forms.
A massive chunk of my family tree had been provided for me in an
instant due to this amazing serendipitous meeting and the following
week I went for a drink with him while we celebrated our shared
ancestry.
I've since traced us back to the late 1600's and that side of the family
didn't move far from Leigh.
It was no surprise to discover the Duttons were Lancashire working-
class stalwarts with a mixture of sawyers; silk weavers; mill and

foundry workers and miners. Grafters in fact. Not skiving actors or pen pushers like some I could mention.

My great grandfather, a tough Lancashire miner called Sam Dutton was born in 1847 and by all accounts was a bit of a mad, bad bugger. Lurid stories about him were handed down through the family and I also found out some really interesting stuff by digging about on the Internet.

I have a bit of a fiery temper which I reckon was passed on by him through DNA (more about the Dutton temper later) but I'm a veritable pussycat compared with Sam's exploits.

There is an horrific family story that he had a dog that wouldn't stop barking. He cured it though. By dropping it down a mineshaft.

He also swung on a lion's tail as a circus parade came through town and once dropped laxatives in the drinks of a brass band playing Christmas carols which forced them to stop blowing. They didn't dare.

He ended up behind bars on more than one occasion but it doesn't seem to have had the same chastening effect on him that it had on me.

Quite bizarrely, he was given three months for obtaining a pair of trousers and a waistcoat from a bloke by false pretences. I would love to have more details about that.

He married a widow, Ellen Green who had been born in Slaidburn, Yorkshire (my God, **please** don't let on I have Yorkshire dna as well as Southern!)

Her dad Steven Simpson moved there when the Fylde Water Board slyly took his village over and flooded the valley to make a reservoir. It's called Stocks Reservoir and is now a beautiful place to pass an afternoon.

When my grandfather Herbert was born in 1881, it meant that along with her two previous sons and two lodgers, the seven of them all lived together in a two up two down terraced house in the romantically named Bag Lane, Atherton, like something out of the socialist tome *"The Ragged Trousered Philanthropists"*.

When Ellen died in 1902, Sam went walkabout all over England and somehow ended up in Plymouth Workhouse amongst other places. He had been hauled in front of the courts on more than one occasion for being drunk and I reckon this was probably at the root of his problems as he ended up a pauper.

More than that, he was colourfully described in the local papers as "a **troublesome** pauper" for his astonishing exploits at the local Workhouse in Leigh.

My Mam used to tell me that Sam had smashed all the workhouse windows and I always thought this was apocryphal until I found the press report of the actual court case.

The newspaper headline is "**Window Smashing Extraordinary**" and reads as follows:

Samuel Dutton, a powerful rough looking middle-aged man, pleaded guilty to damaging the plate glass windows of the Leigh Union offices.

Mr Richard France said that about 1 o'clock on Friday afternoon the prisoner got a prop from an adjoining house and deliberately smashed in succession the seven half-inch plate glass windows in the new offices, doing £10 worth of damage (About £1,200 in today's terms).

The prisoner said the relieving officer would not give him a ticket to go into the workhouse and he had slept out two nights and had had nothing to eat.

Mr Thorpe, presiding, said the prisoner would be able to get something to eat in jail, for he would have to go there for two months.

Once out of jail, he must have persisted in knocking on the workhouse door because they eventually let him in (probably preferable to having to having all their windows smashed.)

I think they must have regretted their decision because once in, he caused them no end of trouble.

Brought in front of the courts again, he pleaded guilty to absconding from the Workhouse with a coat, vest and trousers belonging to them and was sentenced to 14 days hard labour.

He became quite a star in the local press. Another write up told of how he escaped, Colditz style, over the wall of the Workhouse, went on a bender, returned drunk in the evening and was given into custody. He pleaded guilty with nothing to say and got another month in the chokey.

One court case report where he was fined for drunkenness was headlined "**The Drink Craze**".

I reckon he was forced to live rough because no one in his family could put up with his mad, bad and dangerous to know ways.

It is strange to think the Leigh Chronicle reporter who wrote about Sam worked in the same office and the same room I would work in 60 years later when I joined the staff of that old weekly newspaper. I hope he had as much fun as I did.

Sad to say, Sam's tempestuous life ended suddenly in that Workhouse.

A few days after being admitted there under a removal order from the Workhouse in Plymouth, he was working with a fellow inmate in the wood chopping room when he stood up, suddenly turned round and fell forward on his forehead.

His workmate put a jacket under his head and sent for the Workhouse Master but Sam was already dead.

His last few moments had been spent in banter, joshing with his pal who described him as being quite jolly and who told the inquest his last words, quite prophetically, were **"Now we shan't be long"**.

At the hearing, his son – my granddad Herbert – described Sam as "*a man of irregular habits*". I think that's putting it kindly.

For all his faults, I have a soft spot for the old reprobate and proudly possess two Victorian pot dogs which Sam allegedly nicked from the Workhouse.

I'd willingly give them back only it's a housing estate now.

Sam (in typical pugilistic pose) and me. Spot the difference?

Atherton in those days was a typical South West Lancashire town, with a thriving industrial base of cotton mills; coal mines and foundries.

It was a mix of native Lancastrians and "*incomers*" - mainly the Welsh; Irish and people from the Forest of Dean who had got on their bikes to find work.

They were tough folk. Pastimes included "*parring contests*" which involved two blokes in clogs grasping shoulders and kicking each other's shins till one was so badly injured, they couldn't continue. Well, they had no telly in those days.

I recall hearing stories about the mad characters who abounded in the town: such as the man who worried rats to death with his teeth in the pub for money; a joker who painted a sparrow yellow and sold it as a canary and another who drank a pint of maggots for a bet.

It was a hard life. As a boy of 9 or 10, Granddad Herbert was made to work part time in a hot and noisy local foundry and later became a miner.

When he married my gran Frances in 1901, they moved into the terraced house which I'm glad to say is still in the family. Their first two children – Tom and Ellen - sadly died in infancy but they went on to have six more including my Mam Mabel.

It is self evident that the life of a miner was always hard. One day, as my gran bathed one of her babies in a tin bath in front of the fire, there was a dull thud which rattled the pictures on the wall and made ripples in the bathtub.

She knew instinctively there had been an explosion in a nearby mine. This was on December 21st, 1910 when 344 men and boys lost their lives in one of the worst ever mining tragedies at the Pretoria Pit just up the road from the family home. Thankfully, granddad was working down another mine but the event left a black cloud over the community for decades afterwards.

To do his patriotic bit in the First World War Herbert enlisted in the King's Own Royal Lancaster Regiment at the grand age of 34 and went off to fight in France where he was blown up and buried by an exploding shell and after recuperating from that got a bullet through the arm and one through the leg. When he was fit again, he subsequently fought with the Lincolnshires at the Third Battle of the Aisne in France in mid 1918.

While he was on previous convalescent leave, a comrade sent him this chilling graphic letter which I used to take out of his old tin trunk from time to time to read and always found it gruesomely fascinating.

It certainly brings home the real horrors of that time and left an impression on my young mind. Don't read if you are squeamish!

May 29th, 1916 Monday.

Dear Old Pal,

I now take the Pleasure in writing you a few lines as I know how you will want to know my experiences in the boxing ring. (I presume this was his way of describing the war) *Them were the days Dutton. Well, I have been in hospital with swollen feet but it was with standing in the trenches up to the knees in water.*
You know 8 days is a fair while to be stood up and we never got to close our eyes all the time. You might not believe it but it is true

enough and the Germans sent their gas over and 78 were gassed and when the artillery start, they don't send shells, they send foundries over.

What a life Dutton. I could not make you believe what it is like. There was some mines blown up and believe me, I thought it was lights out and the ground trembled like a jelly.

We were only 25 yards from the German trenches, so you will understand why we had no sleep. I had a private in my sentry group. It got on his nerves to such an extent that he went stone mad.

Directly after, a shell came and hit a fellow from Nelson but he was in fragments and I picked up his top lip with his tash on. So you will have an idea of what it is like here.

Harper is here and he is no friend of the men. They do not like him. Swallow is here and Wright. As regards my first coming out here we landed at a place and stayed there about a week and we were sent up the line to another place on the 2nd of April which was a Saturday and on the Sunday, we joined the battalion and at about 4-30 the O.C. came and said we had a trench and crater to take and at 6-30 we set off to our task.

When we had gone so far, we had to get our faces blackened and off we went again. At 2-10 on the Monday morning, we had got to where we had to make the bayonet charge and before I knew where I was, I had fallen into a German trench and of course, I was a bit dazed but I soon jumped up when I heard someone shout "Mercy Comrade".

It was dark and I had a job to find out where the noise was coming from, so I felt with my hand on the floor and I could just feel the head of the German.

He was buried all but his head - wait for it - and then seven came walking towards me with their hands up asking for mercy but they got it.

I can assure you Dutton it is no picnic going into a bayonet charge. It is not like charging sacks. Then after the charge comes the bombardment. That is worse than the charge.

I will draw this letter to a close with best wishes for your welfare. I will tell you what Dutton, I could do with some tackle to clean my buttons as we have to clean them when out of the trenches.

So no more this time from your old pal Whit.

Buck up. Write back soon Dutton as I shall not be here long.

34

Cpl T. Whittaker 16731 K.O.R.L. Regt.

That letter encapsulates in a few words more about the horror of the
First World War than any book. I often wonder if his old mate
"Whit" survived any of this madness.

In recognition of my granddad's brave exploits, the government kept
a pound back out of his final army wages which they said they
would only refund him if he returned his army greatcoat! The
ungrateful sods.

I also have a postcard Herbert sent to my gran from the trenches
bearing a cartoon of two squaddies recklessly sticking their heads
above the parapet as bullets whizz past.

Under a printed heading entitled "*Many thanks for parcel of smokes
received*" he writes:

" *This is a true picture for I was in the same predicament a few
weeks back when three officers and two men were killed by one shell
and some of my pals were shot through the head. So keep this card
to remind me of yours truly*".

He addressed it to Ciss – his affectionate nickname for my gran and
signed it Sammy, which was his nickname.

(There is a spooky link here inasmuch as his father's name was Sam;
Herbert's nickname at school was Sam and for some strange
unknown reason, I was also nicknamed Sam at Grammar School.
And now I have a lovely granddaughter whose name is Sam Daisy.
My son Gareth and his wife Frances gave her that name to keep up
the "Sam" family tradition.)

Herbert Dutton – the brave granddad I never know.

From what my Mam told me, granddad found it difficult to adapt to
civilian life after the war and the terrible sights he had seen must
have affected him deeply as he sometimes took to drink and often,
on his way home sang a mournfully moving song which was a
favourite of his, called Poor Old Joe:

Why do I weep
When my heart should feel no pain?
Why do I sigh
That my friends come not again?
Grieving for forms
Now departed long ago?
I hear their gentle voices calling
Poor Old Joe.

I think he must have been grieving for his fallen comrades.
After the carnage of the trenches, he went back down the pit.
The Germans couldn't finish him but he was cut down by a far more
insidious enemy when he caught pneumonia at the age of 53 after
being soaked in a downpour while watching a football match.

He died far too early. His lungs must have been severely weakened from his time in the foundry, mines and battlefields where poison gas was used against him in France.

I wish I had known him as from all accounts, he was a decent human being who would often bring tramps home to give them a bed for the night, much to my grandma's chagrin. They were probably ex servicemen like him.

Everybody in our family called my grandmother Frances "*Mother*". It was one of those customs I suppose that happened in working-class Lancashire families and even my cousins called her Mother Dutton. (We also had a Big Alice and a Little Alice and a Big Bert and a Little Bert to differentiate between parent and child, even though Little Bert was eventually a lot bigger than Big Bert!)

She was born in 1881 and as a young girl had worked "below stairs" as a domestic servant for the Bradburn family who made their money baking and selling Eccles Cakes in the Lancashire town of that name but, sadly, she wasn't well treated by them.

A large part of my early childhood was spent in her company. She was a Victorian lady and I was a bit of a wild child and consequently these two elements of our personalities frequently clashed.

If I did something to upset her, she chased me round the table in our front room shouting in her broad Lancashire accent "*If I can't catch thee mi dog can!*" - the "dog" in question being a large scrubbing brush which she hurled in my direction in an attempt to hit me on the head. I sometimes retaliated by spitting at her. I was a right brat then.

She always called me a "*neet ullert*" (night owl) because I never wanted to go to bed and when I picked up pencils by curling my toes round them, she shouted :"*He's too lazy to bend his bloody back!*"

When we weren't scrapping, I was frequently to be found with a copy of the Daily Express in my hand reading out the entire race-card for that day's horse race meetings as she liked a flutter but was partly blind.

Consequently, at a very early age I became quite adept at picking winners and was very familiar with the leading trainers and jockeys of the day.

I can remember I was extremely proud of picking a Grand National winner called Teal in 1952 at odds of 100 to 7 but also cried myself to sleep because I hadn't been able to convince anyone to put any money on it!

I was four and a half years old at the time.

The champion jockey Scobie Breasley was a particular favourite of Mother's and she religiously put her sixpence each way bet on two horses called Gudmenaremist and Russian Satellite which, to my knowledge, never brought her a penny in return.

Mother also regularly took me to the local cinema but once had to dragged me out screaming and yelling when the big bellowing Giant appeared in Abbot and Costello's Jack and the Beanstalk.

She used her natural dialect frequently. She used to admonish me never to play in the *cartroad* (the street) and to "*stick to the sidestone*" (the pavement.)

In what sounded like something out of the Middle Ages, she sometimes referred to my Mam as "*wench*".

If I asked what I could have to eat, she'd respond: "*Three run jumps at buttery dooer – and when tha' gets theer, slurr (slide) deawn*".

She was usually very prim but if I lay too long in bed she'd shout: "*If tha doesn't get up, I'll come upstairs and pee in thi ear!*"

She had these funny nonsense phrases. If I was nosy about someone and asked who she was talking about she'd reply "*Icky, t'Fire Bobby*" (fireman) or "*'im in't neet wi't rag arm*".

Inevitably if she thought I was too inquisitive asking what such and such a thing was for, she'd reply: "*Layoles for meddlers and crutches for lame ducks*".

Go figure, as the Yanks say.

Surprisingly for a working class lady, she was a big supporter of Winston Churchill – so much so the regulars at her favourite pub used to call her Mrs Churchill. When I was seven years old he suddenly resigned as Prime Minister in 1955 and I ran all the way home from cousin Alice's to break the news to her.

She was very Victorian in lots of ways. When my cousin Pat had a baby girl, she wouldn't let them over the threshold of the house until our Pat had been "churched" – which involved a blessing in church from the vicar which, presumably, purified her after childbirth.

On Saturday afternoons, our house was usually full of relatives who tucked into the large meat and potato pie Mother used to make, along with Singing Lily: a Lancashire confection of sweet pastry filled with sugar and raisins and slathered in best butter.

One day, when I was about eight years old, I was reading the Beano on the outside lavatory (or petty as we Lankies call it) when there was a loud rat-tat-tat on the back window and a voice at the back door called "*Hurry up will you, someone else wants to use it*".

I marched in a disgruntled manner into the packed kitchen and shouted loudly to my Mam's dismay: "*Can't a lad have a shit in peace?*"

My Auntie Phyllis, red faced and trying desperately to cover for me, stammered: "*Aren't you lucky having all these aunties and uncles?*"

"*Yes*" I replied. "*But look at all the bloody funerals I'll have to go to*".

The room went silent. Mouths fell open. Heads were slowly shaken. I'll never forget the shocked expression on the dear lady's face.

I deeply regret saying that now and sadly, over the years, I have had to attend all their funerals until there were no aunties and uncles left.

It wasn't the first time I'd embarrassed the family. I had not long before marched in from the street, pointed at various body parts and chanted "*Milk, Milk, Lemonade. Round the corner where chocolate's made*".

When asked where I'd learned that, I replied: "*Some big lads*". (They also taught me to sing "*Bum titty, bum titty...play the ukulele*" – with appropriate hand actions)

With Mam busy at the mill, I spent a lot of time at various aunties' homes: mainly my Auntie Alice who fed me her delicious home cooking and with my lovely Auntie Phyllis who was like a second mother to me.

She was a plump, pretty, bighearted and jolly lady who used to smell of the concoctions and medicines that were made at Stothert's, the local manufacturing chemists where she worked.

She died tragically young in her 40's after a heart attack and her dying words to her husband were: "*I feel sorry for you Syd*". That summed her up. She always put other people before herself.

Uncle Syd, a chiropodist by profession, was a decent bloke who became a sort of surrogate dad: teaching me photography and taking us all on seaside trips in his large old banger of a car.

My reaction to her death still bemuses me and makes me feel ashamed. It fell to my Auntie Alice to break the sad news to Mother who rocked backwards and forwards in her chair crying: *"No, no! Not my baby!"*

I'd never experienced anything like this before and for some inexplicable reason, I started to giggle nervously. Auntie Alice glared at me and said: *"It hasn't hit him yet"*.

I loved my Auntie Phyllis deeply and yet it seemed to them I was laughing at this tragic situation. This haunted me for many years until I learned this is a normal response with some people as tears and laughter are closely interlinked (we sometimes cry when we laugh don't we?)

The picture of my distraught grandmother is burned into my memory though and I still feel bad about it.

One other thing I also regret. I was persuaded to see Phyllis in her coffin in the front room of her house. It didn't look like her. She looked so shrivelled and empty: not like the loving, expansive adorable lady who loved me like a son.

This deeply upset me and since that awful day, I've never been to view anyone else in their coffin and I never will.

My beloved Auntie Phyllis. You can see the love between us in this picture. I wish you had stayed with us longer dear lady.

TEMPER TEMPER

Don't worry lad: we all have an Uncle Ned in our family...

I should mention here the genetic curse that is The Dutton Temper. My Mam was a fiery individual. So am I. Even in her last days in a nursing home, she swore profusely and threw pears and custard at the lady who was bravely tried to feed her: testament to the short fuse she had possessed all her life, although her condition magnified her response.

She once upbraided the legendary Lancashire hellraising comedian Frank Randle (a wild guy and one of the highest paid artistes of his day, who had smashed up dressing rooms with an axe and bombarded Blackpool with bog rolls from an aeroplane) because she thought he was tutting at her and her fellow workmates on a night out.

"*Just because we are Lancashire mill girls having a laugh, don't you dare look down on us*" she warned him – not realising then who he was.

"*Eee. I'm from Wigan meself love*" he replied – and gave her his autograph on a Woodbine packet, which I still have.

Once, when I threatened to leave home as a kid of about 9, she threw a suitcase at me from the top of the stairs and said: "*Here, put your stuff in that!*"

I'll put it down to genetics. It probably stemmed from great granddad Sam, although my Uncle Walter's temper was so combustible that on numerous occasions after some imagined slight, he'd yell "***You can all bugger off!***" and then storm out in the middle of the night to walk from our house back home to his wife in Northwich : a distance of around 17 miles!

When he wasn't on his nocturnal perambulations, he was a lovely man who delighted in telling me stories about his days as a professional footballer with teams such as Bolton Wanderers, Reading and Colwyn Bay and the pranks he played with his mates in the RAF.

He told me that during a reserves match at Bolton Wanderers, he had been subjected to a nasty tackle which caused Mother Dutton to rush onto the pitch and hit the offender over the head with her umbrella crying "*Leave him alone you dirty bugger!*"

42

(Just having a mental picture of Lionel Messi's Mam doing the same.)
He liked a tipple. One night I was hanging out of my bedroom
window talking to lovely Linda, who was several years older than
me and lived next door. I had a pubescent crush on her.
I was smooth talking her in my facile manner when, whistling
tunefully, Uncle Walt popped out of the back door, unceremoniously
whipped out his todger and had a copious and noisy pee in the
kitchen grid directly underneath us. Well I supposed it saved him
walking ten steps down the yard to the outside lavvy.
He also had other eccentricities: including concocting his notorious
home-made suntan lotion: a smelly, lethal mix of corn oil and
vinegar which he also persuaded Mam and me to rub over ourselves
when the sun put in an appearance.
We'd never heard of melanomas in those days and we ended up
looking and stinking like overdone chips. When we finally objected
to dousing ourselves in it, he stomped out and made the long trek to
Northwich yet again.
Another of his ideas was to sometimes walk up and down the stairs
with his feet spread wide either side so he wouldn't wear out the
middle of the stair carpet.
He persuaded my Mam to do the same until she saw the
ridiculousness of it. I still do it occasionally in his memory for a
laugh.
I loved to hear him talk because he had a phraseology all his own.
A typical Uncle Walt statement would start:
*"It's a funny thing...I've just seen wotsits up t'Street and we
were havin' a bit of a chinwag about this that and't tuther when who
should turn up but oozits who we hadn't seen for umpteen years
since we all had a drink at wajumacallits together"*.

You just had to nod and pretend you knew who wotsits and oozits
were and what the hell in general he was talking about.
When I took my wife-to-be Lynn to meet him one Sunday, he'd had
a beer or two and stood at the middle door eating his dinner off a
knife and spitting bits of mashed potato as he told her how pleased
he was to meet her. Mam was disgusted but Lynn and I still chortle
about it.

Uncle Walt in a good mood.

Despite me not having a dad, I am grateful to have had so many loving uncles and aunties who thought a lot about me and made up for my dadlessness in no small measure. They were a characterful lot who enriched my early childhood years.

The eldest, Uncle Bert, was a down to earth ex coal miner who was seldom seen without his flat cap and liked a drink or few.

He could sometimes be found with his feet sticking out of privet hedges or languishing in the bottom of unlit street excavations. He was married to dear Auntie Emmy, a typically hospitable lovely Lancashire lady whose kettle was always on the boil to provide cups of tea for her many visitors.

We had to hide the cough medicine when Bertie came round visiting, otherwise he'd neck it in one. For some strange reason, he never referred to me by my real name but always called me Bill. I never did ask him why. He smoked Capstan Full Strength, the fumes off which could choke a dray horse and once gave me a herbal cigarette to smoke on the outside lavatory when I was about nine or ten. At least that's what he said it was. I can still taste that flavour of burning autumn leaves. Nearly all my close relatives smoked and I was an early smoker too.

My habit started when I was a mere six years old. I was the youngest in the gang of kids from round our street and was heartily encouraged to take up tobacco by the big lads in the neighbourhood. I think they call it peer pressure.

We hung about the factory gates and picked up the soggy "dimps" the workers chucked on the floor as they went into the cotton mill, then we passed them round and drew deeply on the frayed damp ends of the cigarette stumps. It was probably a good way of catching TB.

When we were desperate, we also smoked bits of oily wicker skip that they carried the cotton bobbins in. God knows how we didn't all die of emphysema before our balls dropped. We even did fancy tricks such as the "Factory Chimbley" where we turned the cig back to front and put the lighted end in our mouths and blew smoke out through the end you normally sucked on. That took some courage the first time you tried it. Or there was "The Swallow" where you gulped down the smoke then belched it back out in clouds with an enormous "*Burrrrpppp!!*"

My Mam once caught me smoking a cigarette she had left in an ashtray and thought she would craftily cure me. I'd be about eight or nine.

"*Those cigs are no good son: you need to smoke one of these. They're a lot better*"

She handed me one of my Uncle Bert's lethal Capstan Full Strengths and a match.

I thanked her then trooped off to the outside lavvy to light up. I strolled in beaming joyfully a few minutes later.

"*You were right Mam. I bloody enjoyed that! Can I have another?*"

Not the result she was looking for and it wasn't the last time she was to despair of me.

Uncle Harold, who was a spinner in the mill, smoked copious quantities of Park Drive and died with his lungs full of holes and gasping like a fish out of water, crying: "*I'm sick of this...*".

His son, my cousin Norman who was a plasterer and fond of a drink and smoke, died young with throat cancer. His Mam, my Auntie Mary, a very gentle and quiet woman, had a brain haemorrhage and also died young.

My Uncle Ned, who was married to my Mam's sister Alice, was another miner who was hell of a character and I can still remember the night he turned up tipsy at our house when he went up to goofy tv star Ken Dodd, raised his index finger and poked him vigorously in his famous prominent gnashers enquiring: "*Are them yer own teeth Mr Dodd or do you 'ave special ones made for the telly and that?*"

I offered an apology to Doddy afterwards, but he waved it away saying: "*Don't worry lad: we all have an Uncle Ned in our family…*" If you're wondering what such a big telly star was doing at number 9, you'll find out later.

Uncle Ned once took the massively popular American singer Johnny Ray down Agecroft Colliery where he worked although I'm not sure the reason why. He also took me down the mine and I'm glad I went.

I was able to see what the working conditions in a Lancashire coal mine were like: going down the shaft in a cramped metal cage; experiencing the oppressive heat when I got down there; the long trip to the coal face; crouching and walking on my haunches down a claustrophobia-inducing slope for a hundred yards or so and seeing the pitmen working in water with the ever present danger of explosion or rockfall.

It gave me a new respect for those brave men and the many members of my family who had earned their living and provided for their kids in that way.

God bless Uncle Ned. It is said when he once went on a trip to the Isle of Man with his mates, he asked them where he had to go to change his money.

It's also rumoured he once stood in front of Big Ben when it was striking the hour, looked at his wrist watch, looked up and said "*That bugger's wrong. I checked this watch with the wireless this morning*" not realising he had checked it with the chimes of Big Ben!

When not poking Ken Dodd's teeth, Uncle Ned had a part time job impersonating Hitler.
(Actually an end of war street party).

So this was the house in which I was to spend my formative years. No dad, no luxuries but lots and lots of lovely aunties, uncles, cousins, friends, neighbours and Mam and Mother. Oh – and not forgetting Tony our educated budgie who could sing Pop Goes the Weasel while bobbing up and down and alerted us when various neighbours were coming by peering through the net curtains and announcing: "*Mrs Heathcote's here*" - and invariably she was!

Me with our incredible budgy Tony

MY SUPERSTITIOUS MAM

"Scratch your bottom for a pleasant surprise!"

M-A-B-E-L

God how she hated that name.

She told me she had always wanted to be called Eunice. That, to her, was an improvement. She had once worked with a Hungarian lad who charmingly pronounced her name *Mabelle*. She loved that.

It's very hard to sum up my mother Mabel in one line.

The nearest I could get would be to say she was a hard-working; quick-tempered; regretful; wiry; deeply superstitious; nostalgic; worrisome; jittery; caring; loyal; no airs and graces type of lady who was proud of her Lancashire roots. She never lived anywhere else. Come to think of it, neither have I – unless you count Greater Manchester as Lancashire, which I don't.

She was a good mother and loyal daughter who hated snobbery and injustice. She fed the birds; fought for her fellow workers and worked damned hard to feed and clothe me and put me through Grammar school.

Mabel was a true eccentric.

For instance, she always bought herself little presents to wrap in August and unwrap on Christmas Day in the hope she'd forgotten what she had bought herself!

It wasn't that she didn't get any Christmas presents at all; in fact I don't know why she did it to be honest. Perhaps it was the only way of ensuring the presents she opened on Christmas day were ones she actually wanted.

We once bought her an expensive umbrella for Christmas but she never even took it out, saying because it was expensive *"it would be a shame to have it spoiled in the rain"*. That was Mam's logic at work.

She had certain catch phrases such as *"I've been done with me drawers down!"* to reflect the fact she always seemed to get a rough deal in life such as being overcharged for some repair job round the house that wasn't even done properly anyway.

"You'll get paid back" was muttered when she thought someone was doing something they shouldn't be doing. Usually me.

"*You can go off people, y'know*" or "*Oooh, David. You've been brought up different than that*" was usually aimed at me too whenever I broke wind in front of her.

I once went home after a night out to find her shaking on the sofa.

"*What's the matter Mam?*" I enquired.

"*I just heard me Mother shouting me name*" she wailed. (Mother had been dead 25 years by then.)

"*When?*" I asked.

"*A couple of minutes ago. She shouted '**Mabel!**' She must be coming for me*" she wailed.

"*A couple of minutes ago? That was **me** shouting for you through the letterbox – I've forgotten my key!*".

I don't want to give the impression Mabel was a crazy woman: she wasn't. It was all part of her psychological make up and strangely endearing in a way.

While writing this, it struck me how, as children, we accept things that grown-ups say as true.

My Mam used to warn: "*Never stand with your back to the fire or your spine will melt*". This terrified me so I kept well away and ended up with a cold arse. Apparently, doing the same could cause the Devil to jump out at you as well.

Another of her sayings was "*it'll come to ye!*" which meant any late life minor affliction of hers like a sudden arthritic twinge which gave me amusement would inevitably be bestowed upon me in my latter years.

When I was a child, she was also fond of relating to me the strange parable of the Old Chinaman. This was a cautionary tale of an Oriental gentleman whose son was carrying him in a basket to throw him into the sea because he had outlived his usefulness.

Just before the son was about to carry out the dreadful deed, his father popped up in the basket and warned: "*Don't forget to save the basket. Your son will need it for you*".

This I took to mean what comes around goes around. Why he had to be Chinese, I haven't a clue. I still think it's a weird story to tell a very young child.

She detested you sniffing at flowers because she reckoned if you do, "*you'll get creepy crawlies up your nose*".

You had to wear new clothes on Easter Sunday because if you didn't *"the crows will shit on you. "* I often wondered how those crows knew the difference.

If she passed a sheep in the field she always said "*Good morning, Mr Sheep*" as she claimed it brought good luck. Not that she had much.

If, on leaving the house, she had to return for something she had forgotten, she sat down and counted from 1 to 10 with her legs raised high in the air in order that ill fortune would not befall her for the rest of the day. She didn't give a jot or tittle how silly it looked – she had to do it.

Woe betide you if you uttered the word "*pig*" on a Friday or you were sure to bring down the wrath of the gods upon your head. She would put her hand over her mouth and point at you as if you'd come out with the worst swear word imaginable.

My jacket pockets were filled with string "*for luck*" - which usually entailed me frequently having to laboriously unravel it from my keys. I don't call that lucky.

If you threw stale bread on the fire you were "*feeding the devil*" and you had to crush the shells of your boiled egg afterwards to stop witches sailing out to sea in them to drown sailors. Micro witches presumably.

Hell fire! How old were those superstitions?

If you stirred your tea and there were bubbles on top, you had to scoop them up with the spoon and drink them quickly because apparently, it meant you were about to receive money. She frowned if you didn't jump to it when she nudged you and said: "*Quick – bubbles!*"

She believed that a woman being handed a cup of tea that was overflowing into the saucer, meant she would end up with a drunken husband.

Another tea related one of hers – if you find a tea leaf floating on top, put it on the back of your hand and press with the back of your other hand. Say the days of the week, and whenever it sticks that's the day a visitor will arrive.

If the bubbles on your cup of tea go to the side of the cup, it's a sign of rain (as is a quarter moon on its back and the top set of your false teeth falling down.)

When the latter happened to her along with her corns twingeing, she didn't need any weatherman to tell her a downpour was imminent.

She had a reliable weather forecaster right there in her shoes and mouth.

Killing a spider or a worm will also make it rain. So if your garden plants are dry, murder a worm.

If her right hand itched, she rushed to find something made of wood to rub it on because she believed it would bring her money. If the left hand itched though, it meant money would pass out of her hands.

Rub on wood – sure to be good

Rub on brick – sure to be quick

Rub on knee – it will come to me

Some of her superstitions were simply out of this world. There were so many, I persuaded her to write them down one day. I'm glad I did. Take a look at the following…

If she had a loose eyelash she put it on top of her little finger then got someone else to put their little finger on top of hers, then both made a wish and said a poet's name. One lucky person got the wish and the other was left with the eyelash. Where the hell did that one come from?! Who on earth started it in the first place?!

She believed if you saw the shape of a dinosaur in the froth on top of your beer glass you were going to win money! Funnily enough, I have never seen a dinosaur in a pint pot in all the years I have been going in pubs. (*I have to take this back because shortly after writing this, I was having a pint in Manchester when I looked down and saw what looked like a Tyrannosaurus Rex in the froth on the inside of the beer glass. So much so, I put it on Facebook. Still waiting for the money though so I'll put it down to Mabel having a laugh.*)

I swear I am not making any of her superstitions up. God's Holy Bible, as we used to say when we were kids.

Want more? Go on then…

A plane flying directly over your head is a sure sign of good luck. (This must be why she ran outside looking up every time she heard a plane).

If you leave hair in a brush or comb, you will lose a friendship.

If you find money on the floor, pick it up, toss it in the air and kiss it and you'll get more…

See a Woodbine packet in the street, put your foot on it and say this rhyme: "*Wee Willie Woodbine bring me luck, today or tomorrow may I pick something up*" (Although they don't make Woodbines any more.)

If she banged her elbow, she deliberately banged the other one "for luck".

A rhyme she believed in went: "*Never trust a man whose eyebrows meet: for in his heart doth lie deceit*". Fans of the Gallaghers take note.

Sitting on a table or taking the last piece of bread off a plate or weighing something and guessing the weight correctly first time meant you would never marry. She must have done all three.

The following things, apparently, brought **very** bad luck:

 finding an odd glove; leaving crockery upside down after washing and drying it; putting shoes on a table; opening an umbrella indoors; seeing an owl; bringing holly, ivy or playing cards into the house; turning off a tap someone else had turned on; failing to shake the evil spirits out of a coat before putting it on; seeing a cloud pass over the moon; refusing a mince pie; putting red and white flowers together; marrying in green; having chalk ornaments in the home or touching a sailor's collar to make a wish. (I'm certainly not going to try the last one. Can you imagine?!)

She said it was good luck to see a white horse because you could make a wish – but not if you saw its tail first. Obviously.

If you found a hair in your mouth or drank out of a cracked glass it was a sure sign you were shortly going to be drunk.

Two knives crossed? Run them under cold water in the sink. Cold water, not hot, mind you.

You would also be well advised after a haircut to always burn your hair or wrap it up and dispose of it safely for if a mouse makes a nest of it, you will never be rid of a headache.

That's a real Mabel cracker isn't it! If you suffer from migraines, blame that homebuilding rodent.

Perhaps one of the strangest superstitions (and you will have gathered by now there were many) was the one where if she ever got an itchy bottom, she vigorously nudged the person next to her to scratch their own and urged : "*Scratch your bottom for a pleasant surprise!*" and you damned well had to do it.

Even stranger was this adage:" *If you meet a crosseyed person in the street, touch a four holed button or else it's bad luck*".

Woe betide if a bird craps on your windows for that presages sickness within the house (strangely, that seems to happen!) and just about the worst thing you can do is cut your hair or nails on a Sunday for that brings certain doom:

"*My friend Doris did that and her husband dropped dead next day*".

Mabel even had a rhyme for the nail thing.

Cut nails on Monday, cut for news
Tuesday, new pair of shoes
Wednesday, cut for a letter
Thursday, something better
Friday, living to seek
Saturday, best day of the week
Sunday, Devil will have you the rest of the week.

Oh Mam. No wonder you were a worrier and a nervous wreck at times.

Where you got these superstitions from, I guess we will never know. Perhaps they had been handed down through generations of neurotic Duttons.

I'm glad to say most of them ended in the virtual bin when they arrived at me although she passed some on to my late cousin Susan who used to wail "*Oh Auntie please don't tell me any more!*"

This next one is a belter…

She reckoned that if, say, you want to wake up at 7 am the next day, when you get in bed, bang your head on the pillow seven times and you'll wake up at that time. Bang it eight times for 8am and so on. She swore it worked for her.

Here's some more she believed in:

Jump over a bunch of thyme three times and you will meet a lover. If someone shows you an engagement ring, try it on your wedding finger – turn it three times then make a wish.

Your ear is burning? That's left for love and right for spite. If it's the right ear and someone is calling you, they will bite their tongue. Serve 'em right.

Whatever you do, never hang clothes on a doorknob as it's a sign of a quarrel - as is a broken shoelace, a teapot with the lid off or putting your hands in the same water as someone else. If that happens, to rectify the situation all you have to do is spit in the water and count to ten to avoid a quarrel.

She hated the song Auld Lang Syne probably because she had the superstition that linking hands and singing it would cause death to the first person to break the chain.

If a crow circles around a chimney, that presages doom for someone in the house. Other signs of death include a dog howling three times; a peacock opening its tail feathers; someone's picture falling off the wall and hearing three knocks on the door and there is no one there when you open it.

Picking up a sixpence; popping a paper bag; opening a sheet, pillowcase or tablecloth and finding a shape of a diamond in it; a bird flying into a house; accidentally killing a cricket; a black cat meowing in the doorway; a cock crowing three times; hearing a can kicked or seeing a cinder jump out of the fire were **all** regarded by her as a sure sign of impending death.

If death ensued, a window should be always be opened to let out the dead person's soul.

When sewing a garment and the cotton knots, you will not live to old age unless you get the knot undone...

Don't talk or shout under a railway bridge unless a train is going over it then make a wish.

On leaving a table after a meal, always push your chair back under or you might not sit there again.

Never read your own teacup or cards. Don't put salt on celery (she'd put sugar on). Don't wave anyone off until they've gone round a corner out of sight. Don't put an umbrella or shoes on a table or you will die with your feet in the air (hanging).

If you drop a glove on the floor, stand on it before picking it up or you'll have a disappointment.

She never liked us to cross on the stairs. And tripping up going upstairs was regarded as the sign of a wedding.

Whereas tripping up in the street involved having to turn round three times and kiss your thumbs. I bet that looked strange!

If a stray dog walks into your house it means you're going to meet a new friend. And if a moth flies on you, you'll receive a letter. But don't kill a cockroach on a Friday.

She thought it was unlucky for a bride to see herself fully dressed in a mirror before the wedding but to avoid this it was okay to leave one shoe off.

She had loads more weird and wonderful superstitions but that's more than enough for now. I'm getting paranoid.

In Lancashire, there are such things as Boggarts: mischievous little spirits that spill milk and hide things in your house. But to get rid of them, Mam said all you have to do is recite "*Ivy clings. Holly is green. No more in this house will a boggart be seen. Bugger off boggart!* "

And with that thought, I'll bugger off myself to the next chapter which I think you'll find very interesting.

Fingers crossed and touch wood…

But first…..
Here's Mabel in a photo booth, wondering where to look and then failing to grasp that the booth takes four photos.
*That's **four**, Mam, not three.*

THE SUICIDE SQUAD

I will place a curse on you and anyone who wants you!

She was a beautiful young woman who had spent her early working years in the local medicine factory but the advent of the Second World War changed Mabel's life for ever, as it did for millions of other people.

She was born at 15 minutes to midnight on Christmas Eve in 1921 in the family home at number 9 when her father and mother were both about 40 years old and consequently felt she was more of an accident of nature rather than a child who was really wanted. To some extent, this may have coloured her life as it did mine.

She told me her mother always used to take sides against her in an argument with her siblings and hit her across the legs with a strap that was hung by the fireplace and which, typically, Mabel disposed of by hurling it in a temper in a nearby stream.

She sometimes had to wear hand-me-downs which no longer fitted a neighbour's daughter including itchy knickerbockers which fastened with three buttons in between the legs and had navy blue stripes down them.

Other clothes she wore had once belonged to a girl who had died and whose corpse she was made to view in the coffin against her wishes.

She idolised her father Herbert, who she called Pop. He would give her his last penny and she had happy memories of him bringing home toffee fish from the market and other sweets from the pub.

He could play the concertina and used to walk through the nearby fields with a line of local kids in tow singing along to the tunes.

His early death from pneumonia at the age of 53 left her distraught. Ever one for hoarding souvenirs, she kept his last half-smoked cigarette in a matchbox and I still have it.

Every now and then I take the battered cig stump out of the matchbox and pretend to smoke it. It's comforting to know that although I never met him, granddad and I shared a cigarette together. Well, sort of.

With her good looks and full lips, Mabel wasn't short of suitors but she genuinely believed she was hexed after a fair number of them died prematurely. I'll speak more of this later.

She told me that when she was in her teens, she went on the local fair with some friends and caught the attention of a young curly haired gypsy boy called Duddy Boswell who travelled with the fair. He begged her to go out with him but she declined and in a rage he yelled "*If you won't go with me, I will place a curse on you and anyone who wants you!*"

Knowing how superstitious Mabel was she would have taken this threat very seriously indeed.

Whether the curse worked or not, it cannot be denied she didn't have much luck with men.

In those days she didn't smoke; drink; listen to dirty jokes and if any boyfriend tried to go further than a kiss, she chucked them right away. No messing with Mam.

After she died, I found a small diary in which she had listed her boyfriends and her thoughts about them.

One lovesick lad proposed to her when she was only 16, declaiming "*You take my breath away*". She turned him down and he married someone else in a fit of pique. Another rejected suitor smashed his fist into a wall and broke bones in his fingers when she finished with him.

One night, she was coming home from a date with a boy who pretended to tie his shoes and then suddenly (and foolishly) made a grab for her. "*I kicked him in the gob and ran home*" said the pithy diary entry.

In 1935, she started a job at Stothert's: a local manufacturing chemist making everything from rubbing oils and sticky fly bands to cough medicines.

You could usually smell someone who worked there before they came round the corner with the scent of the oils and powders impregnated on their clothes.

When war broke out in 1939, at the age of 17 she was put on fire patrol duty on the roof of the factory armed only with a stirrup pump and a bucket of water to douse any incendiary bombs that might be dropped by the Germans and she had to sleep on a camp bed inside the building.

There was an air-raid shelter facing number 9, which, being near to the Luftwaffe-targeted Manchester conurbation, the Dutton family made good use of.

She told me "*We seldom got a good night's sleep. Sometimes the siren went off four times a night and just as you were dropping off, you had to rush out again.*
Mother panicked and sat on the top of the stairs shouting 'Oh God have mercy on us. Wheer's me gas mask?!'"
The younger workers had to leave Stothert's to go on war work. Originally, Mam was supposed to work at a local engineering factory but when she went to the local Labour Exchange, she was told she was being sent to the Royal Ordnance Factory at Risley, near Warrington which was 11 miles away. That
was heartstoppingly bad news.
Under the tuition of experts from Woolwich Arsenal, hundreds of thousands of bombs and mines were made there, mainly by young women conscripted from surrounding towns who packed the bomb cases with explosives.
It was a massive countryside site covering around 1,000 acres which had taken 18 months to build and was chosen because it was on Risley Moss and often covered in mist: thus providing cover from the German bombers who amazingly never managed to find it during the whole course of the war.
At the tender age of 19 she was thus forced by law under threat of imprisonment to work at this virtual hellhole of a place and, even worse, was allocated Group One which was nicknamed the **Suicide Squad** on account of the many poor unfortunate girls and women who had been blown up, killed; maimed or blinded in that department.
She didn't realise that she had been sent to the worst place possible in Risley.
There, she was given the task of working with highly volatile explosives making detonators. She noted that the woman who accompanied her as a guide on the first day only had one hand and a finger missing off the other one!
On young Mabel's first afternoon there, she was put in the Experimental Shop where she had to test the powder by weighing it on brass scales and sealing detonators one at a time, wearing only goggles and leather gauntlets for protection.
Think of that for a moment.

A teenage girl, miles away from home is given a job that could blast her to bits at any moment with only gloves and goggles to keep her "safe". Health and Safety then? Forget it.

She was just a kid who, like many others at the time, was **forced** by the Government to work in munitions because had she refused, she would indeed have been thrown in jail. She told me she often fretted if the bombs she had worked on had killed innocent women and children, which they probably had.

One day she was given a mysterious red box to carry while one person walked in front of her and one behind waving red flags to warn people to keep their distance.

She revealed:

"I didn't know what I was carrying. There was a massive explosion from an adjoining room. I dropped the box in shock and was horrified to see a young woman thrown through a window with her stomach hanging out. I was sickened.

Luckily, for some reason, the box, which contained detonators, did not explode or we would have had our legs blown off".

When she got home that evening, she told her sisters Alice and Phyllis she was never going back to Risley. They laughed sardonically because they knew she had no choice.

Sometimes, German planes flew over Risley speculatively dropping incendiary bombs and flares to light up the sky for the bomber planes. Mam had the job of banging furiously on a big metal triangle to warn everyone to hurry into the shelter, then follow them all in afterwards. The last person in.

The pressure proved too much for some of the young conscripts. One poor girl went mad and put detonators under her fellow workers' lavatory seats. Luckily, Mam said they had been told to lift the board up with their feet for hygiene reasons and in this way a terrible fate was avoided.

Strange things happened there in the dark and mist. There was a resident ghost of a lady called Madam Weatherby, who had been murdered centuries before, which was seen on many occasions.

She also told me of two Irish girls who ran in one night very upset claiming they had seen two banshees wailing on top of a workshop. These were spirits which presaged a disaster. Sure enough, shortly afterwards, that building had been blown up with the loss of the life of a young man from Mam's home town and many others were injured.

The Risley women wore smart functional uniforms consisting of white trousers and a coat with a mandarin collar and buttoned down front. In the canteen, they had lunchtime concerts to relieve the stress and some of the bosses joined in.

Once, as a treat, some Max Factor makeup artists came over from Hollywood demonstrating the latest lipstick and pancake makeup and gave free samples to the very grateful young ladies.

But these lighter moments could have hardly compensated for the constant threat of death and injury.

If there was an explosion in the magazine or workshops, they had to go immediately to the canteen for a cup of tea and two cigarettes while clearing up operations took place.

The other girls begged Mabel for her fags as, up to then, she didn't smoke.

One day, a young girl came into Mam's workshop to sharpen a pencil. She had just gone out when there was a loud explosion. Everyone except Mabel rushed out to see what had happened.

The girl had just walked in through the door of the other workshop when the explosion happened and to steady herself, she put her hands in the wall.

One hand dropped off, along with the fingers of the other hand. She was also blinded.

As they wheeled her past on a stretcher, Mabel saw the young girl's curly auburn hair had turned straight and white.

Seeing how shocked Mabel was, a group nurse lit a cigarette and told her to smoke it to calm her nerves. She did the same the following day after another explosion.

It was the start of a lifelong habit.

One night, a very tired Mabel was desperately trying not to nod off and was spotted by a fellow worker.

"*Here luv. Take one of these*" she hissed – slyly slipping Mam a tablet.

"*What is it?*"

"*Get it swallowed. It'll help you keep awake*".

It was an amphetamine wakey-wakey pill which RAF bomber pilots took on missions to keep them alert.

She said it kept her awake for days afterwards and as far as I know, that's the last time she ever "dabbled".

Mabel and sister Phyllis. Two real beauties. I can see what my dad saw in her.

MABEL: UNLUCKY IN LOVE

"This is the last time you will ever see me. I am going to drown".

Mam told me when she was at Risley she had 10 boyfriends on the go. All of them were in the forces and she used to write constantly to them but if they got serious and spoke about getting engaged, she dropped them immediately and refused to have anything further to do with them.

One persistent suitor was a handsome young man from Atherton by the name of Fred Knight.

He was always asking her to go out with him but she constantly refused.

One day, his mother who he was deeply attached to, committed suicide by drowning herself and he was heartbroken.

Feeling sorry for him, Mabel agreed to go out with him which was probably for the wrong reason. One day, they had a lovers' tiff and she, unthinkingly, told him to go and drown himself and bitterly regretted it afterwards.

"I really thought I loved him after that but things weren't the same and I wouldn't go out with him" recalled Mam.

He told her in order to forget her, he had volunteered to join the Fleet Air Arm and as he was being posted to HMS Goshawk, a training station at Piarco in Trinidad, he gave her a poppy to remember him by.

On their final conversation together he told her: *"Take a good look at this ugly face. This is the last time you will ever see me. I am going to drown"*.

Mam replied defensively and sarcastically: *"Do you want me to cry or something? You're not going to drown. You're a champion swimmer"*.

This was another remark she was later to regret.

But poor Fred must have had a premonition which unfortunately turned out to be true – indeed, I have a letter from him to Mabel in which he writes: *"I do fully realise what I'm in for. A short life and a merry one, I say"*.

A few weeks later, Mam was walking home from the pictures with her niece Marjorie when a neighbour stopped her and said Fred's sister Edith had received a telegram informing her Fred had died on October 30th 1942 at the age of 20.

The plane he was in was struck by lightning and although some of his colleagues had been able to bail out, Fred was trapped in the back of the aircraft which had nosedived into the sea. Unable to escape, Leading Airman Fred Knight, as he somehow foresaw, drowned in the ocean.

His name is engraved on the Memorial on Marine Parade West in Lee-on-Solent.

Tragically, two weeks after Fred's death, Mabel received a letter from him written just before had gone on that fateful flight.

In it, he told her the weather was squally with thunder and lightning but he had to go up in the aeroplane as part of a test he was doing.

Eerily, Fred was not the only one who had foretold his death.

Mam had a sister-in-law called Mary whose mother was a medium who used a crystal ball for divination.

Some weeks before Fred's death, she told my Mam to look into the crystal and tell her what she saw.

It chilled her.

She told me she saw a vision of Fred with a black hatband instead of the usual white one around his service cap.

The medium told her that was a sign he would drown.

"I didn't believe her at the time, or want to believe her, but she was right " said Mam.

At the same sitting, she also saw a scene containing two gates and a path going up to a big house with poplar trees on either side and a little white-haired old lady sitting in a rocking chair inside with a cat on her knee.

"The medium told me to take notice as I would go to such a house and there would be water flowing past it.

My brother Harold used to make fun of it all and made silly noises to try and scare us but Mary's mother asked him to take the crystal ball in the dark under the stairs and look for himself.

"He came out white as a sheet with his black hair standing on end. When he looked in the crystal ball he had seen our cousin Jack Horrabin, a trooper in the Reconnaissance Corps, in his army uniform with his cap pushed to the back of his head, leaning on a fence and looking weary and defeated.

We later found out Jack had been taken prisoner by the Japanese in Burma and was shot in the back trying to escape in July 1943. Our Harold never scoffed again".

(I looked on the war graves site on the internet. Jack indeed lies buried in the Burma-Siam Death railway prisoner of war cemetery in the village of Thanbyuzayat.)

Although she didn't like to talk much about it, she claimed something bad happened to a lot of the men she went out with and she truly believed she was jinxed.

Her diary recalls a boyfriend called Bob who was shot down and killed in his fighter plane after she had refused to go out with him before he returned to active service.

I remember in later life another suitor being found dead of a heart attack in his bath, getting ready for a date with her, so maybe there was something in that.

Did the gypsy's curse that had been placed on her come true? I'm sure she thought so.

Out of the 10 boys she had been corresponding with, no less than five lost their lives in the war. Thinking herself ill-fated, she stopped writing to the rest of them.

Shortly after, her life was to change in a big way when into it came a man who she hated and feared.

Mam, second left with her Risley workmates who later became lifelong friends.

MR GRANT

"Bloody Hell Alice!"

One morning, Mam was walking along a concrete path at Risley.
It had been raining and it proved so shiny and slippery underfoot she
had great difficulty in keeping her balance.
As she tiptoed gingerly along, a deep commanding Southern voice
boomed out behind her:
**"If you put your feet down correctly, you would walk much
better!"**
Struggling not to fall over in shock, she slowly turned round to
confront the owner of the fearsome voice.
To her horror she saw it was the Group Manager, Mr Stanley Alfred
Grant. Now here was a man she hated with a passion.
With his secretary and foremen in tow, Grant, as she always called
him, paid flying inspection visits to the workshops and woe betide
anyone if he found anything untoward.
Barking instructions to his underlings, he peremptorily disappeared,
leaving them to chastise the errant workforce.
Understandably, being in charge of such important and dangerous
work, he was there to ensure everything was done properly and
according to his orders.
Everyone was scared of Mr Grant who stood over six feet tall, came
from Plumstead and was one of the experts from the Woolwich
Arsenal who had been sent North to oversee operations at Risley.
His expert knowledge of caps and detonators meant his advice was
often sought by bomb disposal squads.
This was the first time he had addressed Mabel personally and she
was so terrified, she could not utter a word in return and off she
tottered as quickly as her balance would allow. She was a shy young
girl, completely out of her depth.
But from this inauspicious beginning was to start a love affair which
affected the rest of her life. Without it, I wouldn't be here to write
this book.

Stanley Alfred Grant. Aka Dad.

WHEN MABEL MET STANLEY

"We didn't think he was human"

In the Spring of 1943, Mabel was persuaded to go to a cabaret dinner specially organised for all the factory overlookers. She had just been promoted to that position – putting her in charge of the workers in her department.

Donning a beautiful blue dress embellished with black lace (costing four guineas from London House, Leigh) she went along and was fuming when the dinner didn't start on time because the big boss Grant had arrived late. This didn't sit well with Mabel and I can imagine her getting more and more irate.

He finally showed up and as she and her workmates sat talking at their tables, she noticed Grant kept staring over at her and Mabel being Mabel thought it was because he was weighing her up and thinking she was too young to be an overlooker.

His piercing eyes followed her round the dance floor all evening, making her somewhat unnerved.

As she waited alone for the bus to take her home afterwards, Grant came outside and to her astonishment, he was singing to himself. *"We didn't think he was so human as to sing"* remembered Mam. *"It didn't seem like something he would do"*.

He walked towards her and her heart started hammering faster. *"What's your name?"*

"M...Mabel" she stuttered...

He asked her which part of the factory she worked in and the conversation slowly developed.

Scared of such an approach from the authority figure who she detested, Mabel could hardly get her words out and he offered to call a taxi for her in case she missed the connecting bus home at Leigh.

Next day, when she told her best friend Doris Hill and the other girls at work how helpful Mr. Grant had been, they didn't believe her. Helpful? Not him.

Naive Mabel hadn't realised he was making a pass at her.

Later that morning, the phone rang. It was Grant's secretary informing Mabel he wanted to see her immediately in his office. She went along, dry mouthed, quaking in her shoes and not knowing what to expect.

He told her he was living just a couple of miles away from her in the Greyhound Hotel on the East Lancs Road and would like to meet her on Saturday.

This hit her like a dropped box of detonators. Again, she was dumbstruck.

"I didn't say anything. I just shot out of the office. I couldn't believe it".

Undeterred, Grant persisted over the next few days until she hesitantly finally agreed to meet him in front of the hotel.

She borrowed her sister Phyllis's brand new coat and shoes and nervously hopped on the bus. He was waiting for her in front of the Greyhound. She must have felt like a serving wench called into the presence of the King.

He suggested a stroll and they walked down a nearby lane full of May blossom then had jam and scones for tea in a small café before going to see a film at the Odeon Cinema in nearby Leigh. He escorted her to the bus and she went home in a total daze.

The attention paid by the big boss from London to a small-town young Lancashire lass was somehow beyond comprehension to her.

In spite of all this, the relationship developed over the next few weeks as Grant gave her the key to his office and they began to write love letters to one another.

They went out together to the cinema; to the pleasure gardens at Manchester's Belle Vue Zoo and to Old Trafford where Mabel became bored watching her first ever cricket match and naively asked why one of the players had been sent off when in fact he had just been bowled out.

Stan laughed loudly and uproariously in a manner she found daunting and embarrassing. She walked off and left him and he followed her out of the ground.

His attentions towards her never wavered and eventually he received an invite to Sunday dinner with the Duttons.

Mother Dutton told the family to be on their best behaviour and warned the lads not to swear but as luck would have it, as big sister Alice was shaking a brown sauce bottle to put on some beef, the top flew off and covered everyone and the tablecloth with blobs of brown sauce.

"*Bloody Hell Alice!*" yelled Mother to red (and brown) faces all round.

You could hear a pin drop but Grant thought it was hilarious and laughed immoderately and earsplittingly loudly.

Invites were extended to weekend stays but young Mabel was embarrassed because the house had no hot water or a bathroom: only the lavatory at the bottom of the back yard.

This didn't seem to bother Grant who, as we now know, had had a hard upbringing in the workhouse and children's home.

He and Mabel sat listening to the wireless downstairs in the evenings while sister Phyllis sat nearby curling her hair.

Thinking the couple were alone together unchaperoned, Mother crept downstairs on the pretext of getting a glass of water in order to spy on them. Don't forget – she was a Victorian lady.

If they stayed in the house alone, brothers Harold and Bert would be sent in the room ostensibly to pick up a hanky while making sure there was no hanky panky.

Grant had a party trick which involved leaping over billiard tables in pubs. One day, he didn't make it and caught his leg on the edge of the table causing a big black bruise at the top of his thigh. When Mabel related the story, Mother accused her of having seen it - which she hadn't - and called her brazen.

Mother needn't have worried at that stage. The lovers' first kiss was a full six months after their first date.

Grant embraced Northern ways and mother grew to like him. She even taught him how to make chip butties, which he'd never had before and which became a firm favourite.

He had difficulty understanding Mother's broad Lancashire dialect and she couldn't make out what he was saying in his London twang when he enquired: "*Has the piper cam yet Mather?*" when he needed to know if the newspaper had been delivered.

Love deepened for Mabel and Grant. He was very caring towards her.

"If I didn't turn up for work, he would be round like a shot feeling my forehead and my pulse and telling Mother not to let me return until I was better. One day, he picked me up and squeezed me so hard I thought my ribs were going to break. The following day, the doctor diagnosed pleurisy. I had to sleep in a bed downstairs. I told Grant not to keep coming to see me but he wouldn't keep away.

"I was horrid to him. At times I would have him in tears. Once, he put his arms round me in front of Mother and I was so embarrassed, I told him to let go. When he didn't, I burned him on the back of his hand and cheek with my cigarette. Phyllis went mad and so did Mother but I wouldn't give in".

On several occasions after a row, she even threw hot food over him. It's a wonder he still wanted to keep seeing her but she broke off the relationship and told him not to bother her again.

This time, he took her at her word and didn't contact her. She couldn't believe it. Perversely, exhibiting signs of lovesickness, she missed him so much she began to lose a lot of weight and couldn't get to sleep.

He kept out of her way at work until one day as she was leaving the canteen, he saw her and enquired: *"Have you been ill? You've gone thin".* Again she ignored him.

Undeterred, he asked her friends to speak to her on his behalf and when they went to the same works concerts, he asked the band to play their favourite songs, such as *"You'll never know just how much I love you"*, *"You are always in my heart"* and the Ink Spots' *"Whispering Grass".*

I have a letter from my dad to Mabel which ends *"God bless you and ours. All my Love to you. YNKJHMILY "* (Their song).

A former colleague of my Mam told me recently that Mam was always singing *"You'll never know"* as she went about her work in the cotton mill decades later. I think he was permanently on her mind.

Eventually after such sustained attention, she gave in and they started to go out together again, enjoying favourite walks over the West Pennine moors at Belmont near Bolton where they sat near a stretch of water called the Blue Lagoon and watched the rabbits play.

Well that's what Mam said they did anyway. It was still a favourite spot of hers many years later and I often took her to it. I wonder if I was conceived there? She would never have said.

They went to see the variety shows at Bolton Grand Theatre where Grant roared with laughter at the comedians and when he laughed, Mam said it was like a clap of thunder and soon all the other rows would be laughing at *him* laughing.

She told me he once laughed so loudly at work that a cleaner jumped in the air and knocked a bucket of water over: causing him to hoot even harder.

I have inherited his mad loud laugh. My lad Gareth has too. We embarrass ourselves sometimes when we catch ourselves laughing so deafeningly that people in the next dimension turn and look at us.

Once, Mabel had booked a holiday in Blackpool with her workmates and Grant wanted to join them but she wouldn't let him. When they got there, he was waiting for her with a diamond engagement ring which he placed on her finger and told her never to take it off.

As he was still married, it could only have been a statement of intent. She wore the ring to work, covered by a piece of leather.

Mam's attention had been caught by the photograph of a young girl on Grant's desk. She mistakenly and jealously assumed it was a girlfriend but it was his beloved daughter Joyce: my half sister, who I later met and formed a relationship with.

I'll tell you the circumstances later.

Grant felt it was time his mother was in on the secret. When told about the affair, she graciously invited them both to a meal at her house in Stafford Road near Stockton Heath in Warrington.

When she got there, Mabel had the shock of her life.

The house was the one she had seen previously in the crystal ball: complete with path, poplar trees and the flowing water as predicted by the medium, which was the nearby Manchester Ship Canal.

There was a cat and a rocking chair in which Grant's mother sat: a white-haired elderly lady, exactly as foreseen.

She was soon to be my grandmother.

I still find it hard to come to terms with this sort of supernatural happening. If a snapshot of the future can be seen in this way, does it mean our lives are pre-ordained? What strange force enabled my mother to be able to tune into the future?

(To digress, my own belief in the supernatural was reinforced when I attended a funeral of a friend who had dropped dead in his 50's.

As we were waiting for the church service to start, I looked across at the rows of candles the mourners had just lit in his memory and for some reason I said in my mind to my dead friend: "*If you can hear me mate, extinguish the end candle on the top right of the row*".

A split second later, that very candle went out as the other 40 or so candles kept on burning. I was totally shocked. I stared in amazement at the flameless wick and then I smiled and muttered: "*Well done mate*" to my dead friend.

I like to think he was bringing me proof as he was a fun-loving, mischievous sort of guy. And after the service, his son who was walking down the aisle of the church with his mother suddenly stuck out his hand as he passed me and shook mine for no apparent reason as he walked past all the other mourners, family and friends who had packed the church.

Even stranger, at the same time his Granddad George died in the middle of the night, my son Gareth suddenly woke up to hear the sound of a clock ringing Westminster chimes, despite there being no timepiece of that nature in the house. The only one in our family was the one on George's mantelpiece – and that was 200 miles away.)

Whatever Mabel was thinking at the time about her strange crystal ball preview, she was brought back to reality by the fact that Granny Grant, as she came to be known, had decided to serve them kippers which Mabel abhorred but somehow managed to force down with the help of large chunks of bread. After that, meals with Granny became a regular event.

She got on really well with Granny and it was the first of many visits to the house she had first seen in the crystal ball.

Eventually Mabel got "caught" as they say in Lancashire and I was the result. Stan was summonsed and ordered to pay ten shillings a week maintenance until I was 16.

He had wanted to leave his wife to marry Mabel but, as the youngest offspring, she loyally refused to leave her mother alone. That was the reason she claimed, anyway.

He sent her many love letters in an attempt to persuade her but she wouldn't give in.

I really can't understand why they didn't get together. I wonder what lay deeper in Mam's mind to prevent her from getting together with him? She took the secret to the grave.

My father was the love of her life and even decades after they parted and she became an old lady, she slept with his yellow woollen scarf and his fading handwritten love letters under her pillow.

As I had nothing that had belonged to my father, I thought about keeping the old scarf when Mabel died, but thought it more fitting to have it placed in her coffin to bring closure to their long-time unfulfilled love affair. I think she would have wanted that.

At her funeral service, we played "*Whispering Grass*" by the Ink Spots and "*Some Enchanted Evening*" from South Pacific which she loved, mainly because of the handsome Italian star Rossano Brazzi who sang it in the film and whose appearance made her go all gooey. Sometimes, my wife Lynn catches herself humming "*Some Enchanted Evening*" for no reason at all and says smilingly "*Mabel's here*" ...which she may very well be, as this next story shows...

Cabaret for Overlookers at Risley ROF April 1943. Mabel 4th right 2nd row. Grant 10th right same row.

MABEL RETURNS

I'm so proud

I don't know whether you will believe the next part of the story but there is an eerie postscript.

Five years after my Mam died, my son got married to Frances in Sir Christopher Wren's old house (now a hotel) on the banks of the Thames in Windsor.

It was, as you can imagine, a joyous occasion packed with those closest to Gareth and his wife-to-be Frances.

After the celebrations were almost over, a few of us sat at a table mulling over the day's events. Facing me was my friend Johnny who had been best man at our wedding.

Mid conversation, I saw him stare over my shoulder and his expression changed to a look of shock. After a few seconds, he laid his head on the table and cradled it with his hands.

I asked him if anything was the matter and, visibly shaken, he looked at me and stuttered: "*I've just seen your Mam...*"

The words didn't register at first but then I asked him what he meant.

He said Mabel had been standing just behind me and had looked at him smilingly and said: "*Oh Johnny, I'm so proud*". Then she disappeared.

I thought he was joking at first but it was evident by his state of shock he had witnessed something out of the ordinary.

Johnny wouldn't lie and he is a down-to-earth level headed Lancastrian, not given to fantasising. Mabel thought the world of her only grandson and it seems she hadn't wanted to miss his big day.

Johnny, seconds after seeing Mabel. I took this pic, not realising what had just happened.

It wasn't the first time Johnny and I had experienced a strange supernatural event.

We were in our 20s and Johnny had paid a visit to our house one night. As he was leaving, we chatted on the doorstep and for some reason John, a Catholic by upbringing, brought up the question of the existence of the Almighty.

"*Don't be daft, Johnny*" I responded "*there is no God* ".

No sooner had the words left my lips when in the middle of the street directly behind Johnny, there was a blinding blue flash and a loud bang which immediately caused me to involuntarily slam the door in his face!

A few seconds later I tentatively opened it and a shellshocked Johnny "thanked" me for leaving him in the presence of the unknown.

I don't know what caused the phenomenon but it wasn't Bonfire Night or thunder and lightning as there was no sign of rain and the flash happened only a few feet behind Johnny. The timing of it was perfect. Perhaps my flippancy had angered a Higher Authority.

I suppose it was a Damascene moment and perhaps I should have become a priest: but then again, thinking back to that miserable old sod who refused to baptise me, perhaps not.

While we're at it, I'll throw in another couple of spooky stories...

One night I dreamt out of the blue about a guy who used to be a regular in a pub I went in some 35 years previously. He was always a miserable sod and he spoke in his normal grumpy manner to me in the dream. I'd never even thought of him in the intervening years.

A couple of hours after I awoke, I had a friendship request on Facebook: it was the daughter of the landlord of that pub. I hadn't spoken to her in all that time.

As we chatted online, she asked "*What was the name of that grumpy old sod who used to hang me up on the coat hook in the tap room when I was a little girl?*".

It was the bloke from long ago who I'd dreamt about that very night. How the hell did that happen?

I also once dreamt about an acquaintance I had known since I was a child but who I hadn't seen for years. In the dream, I was sitting on his chest and he was having difficulty breathing. I learned he had died of a heart attack a couple of days later!

While I'm on a roll. I'll throw in a few coincidences for you.

Once when I was travelling down to London on the train to attend an audition, I found my reserved seat was next to an attractive young lady in her 30s.

She told me she had been in Manchester to publicise a play she had written. (Coincidence number one: Actor sits next to playwright). She turned out to be Amy Rosenthal, the daughter of the late Jack Rosenthal, the brilliant award winning film and television scriptwriter and husband of actress Maureen Lipman. (Coincidence number two: her parents and I had mutual friends: a reporter I used to work with. I frequently stayed at his home near Blackpool many years ago and one day Amy's dad Jack gave me a lift into town to catch a bus home to Manchester).

Just a few days later came coincidence number three. Completely unrelated to the chance meeting with Amy, I got a call from my agent Debs to ask if I would be interested in doing a play in Manchester based on three Coronation Street scripts from the 1960s written by none other than Amy's dad - Jack Rosenthal.

As I love Coronation Street and given my history in it, I leapt at the chance to play the old Rovers' Return landlord Jack Walker.

Playing Jack Walker in Corrie '68 with Christine Barton Brown as snooty wife Annie.

To the delight of the cast, Jack Rosenthal's widow and Amy's Mam, Maureen, came to watch the play and I found myself sitting next to her as we watched another play at the Lass o' Gowrie pub in Manchester where our Coronation Street production was taking place. (Coincidence number four- although I knew none of them personally, I had now sat next to all three separate members of the Rosenthal family on three different occasions.

Maureen was very moved by the production and very complimentary to our cast. We spoke together on the last night and I told her about the various coincidences and she leaned towards me conspiratorially and said "*I have to tell you there is another coincidence you might like to hear about – a couple of days ago, I did a gig for charity in the Midlands and the man who organised it was called....Dave Dutton*". Hey up - coincidence number five!

Here's another…When I was front man in the comedy folk group Inclognito, I wrote a comic song called "*The Lancashire Astronaut*". This was about a guy called Albert Clegg from Wigan who built a rocket in his shed out of dustbins in order to explore outer space. Shortly after, I went up for a part in Emmerdale.

It was a whimsical one about a man who built a rocket out of bits and pieces in his shed in order to explore outer space! I didn't get the part – it went to my mate Bernard Wrigley the Bolton Bullfrog. The name of the character who built the rocket was… Barry Clegg! (Presumably Albert's brother).

I later got a part in Emmerdale as a crazy UFO spotter. That's to come…

MAMA'S PICANINNY

"Clap hands, daddy come" (He didn't)

Some people claim they can't remember much about their early years.
Others like actor Brian Blessed and the writer Ray Bradbury have
said they could even remember being born.
I can't claim that but I have a definite memory of being weighed as a
baby in a big white enamel container on the counter of a local
chemist's shop, looking up at the windows and roof of the shop
opposite and feeling the coolness of the metal on my back.
I also recall standing up in my cot and scraping the paint off the top
bars with my teeth. I must have been teething at the time but I recall
the satisfying feel of the wood against my teeth like some giant
wooden teething ring.
Being pushed in a pram round the local market by my cousin Alice
is another picture I have in my mind and I can also remember
screaming in pain after some sort of operation on my willy which I
presume was my circumcision. I remember Mam carrying me
howling up the stairs. Bradbury also remembered his circumcision.
Well, it's quite a traumatic event when you think about it.
To lull me to sleep at night, Mam always sang to me a very strange
but melodious song which, to the best of my recollection went:

"Go to sleep, Mama's picaninny,
Mama's going to smack you if you don't.
Hush a bye, rock a bye, Mama's little baby,
Mama's little Alla Balla Coo".

That was her version. Curious, I looked it up on the internet and
found out this was a not very politically correct song of the Deep
South from 1899 entitled Mama's Little Alabama Coon (alternatively
titled Stay in Your Own Back Yard), an alleged Southern Lullaby
about a little black boy who gets upset because the white kids won't
play with him!
She wouldn't have known that because her version was nothing like
the original and she would probably have been horrified.
How it ended up as a lullaby being sung to a Lancashire baby I'll
never know but the strange thing is, I still remember the words even

81

though she must have sung it to me when I was but a babe in her arms. So be careful what you say in front of your babies – they remember stuff.

She also sang "*Beebo a babbyo, Mammy's little laddyo*" but I can't remember the next line although I'm certain the last one was "*Cos he hasn't got a daddyo*" which seems a bit bizarre given the circumstances but another equally bizarre rhyme, now I come to think of it, was:

"*Clap hands, daddy come
Bring our David a cake and a bun*"

What was the point of singing that? Daddy was never going to come and bring our David a cake or a bloody bun was he? All that distant Daddy was ever going to do was send the bloody maintenance payments once a week. Apart from the times he couldn't afford it. Another bedtime favourite of hers that I remember was the kiss routine.

Mam recited:

"*Butterfly kiss*", then she fluttered her eyelashes next to mine.
"*Eskimo kiss*", then rubbed her nose against mine.
"*Horse kiss!*" (and this was the bit I never looked forward to) then she'd bite me on the cheek.

It was a playful bite and meant to be a bit of fun but it never failed to unnerve me.

You wouldn't think so looking at me now but I had quite angelic features and a shock of blonde curly hair when I was a toddler.

I can still remember the disappointment of sitting on Father Christmas's knee at Lewis's in Manchester and being given a doll because he thought I was a little girl. I was most upset.

You can see why Father Christmas might get it wrong...

According to an old diary of my Mam's, I contracted whooping cough, pneumonia, measles and mumps at various stages of my early life keeping Doctor Smythe quite busy. He was a lovely man who I later ended up having a drink with : not after he cured me of the mumps, I mean when I was old enough to be able to go in pubs. He drank halves of lager with a whisky chaser and when he'd almost emptied the glass, he shook the drops of whisky into the lager.

I remember him laughing uproariously once when I was a toddler after he put his stethoscope on my chest in his surgery and I yelled: *" Bloody hell – that's cold!"* Mam was mortified.

Music played a big part in our lives. Like most people in our town, we couldn't afford a telly but there was always the wireless and the gramophone. We had stacks of old 78 records. By the time I was three, I was already a performer: singing Teresa Brewer's hit *"Music. Music. Music"* from behind the couch for the benefit of visitors and relatives (even if I had no idea what a nickel or a nickelodeon was that was mentioned in the song).

My grandmother also used to sing me funny little rhymes such as: *"Go to bed Tom, Go to bed Tom. Father and Mother and everyone..."* - accompanying herself by rapping out the rhythm with her fingers on the arm of her chair. It used to fascinate me.

She also taught me *"Three Men They Went A-Hunting"* which included the verse:

"Three men they went a-hunting
To see what could they find
Till they came to a cow pat
And that they left behind
The Englishman said "it's a cow pat"
The Scotsman he said "nay"
And Paddy said, "it's a custard
And the crust has blown away"

I loved all that. Even wrote a song about it called *When Granny Sang Me Songs* which was recorded by several artistes.
Chorus goes:
Now the kids have television and they've pockets full of cash
They don't go short of anything but love.
And though I'm just old fashioned – I don't know the rights or wrongs
But I'd rather be back in the days when Granny sang me songs.
Just about sums it up.
She also taught me Music Hall songs from her younger days like *Put A Bit of Powder On It Father; There Was I, Waiting At The Church* and *The Little Shirt Me Mother Made For Me* and we listened to records of old stars such as the whistler Ronnie Ronalde; comedian Sandy *"Can You Hear Me Mother?"* Powell and Irish tenor Joseph Locke.
In her younger days, Mabel loved the stars of the day such as Nat Gonella and that un-PC named American black singing group The Ink Spots.

My gran, Frances Dutton and friend in a pub in Chester. We used to joke with her – which one is the bear?

One of the greatest experiences of my childhood was when Mabel took me to see the variety shows every Saturday night at the Bolton Grand Theatre.

I revelled in the excitement of it all: the lifting of the big safety curtain with adverts for Magee Marshall's Nourishing Oatmeal Stout on; the dimming of the lights; the orchestra overture...then we were off into a magical world of speciality acts.... exotically dressed knife throwers; amazing jugglers; acrobats balancing on piles of furniture; performing dogs playing football; horses that could count; sea lions juggling beach balls on their noses and clapping at their own cleverness; a man who made strange shadow puppets on the backdrop and an Indian maharajah magician producing hundreds of gold coins out of thin air.

We saw famous performers of the day such as Jimmy James; Hylda Baker; Donald Peers; Reg "Confidentially" Dixon and many more who held the audience in the palms of their hands and I often wonder if this is what sowed the seeds of the performer inside of me as, to the best of my knowledge, no-one in my family, immediate or past, had even the slightest inclination to perform in public apart from my grandfather with his concertina.

We also had two local cinemas where I went at a very early age, held spellbound by the colourful splendours of the Roman sagas such as The Robe, Quo Vadis and Demetrius and the Gladiators- all of which which made a big impression on me.

All this must have been stirring the soup of the subconscious to urge me on as a performer, resulting in my first ever public appearance aged about eight at the local Independent Methodist Sunday school pantomime where, marching up and down as a soldier in Cinderella singing *"When the guards are on parade, in their uniform so gay"* my trousers suddenly fell down and the audience burst out laughing, thus confirming Ken Dodd's old adage *"If you can't get a laugh, get 'em off!"*

My first stage performance. That's me trying to keep my hat on – shortly before failing to keep my trousers on.

I had quite a while to wait for my next stage performance though…

TIN BATHS AND DOLLY TUBS

Oooh eck! T' babby's had a cack!

It would seem very bizarre to a child these days to live the life we led then. In winter, our house was so cold there were those frost patterns that looked like leaves on the sash windows.

They were very beautiful and somewhat mysterious but that was cold comfort to us.

We had to make a fire every morning from scratch by putting up a shovel against the opening and covering it with newspaper until the updraught got the fire going.

When things went wrong, it was great fun watching Mam jumping up and down on a burning newspaper in the hearth to stamp out the flames.

Just over the fire in the living room was a clothes rack which was raised and lowered by a rope attached to a pulley. The room itself was about 16 square feet with a sofa, an armchair; a round table with some fancy inlay; an old Victorian sideboard with mirrors; a wireless and a gramophone that had seen better days – and so had the performers whose records we played.

The kitchen had all the latest "mod cons" - a gas cooker; a boiler and a big white "slopstone" sink with a cold water tap. At least our house was lit by electricity, unlike my gran's sister Betsy Alice's house which had gas mantles. I found that astonishing.

Mother or Mabel used to "donkey-stone" the steps to the house (this made them white or creamy) as to have dirty steps was frowned upon by the neighbours. There was a great pride about then that is sorely lacking these days.

People still wore their poshest clothes on Sundays – not the scruffy stained grey jogging bottoms and hoodies that pass for attire nowadays.

Sometimes the outside lavatory froze up despite our pathetic attempts to keep it usable by putting a paraffin lamp inside overnight to keep it warm.

I was always very wary of the lamp after a similar one blew up in a playmate's face and melted half of it away.

Thank goodness then for the "jerry" under the bed which saved us from taking an icy trip down to the end of the yard but which had to be slopped out in the morning like something out of Strangeways. With no proper bath in the house, we had to make do with the old tin bath which hung on a nail in the backyard. This was filled by water heated in the old gas boiler and the water sometimes had to be shared to save money. It wasn't very comfortable in there as it was more like a tin coffin than a bath and the bottom scratched your bum.

I remember Mam telling me she was once having a bath in it in front of the fire with a wooden clothes "maiden" shielding her to keep off the draught when the insurance man, Mr. Hartshorn, walked in one night without knocking. He flew down the road when she started screaming the place down.

As well as the insurance man, there was always a constant stream of people at our door in those days:

*Jean, the office girl who came for the weekly rent as the house then belonged to the mill owners.
*The gas and electricity men who came to check the meters although in those days we had to feed the meter with coins and frequently the electricity ran out causing us to fumble round in the dark for sixpence to restore the light.
*The coal man.
*The window cleaner.
*The paraffin man.
*The mobile grocer, fishmonger and butcher.
*The milkman.
*The religious types.
*The gypsy woman selling heather and offering to tell your fortune. Then allegedly curse you if you didn't buy anything.
*The Sikh salesman with his turban and large brown suitcase full of ties and silk scarves who also muttered imprecations if you failed to buy anything off him.
*The Betterware man with his "useful" household knick knacks like egg separators, salt pourers and towel holders.
*The tramp trying to obtain money usually under the pretext of asking for a glass of water.

*The knife and scissors sharpener man who had a fascinating contraption which was part of his bike and had a grinder attached to it which worked by pedal power.

*The street singer who was probably some poor war veteran and who pitifully wailed his song in the street until you paid him to move on.

*The travelling tally man who sold clothes and shoes that Mam paid so much a week for until the cost had been met. (One of them, a nice round jolly man called Mr Dawson, kindly made me a pair of stilts when I was small and I learned to parade proudly up and down our street on them).

All these people along with our many relatives, friends, playmates and neighbours came and went in a constant flow. It's a wonder the door had any hinges left.

One memorable evening a friend of Mam's called Doris Trungle popped round with her toddler. She was sitting on the couch dandling it on her knee when it suddenly did a massive shit. *"Oooh eck! T'babby's had a cack!"* she exclaimed and without further ado, insouciantly picked up the turd, wrapped it in newspaper, jumped up and threw it on our blazing coal fire!

Mam and I looked on in horror as the flames enveloped the jobby, filling the room with an eye watering foul aroma which still lingers in the memory.

Could have been worse I suppose. Could have been an electric fire.

As well as the old tin bath, I was also dunked sometimes in the old dolly tub that my Gran had previously wanted to drown me in.

This was a big round and deep metal receptacle in which clothes were washed and agitated by hand with a poncer or posser as some people called it: a long stick with a perforated metal cone on the end which crudely simulated modern washing machines.

They were then put through the mangle several times to squeeze the water out before being hung on the line.

Thankfully I wasn't mangled - although soon, life had something in store that left me feeling like I had been...

NURSERY BLUES

Oh, please take me out of here Auntie!

Mother (i.e. my gran) looked after me for a while but as she was around 70, I must have proved too much of a handful for her because it was decided I had to go into the Atherton Day Nursery while Mam worked her long hours at the Howe Bridge Cotton Mill.

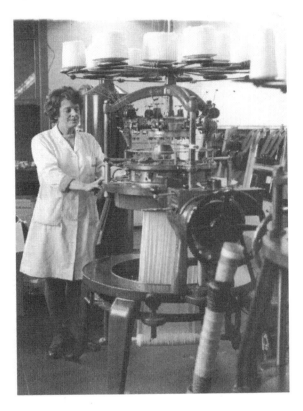

Mam at the mill

I don't know how boarders feel when first sent away to public school by their posh families but I found the whole experience traumatic to the extent that during the forced afternoon nap on the nursery camp beds, I peed myself on numerous occasions.

There was nothing wrong with the nursery: it was probably because I'd been torn away from home for the first time that caused me to wet the bed. I wasn't alone in doing this.

I recall pressing my tearstained little face against the iron bars of the nursery gates as my Auntie Alice went past on her way home and pleading: "*Oh please take me out of here Auntie!*"

She didn't. I think she was still employed at the mill.

So there I had to stay because Mam was working from 6am to 6pm to keep house and home together.

My life was made even more traumatic when one of the other "inmates" who was dressed as a cowboy kicked me between the legs shouting "*I'm Tom Mix!* " (A famous film cowboy of the time) Unfortunately, he had a clog on his foot and I felt the after-effects for some days, though thankfully no lasting structural damage was done. (Hi son)

Yes, we still wore clogs in those days and so did lots of the Lancashire millworkers. They were comfortable, hardwearing and easily repaired. They had to be as we kids spent most of the time kicking shit out of them against the pavement trying to make sparks fly off the clog irons.

After a year in the nursery and shod in natty new red clogs, I started at St. George's C of E Infants School, which I can't remember much about apart from one morning when we were ordered to gather in the school hall and the headmistress came in with a very sombre expression on her face.

"*Children, I have some very bad news*" she solemnly intoned.

"*His Majesty The King has died*".

This was King George the Sixth of course. I don't think any of us burst into tears exactly but we knew it was serious shit by the look on her face and we were more concerned about getting back into the playground to play "What Time Is It Mr.Wolf?"

Shortly after, we were all given lovely Coronation Mugs with a likeness of the new monarch on, so that was okay. I still have mine.

The only other thing I remember about my time at this school is one of the girls in my class shitting herself and the teacher going round smelling everyone's bottom in order to suss out the culprit. (I've seen that selfsame girl around town a few times and although she may be a great gran by now, I still think of her as "*that girl in our class who shit herself*".)

Not long after when halfway to school, I followed through myself and a kind lady who had spotted me through her window waddling like a ruptured duck, took me in, wiped me bum and sent me on my merry way. It must have been all that castor oil they gave us.

For what reason I do not know, but I have always instinctively disliked meat.

I've been a vegetarian for well over 45 years but even as a nipper I must have had the makings of one as I remember the school dinner lady trying to force feed me some deceased beast.

"Come on now. Don't be silly. Eat it or you'll never be a big lad".

Well I didn't eat it and I **did** become a big lad Mrs Dead Dinner Lady.

In those much safer times there was no school run because nobody had a car and I walked on my own to school, which was well over half a mile away, from the age of five.

I was reasonably happy in the infants' school but when the time came to go up to junior school, St. George's didn't want me (not a clue why) and I was assigned to Howe Bridge Junior School - a trolley bus ride away in a neighbouring pit village.

It was an old Victorian building and the first thing that hit you in the eye as you walked through the main door was a beautifully tiled fireplace bearing the suitably stern Victorian inscription "*Manners Maketh Man*" in ornate lettering over the mantelpiece. Mabel had been a pupil there in the 20's and, incredibly, Mrs Phyllis Hodgson, one of her teachers, also taught me. She even remembered my Mam. Although next to a main road, there was an ancient farm next to the playground and fields behind, in which we lay and held buttercups under each other's chins to "*see if you like butter*".

We played children's games like In and Out The Windows, Hopscotch - not forgetting the age old lads' challenge - "*who can wee highest up the lavatory wall?*"

I joined the school recorder group but was hopeless at it as I couldn't get the hang of reading music no matter how it was taught.

I took part in the big school concert and mimed the whole way through it with my Mam looking on beamingly and blissfully unaware.

My mate Incey was as bad as me and could only mime too but he got found out by the furious headmaster and was caned. I lived in constant fear of being the next victim.

The stage beckoned yet again when I was persuaded by a young lady from theatre in education to play an Eskimo – ok, ok, an Inuit - singing "Hills of the North Rejoice" for a school play.

To allay our stagefright, she told us to look at the audience and imagine they were just cabbages. I've played to a few of those since. I was really looking forward to the big night but a mass outbreak of chickenpox temporarily wiped out most of the cast.

I turned my creative endeavours towards writing dirty poems about girls and knickers and suchlike but the teacher caught me passing them round and sent them to my Mam who gently chastised me.

All seemed set fair for my next phase of schooling but life was about to hand out a lesson of its own. A kick in the bollocks with a clog, as it were.

What I learned at school next was that I was "*different*".

Christmas 1951 Atherton Day Nursery. I'm first kid on the right, third row, standing next to the kid who kicked me in the goolies with his clog.
I'm probably thinking, he's better beside me than in front of me...

BASTARD

"He's spurious. He's false!"

It's playtime. Best time of the school day, apart from going home time.
A few of my classmates and I are hanging round the school entrance.
I take an old dictionary out of my pocket and say:
"Hey lads. Let's have some fun. I've brought this dictionary from home. Let's look up some swear words!"
They're up for this. So we do. A seemingly innocuous way of passing the time and probably something done by curious schoolkids since Dr Johnson wrote the bloody thing.
How was I to know that as a result of this simple act, a few moments later, I would suddenly become an outsider. Well that's how I saw it.
I was nine years old and it was a long long time ago but if I close my eyes, I can still visualise that battered old red family dictionary.
We jostled eagerly together as we looked up the so called rude words.
After sniggering over the explanation of "prostitute", I daringly suggest we look up the word "bastard": an expression some of us had heard being used by the big lads.
"Yeah. Go on. Look that up. That word. Bastard" they urge, nudging one another in anticipation.
Thumbing down the words beginning with B, I finally alight on it.
"Come on. What does it say?" shout my mates. *"Oh, er, nowt really"*, I reply attempting to shut the book.
"Eh? Nowt? Must mean summat. Give the book here" shouts one and snatches it out of my grasp.
The others crane their necks over his shoulder.
"Well? Come on. What does it say?"
He looks at the definition intently; furrows his brows and speaks haltingly but loudly.
"It says: *'Spurious...false...fatherless...born...out...of...wedlock.' That's what it says*".
He narrows his eyes and slowly points at me.
"Hey. *Dutton's no dad has he? That's fatherless innit? That means HE'S one of them - a bastard. He's spurious. He's false! HE'S a bastard!*"

Then he throws the book back at me and they all run away laughing and shouting.

Leaving me alone.

Very alone.

I stand in that corner of the playground, dazed and confused, trying to take in what has just happened.

A fundamental change has taken place.

From being part of the gang, I suddenly feel like a stranger in a cold, unfriendly world. What certainties I had up to then are all shattered in that cruel moment of revelation.

There is a line in a poem by Philip Larkin that asks *"what was the rock my gliding childhood struck?"*

That moment was the rock my childhood foundered on. From being a part of everything, I felt apart from everything.

Whether imagined or not, after this incident I felt like everyone was behaving differently towards me because that's what I now understood myself to be. Different. Not like the others. If someone threw a snowball at me, I thought it was because they didn't like me. If someone wouldn't join in a game with me, I thought it was because I wasn't like them. I was the kid with his nose to the window looking at everyone having a good time outside.

Imperceptibly, I began to change. At an age when self assurance is needed most, I began to lack confidence and that remained with me for many years. I became shy and introverted.

I tentatively approached a neighbour called Eric who was only two years older than me and told him what had happened. I asked him why I didn't have a dad.

He reasoned: *"Well everybody has a dad. Yours isn't here but somebody must've shagged your Mam. Go and ask her"*.

So I did.

I confronted her in the front room of our house: *"Why have I not got a dad and everybody else has? Where is he?"*

My Mam's face fell. She turned slowly to Mother.

"I've been dreading this" she said sadly.

"Well?! Where is he?!"

My Gran wrung her hands together...

"Tell him Mabel tell him!"

The strange thing is, I have no recollection of what happened next. I was in such a state, it's all a haze. She muttered some sort of explanation but I couldn't take it in.

I can't even remember the time that my dad's name was revealed to me by my mother but strangely, whenever he was mentioned in our house, it was always by his surname.

She never referred to him by his first name: it was always Grant. At one time I thought that was his first name as that was the only reference she ever made to him.

Not long afterwards I called her a slut. I'm sure it was in the wrong context and God only knows where I got that word from: probably that bloody family dictionary; but it hurt her immensely.

I know now that what she and my father had together wasn't just an affair. It was a love affair and she adored him until the moment she died but I wasn't to know that then.

I was an angry, sad, confused, bitter, fatherless kid who needed answers in a world that wasn't so cosy any more.

My behaviour took a turn for the worse. It wasn't helped by further events at the school.

The exact spot where we looked at the dictionary all those years ago

MR NOBODY

"I can't hear you Mister Nobody"

Shortly after the dictionary incident, a pair of relief teachers who were husband and wife step into the classroom. As is the way with useless, lazy teachers, they tell us to read something from our textbooks and not to talk in class. They then leave the room together. When the woman returns unexpectedly, she catches me talking and decides to stamp her petty authority on the class by making an example of me.
She stops, narrows her eyes and points directly at me.
"You there. Stand up!"
I slowly stand.
"I said there was to be no talking in class. Don't you think it applies to you? Do you think you are someone special?"
I stare down at the floor.
"Well do you?"
"No Miss"
"Well I'll tell you who you are. You're Mister Nobody".
She spits out the last two words with such bitter emphasis that it shocks me.
There is sniggering in the classroom.
She opens a drawer and pulls out a sheet of paper with some words on. She must have been saving it for such an occasion.
"This is a poem called Mister Nobody. You'll write it out and keep writing it out until I tell you to stop. Have you got that Mister Nobody?"
I nod.
"I can't hear you Mister Nobody"
"Yes Miss" I croak, my head bowed towards the floor and tears starting to sting my eyes.
"Well get on with it", she snarls and leaves the room.
I can still picture her podgy, uncaring blancmange of a face and that of her skinny weasel-featured husband.
It's well over half a century ago but it blasted the confidence out of me. If someone in authority tells a nine years old you that you're Mister Nobody then that's who you must be.
Everyone was looking at me.

Me. The Bastard.

Me. False.

Me. Mister Nobody.

Obviously I look at myself differently now but at the time it helped to re-emphasise my lack of self-worth. With such muddy daubs is the canvas of our early life besmirched by those who should know better.

Unwittingly though and a lot further down the line, this crass individual may have helped this particular Mister Nobody to want to become a Mister Somebody by shaking off that unwanted title.

In a strange way, much later in life, it probably made me want to do as well as possible and sent me down another track which emphasised my "differentness". I have never really wanted a 9 to 5 normal existence or to be like other folk. I probably have that dictionary to thank for it.

Unsurprisingly, I started to really hate school after this.

There was a print on the school corridor wall of a painting by Victorian artist William Frederick Yeames about the English Civil War in which a fearful Royalist child is being quizzed by a stern Parliamentarian who asks: "*When did you last see your father?*"

I passed it all the time and used to think well at least he had a bloody father. It was yet another reminder I could have done without.

The smallest thing could have an affect on me in those days.

I remember Des O'Connor making a joke on the telly which went: "*Did you hear about the illegitimate Rice Krispy? – He had a snap; a crackle but no Pop*".

To a sensitive kid, making a joke about having no dad didn't seem right.

Likewise, the song "The Little Boy that Santa Claus Forgot" which had a line about feeling sorry for the laddie cos he doesn't have a Daddy and that's why Santa forgot him. That didn't seem bloody fair either.

I began to stay away from school at the slightest excuse. I used to go missing from home, sending my Mam frantic with worry.

One day a parent of a schoolmate found me on a freezing Winter morning trudging aimlessly up to my knees through a field full of snow in the middle of nowhere. She took me to her home and dried me out.

Another teacher by the name of Mrs Land took a dislike to me. She was a big fat overbearing, white-haired bully of a woman who was hated by most of the children to the extent that 40 years later I met an old schoolfriend whose eyes blazed and mouth foamed at the mention of her name.

During one lesson she slapped me and Mabel marched down to deal with her the following day and it was all they could do to stop her slapping the old cow back in return.

When the headmaster Mr Dagnall gave me a beating with the cane for merely replying to someone who had spoken to me in the class lineup, I decided I hated the lot of them even more.

My attendances became fewer and fewer. Sometimes I hid in the back yard of our house and on one occasion I spent most of the day lying still on top of the shed. My half blind grandmother thought I was a cat.

I hid in the back midden when it was the funeral of Mr Hughes, a lovely old next-door neighbour and watched through a hole in the wall as the funeral party gathered in the next yard. I remember being upset because some of them were laughing and it didn't seem right to do that when someone had just died.

I started to steal. Lots of kids did. Not big stuff: I sometimes nicked marbles from Woolworth's or sweets from the toffee shop. I lifted money from my Mam's purse in order to go on the fair. I kept money from my grandmother's change when I did errands and told her I had lost it down the grid. I suppose that's how Al Capone started! Small stuff.

On many occasions, I disappeared until late at night, sometimes associating with older boys who were bad influences, including one who later "got sent away".

I can see now how easy it is for good kids to turn bad.

UP ON THE ROOF

Please God, don't let the Devil push me off...

I'm not saying I was really bad but I freely confess I got up to all
sorts of mischief which landed me in trouble: but not big trouble.
Okay, there was the time the local fire brigade had to rescue me off
the roof of a local cafe...
It was a warm autumn evening in 1956. Crowds of people are
making their way home from Atherton's two cinemas - the grandly-
named Savoy and the Palace.
Suddenly, attracted by the sound of a fire engine, they make a detour
down a cobbled back street.
Most of them are holding bags of hot chips which they feed one by
one into their mouths as they gaze spellbound towards a rickety
chimney on the roof of an old Victorian building called The Coffee
Pot Cafe. They can't see me. I'm hiding behind that chimney.
I had climbed up a drainpipe with two of my mates (one was my
friend Sandra, the other was a fireman's son called Derek) just
because like Everest, it was there.
Recalling the incident, Sandra told me years later:

*"Derek and I climbed the pipe but you couldn't so I came down and
gave you a peg up.*
*When you got to the top you got scared (the guttering appeared to be
moving away from the roof) so we put you behind the chimney.*
*Derek came down but you couldn't so I said I would put you on my
back.*
How stupid was that? We could both have been killed!
My Mam came round the corner and shouted **'Put that child back
behind the chimney!'**
She slapped me all the way home for taking you up there.
*Derek must have told his dad as the fire engine arrived shortly
after..."*

Indeed they did. A fireman slowly climbs a ladder towards me as I
suddenly discover religion - praying fervently and pleading: " *Please
God, don't let the Devil push me off the roof* "...

"*Come on son - let go of the chimney*" urges the kindly-faced fireman, reaching out towards me. "*I've come to get you down*".
"*I can't. I'm frightened to let go*" I sniff tearfully.
Slowly, he coaxes me towards him down the sloping slate roof then suddenly grabs me tightly and puts me over his shoulder in a classic fireman's lift.
I see the upturned faces of the chip-eating crowd as he backs down the ladder step by step..
When he puts me down on the ground, the crowd applaud and I am whisked into a nearby house where my name and address are taken.
"*Please don't tell me Mam*" I beg tearfully.
"*We'll have to son*"
"*Oh no!*" I wail.
They also told the papers.

It's still there. The drainpipe and the chimney I hid from the Devil behind. Might give it another go…

The following day, I was at my Auntie Phyllis's when along came a local reporter wanting to interview me about my rescue.

"*Tell him to bugger off!*" I yelled as I threw myself face down upon my bed.

He buggered off but they still put a story in the next edition of the Leigh, Atherton and Tyldesley Journal. Now the entire bloody town knew as well as my Mam.

Mam picking me up from Auntie Phyllis's the day after my rooftop rescue. Thank goodness she's still smiling.

It was the first of many times I appeared in that publication but as the years went on, it was for more positive reasons.

More and more I seemed to be getting into all sorts of scrapes.

My best mate then was the aforementioned Eric who lived in our street and was two years older than me. He taught me lots of very important things, such as the facts of life; how to fish and the ancient art of the five knuckle shuffle. *winks

103

Eric and I went fishing a lot and on one occasion, he saved my life when I slid down the steep muddy bank of the local Perch Pond (actually an old mine working) and went straight under the cold, murky brown water.

He had the presence of mind to grab the overhanging branch of a tree, lean out and hold out his fishing rod which I managed to grab the end of, enabling him to haul me to safety. I stripped off and hung my clothes on a hawthorn bush to dry while Eric blithely carried on fishing for perch.

They didn't dry properly and my Mam wasn't best pleased when I arrived home in stinking, soaking wet clothes. Neither was she exactly delighted when, in another escapade with Sandra, I stood in some quicksandy stuff (or sink slutch as we called it) near an old pit slag heap and lost a pair of brand-new sandals which were sucked into the quagmire. They had cost Mam a lot of money she could ill afford.

I turned up at her workplace soaking wet again shortly after when I fell off my bike after attempting to ride through some flash floods: completely ruining my clothes.

I even fell in the River Dee at Chester. I was reminded of this by an old schoolmate, Susan Knowles who was at junior school with me. She told me

"We were having our picnic by the Dee and - of course - messing about, one minute you were dry next minute ABSOLUTELY drenched! Think it was our form teacher Mrs Hodgson who wrapped you in a coat.

You must have slipped and gone full length in the river. We were on Dee banks by the pedestrian bridge - we are not far from Chester and I always think about that day when walking by the river".

After water, it was fire's turn to feature next as a mate named Geoff Ince and I, going through our junior arsonist stage took perverse delight in setting light to fields: the favourites being the ones behind what was called the Top Field at the edge of town.

We watched on with glittering eyes as the tinder dry grass blazed spectacularly and the conflagration could be seen from quite a distance.

Indeed it was spotted by the acutely-sighted and brilliantly-named PC Baskeyfield, a big bear of a bobby on a bike who sneaked up behind us and shouted "*Gotcha!*"as we gazed proudly at our incendiary handiwork.

Incey and I shot off in opposite directions and Big Bobby Baskeyfield gave chase. After a few hundred yards, Incey yelled and flung himself prostrate in the grass hoping Baskeyfield would leave him for dead and chase me.

Instead, being no mug, the wily bobby grabbed him by the scruff of the neck and proceeded to wring my identity out of him. The snitch.

Thinking I was safe, I ran all the way home and hid the incriminatory matches on the windowsill and had my tea.

A little later there was a knock on the door and my Mam opened it to find the light blocked by Big Bobby Baskeyfield.

"*Mrs Dutton?*" he enquired.

"*What's he done now?*" she asked apprehensively.

"*He's been setting fire to things*" he said.

"*What?! Our David wouldn't do that! You'd better come in*" she sighed.

I didn't crack. Even though he offered to belt me ("*Yes, you do and you'll get one back*" said Mam) I didn't admit guilt.

He tried for ages but I denied all knowledge of the fires.

Thus defeated, he went but not without giving me an "*I-know-you-are-bloody-well-guilty-and-this-is-not-the-last-you-will-hear-of-this*" spine chilling sort of glare.

My Mam shut the door, turned to me and said: "*Tell me the truth David. Did you set fire to those fields?*"

"*No Mam. Honest*" I convincingly lied.

"*I believe you son*" she said, proudly patting my shoulder. "*He's nowt but a bully that Baskeyfield*".

Next morning, she was cleaning the front windows when she found the incriminating box of matches on the windowsill.

"*You're nowt but a bloody little liar*" she screamed, now totally unconvinced of my honesty.

I couldn't deny it but in case you're wondering, that's the last time I set light to anything I shouldn't have. Apart from toast. Underlying all these shenanigans though was my feeling of being different and the way it had affected me due to the events at school.

There's a big difference between being adventurous or naughty and being bad. There definitely was a time when the chip on my shoulder could have turned into a log.

A wrong word; a perceived slight that gets blown into a major event in an impressionable young mind and mixing with the wrong company has sent many a kid down the wrong path. My mother was a good woman and I bitterly regret now the hurt I must have caused her at that time.

Mabel despaired of me so much she attempted to frighten me out of my errant ways by dragging me off to that local police station in Water Street which was a formidable old brooding Victorian building with a cell.

She told the bobby she was at her wits' end and asked him to speak to me. That is when he slammed shut the door and locked me in the cell to stew in my own thoughts for a while.

I have often wondered what the turning point in my young life was and I think this may indeed have been a pivotal moment for me.

It pointed out a possible future and a bleak one at that. It must have flicked a switch in my mind which diverted me from the wrong path in life to the right one.

Nothing else I can think of had such a powerful effect on me. The short, sharp shock worked in my case. Thank God or rather that old Bobby way back then.

I no longer stole or stayed off school or mixed with the bad guys. My mate Eric and I even joined the church choir though that didn't last long, as the initiation into the choir entailed being chucked into the middle of a holly bush by the rest of the choristers and the choirmaster was an evil old sod who used to rap your knuckles hard with a ruler if you sang out of tune. Which in my case was often.

Oh and after choir practice Eric and I also used to nick apples from the vicar's garden but that's not proper stealing is it?

We were asked to paint "The view from my bedroom window" at junior school. This was mine – all I could see was the sodding factory. Very abstract though, eh?

A FIFTIES KID

I draw a snake upon your back...

I was one of the last generation of those kids who could play games in their own street.
There were very few cars about, the cobbles were our playground and our joy was in playing out till it went dark.
The names of the games we played have a Proustian ability to conjure up those times again: British Bulldog; Queenie; I Draw a Snake upon your Back; Red Rover; Kick out Ball; Sheppy Custard; Rolly 1-2-3; Jack Jack Shine Your Light and Piggy - an ancient game played with a stick and a piece of wood shaped like a pig that you flicked up in the air and hit as far as you could.
We made bogeys. Yes I know most kids make bogeys but these were very special ones with wheels on.
They were two short planks of wood loosely bolted together on top of four old pram wheels and dexterously steered by the use of your feet and a length of twine.
We raced one another down the steepest embankments that we could find: not caring if we were thrown headlong and headfirst into the ground.
We wore our scars with pride and all kids then had scabby knees.
We loved our bikes. They were to us like Trigger the horse was to Roy Rogers: indispensable for getting around on.
Mine was an old "sit-up-and-beg" BSA bike that Mam had bought second hand.
The other kids in our gang had fancier bikes but that didn't stop me joining in and customizing mine by folding up a fag packet and placing it so it made a whirrrrring noise as the spokes rattled on it.
We regularly went on our bikes to a local beauty spot called Rivington Pike: a round trip of over 20 miles.
No wonder we were fit. One day I had wagged off school to go "Up Rivvy".
A photographer snapped us and it ended up in the local Journal.
Rumbled! I got a right bollocking from Mam over that.

Here's that damned pic that got me in bother. L-R Kenny Hall; me looking like Just William; Bernard Atherton; Anne Shaw and Sandra Marquick. Like the Famous Five, only there's six of us. We were concentrating on the camera and seconds after this photo was taken, we all collided and ended up in a heap. It was me I'm afraid – you can see my handlebars edging towards Bernard's.

We spent ages in the local swimming baths. If you didn't have a proper bath in the house it was a great way to get clean if you could put up with the acrid fumes off the skin-blasting red carbolic soap they gave us.

I became a good swimmer and even represented the school. Swimming made us ravenous and we stuffed our faces with Jammie Dodgers or Wagon Wheels which, incidentally, seemed 300 times bigger than they do today.

Although no-one could ever match up to Stan in Mabel's eyes, she did have a few boyfriends (and potential dads for me I suppose) when I was growing up but they never seemed to last long.

One of them, a nice enough quiet sort of chap, took me to the baths one day.

When I got home, Mabel asked how we'd got on together.

"Oh great Mam" I replied. *"Although he has got a lot of hairs round his willy".*

She binned him shortly after!

I used to love sweets such as Spangles; Cherry Lips; Toffee Fish; Blackjacks; Chocstix (hollow barley sugar filled with chocolate); Refreshers; Swizzles; Kali and Spanish and my particular favourite –

Flying Saucers which were rice paper shaped like UFOs and containing fizzy sherbet that sent your teeth to an early grave.

When we couldn't afford sweets, Mam made a cone out of a bit of paper and filled it with cocoa mixed with sugar which I dipped my finger in and licked as I watched the cowboy films at the "Saturday Rush": the matinee performance at the local cinema especially for kids.

We took our peashooters to the flicks, filled our mouths with maple peas and let fly a barrage at the fire extinguishers at the side of the stage, making a satisfying noise like a machine gun. Ratatatatatt!

I remember dropping mine one Saturday and bent to pick it up to find it covered in piss from where the kids in the higher seats had urinated. Undaunted, I wiped it on my sleeve, put it back to my lips and carried on firing it.

Some of us aimed at the cinema screen because there was a myth that if you hit it hard enough, it would burst into flames. That's all it was – a myth I'm afraid. It never erupted no matter how hard you blew and believe me we all tried.

Although I was skinny as a child I was rarely picked on by others. The only serious bullying I got was from a lad aptly named Crook who used to waylay me every time he saw me and give me a few sly digs in the ribs. This happened over a few weeks so I told Mabel about it.

"If it happens again, give him a good hard punch" she advised.

I remonstrated with her because I was a swimmer not a fighter but she insisted I do it otherwise he would just keep picking on me. So I did.

I bumped into him round the corner from our house and sure enough he started to jab me so I pulled back my fist, aimed for his guts and let him have it with all my might. Only I missed.

My fist crashed right into the wooden railings outside the factory causing me to yell out loud. Instead of taking advantage to finish me off with an uppercut or whatever, young Crook was most solicitous. He checked that I hadn't broken my knuckles before going on his merry way. After that, he was always nice as pie. I think the fact I took à swing at him gave him new found respect for me and he always greeted me like a long lost friend.

I read every comic I could get my hands on.

My Auntie Alice bought me the Dandy and the Beano every week even until I was into my 20s. My cousin Norman passed onto me his copy of the Eagle which was a graphically brilliant with cutaways of all the latest aeroplanes, liners, tanks etc showing their inner workings.

Among my other favourites were the Hotspur; Wizard; Lion;Victor; Rover and Adventure comics.These had proper stories in them that fired the imagination and you had to be able to read properly to understand them: in fact it's probably a misnomer to call them comics in the first place.

A working class lad like me always identified with Alf Tupper the Tough of the Track: an amazing athlete who was a welder and usually beat a load of toffs to the finishing line just after finishing his pile of fish and chips.

I also devoured piles of American imports like Batman; Superman; the Green Lantern; Sad Sack; Archie; and scores of others probably each worth a fortune in its own right now.

There was Film Fun; Radio Fun; Buster; Beezer; Whizzer and Chips... the list seemed endless.

Like many of my generation, I was a voracious reader. I suppose it was because we didn't have any televisions early on to distract us.

I read everything I could get my hands on including classics like David Copperfield; Treasure Island; Kidnapped; The Black Arrow; Coral Island; Children of the New Forest; Robinson Crusoe and many more.

The strange thing was lots of us working class lads were also attracted to books about posher kids such as William Brown in the Just William books who came from a middle-class family and we adored reading about Billy Bunter and his upper class chums at Greyfriars public school. It was another world to us and we were fascinated by it.

One character from the comics I didn't like was Limp along Leslie who was a young amateur footballer with a gammy leg.

When I broke my leg and returned to school one wag used to call me that on account of the way the break had left my foot sticking out slightly.

That wasn't as bad as "toady" which was what one jealous female friend of a girlfriend used to call me. She even scrawled it on our back gate which I suppose was the equivalent of being trolled on Facebook today.

The Factory Street (East) Gang.

GIVE US THIS DAY

Chips with (almost) everything...

Food was basic but filling and Mother made delicious cakes called Maids of Honour containing jam and ground almonds and my particular Lancashire favourite called Singing Lily: a flat cake made of shortcrust pastry, crammed with raisins and delicious served hot with best butter slathered over it.

Equally delicious was the Bobby's Helmet (stop it!) which I think was made from shredded coconut and condensed milk and shaped like a policeman's hat.

I'll tell you what wasn't delicious – the raw egg beaten in milk that Mam used to make me gulp before I went off to school. She also put sherry in it if I was ill.

I think it was supposed to build me up but it merely made me feel nauseous. Malt off a spoon was another health craze of the time which was supposed to make kids grow into strapping adults.

Another fad was the Ginger Beer Plant. Every home seemed to have one of these weird things which was yeast fed with sugar, lemon juice and ginger and which grew in size like some alien blob then was split and passed on to a friend or relative – hence the proliferation.

Food was basic because the choice was limited although every Sunday we inevitably had tinned salmon, followed by home made potato cakes and celery then pineapple chunks in tinned milk.

Food rationing only ended completely shortly before my seventh birthday with the lifting of restrictions on the sale of meat and bacon. I can remember queuing in a church hall with my auntie Alice to receive ration coupons.

Mother liked a bit of tripe now and again as a treat. Some treat. She tried to get me to eat it and it tasted like a wash leather soaked in vinegar.

There were also Savoury Ducks (nicknamed Slavvery Ducks) which were a faggot like concoction but god only knows what went into them – butcher's floor sweepings I reckon.

We didn't have a fridge: we kept perishables in a curious thing called a meat safe which was a small cupboard with a grille on the front.

The chip shop was a focal point of the community and a very handy feeding station for working-class families in those days.

If we weren't feeling flush, we could have a "Threepenny mix" at the local chippy which was three penny's worth of chips covered in peas to which could be added a plentiful helping of "scraps" - bits of batter left over from battering the fish and which were deliciously crispy and cost nowt.

People wanting something more substantial asked for "babby's yeds" (baby's heads) - the colloquial name for a steak pudding which was placed in a bowl and covered in gravy.

When we were kids we used to loosen the tops on the condiment bottles then skedaddle before the next unfortunate customer ended up with his fish and chips swamped in salt or vinegar.

Our chippy was taken over by a cockeyed man who confused customers by looking at them and enquiring *Next?* —and everybody looked at one another because nobody could figure out who he was talking to.

The taste for foreign food came in when people started to travel abroad but the furthest we usually got was Blackpool or Rhyl where my "Auntie" Nellie (Mam's godmother actually) had a caravan.

The caravan site was a converted farmer's field in Towyn. It had no toilet block which meant we had to use the chemical bog next to the caravan.

I dreaded going into that dark pungent box where everybody else relieved themselves and can still remember the eye-watering pong even today. We went year after year to that caravan and, despite the smell of the loo, I loved it.

Mabel and me in Towyn, N Wales

Not a crab. Cheeky. It's me on the beach at Towyn...

Blackpool illuminations brought a special magic into a child's life at that time and sometimes neighbours hired a coach and travelled together on a "chara trip"and gave sixpence to the kid who was the first to spot the Tower – singing popular songs of the day there and back. Do you even know your neighbours these days?

We didn't have a television so I used to enjoy staying overnight at my Auntie Phyllis's house to watch hers. Not that there was a great deal to watch because there were no programmes at all broadcast between 6 and 7 PM in order to get kids off to bed to fool them that the BBC had shut down for the night!

In between programmes, were "interludes" where you could watch such fascinating subjects as an old woman working a spinning wheel; kittens playing with a ball of string or someone making something sloppy on a potter's wheel. And you think telly is crap today!

When ITV finally arrived in 1955, I lapped up the American imports such as Dragnet; Maverick; Hawaiian Eye; Cheyenne and 77, Sunset Strip. The latter featured a cool dude called Kookie who was always combing his hair and was a prototype Fonzie. We all wanted to be Kookie.

America seemed like another planet to a lad from the backwaters of Lancashire and when I finally got to visit New York, I felt like I was on some fantastic film set.

I can also recall being scared shitless by such sci-fi classics as Quatermass and the Pit; The Trollenberg Terror and the Strange World of Planet X – sometimes hiding behind my Auntie's couch during the really frightening bits.

I was reasonably healthy as a kid: apart from a prolonged spell of impetigo which my Mam swore I had caught off the dirty Noah's Ark ride on the fair. Kept me off junior school for quite a while and none of the other local kids were allowed to play with me.

The odd cold was cured by mysterious little round grey pills called "lung healers" in which Mam had great faith and Mother kept herself regular by the use of Andrews liver salts and some quackery called Bile Beans which apparently were essential to inner health.

A feverish head could be cured by the application of a piece of cloth soaked in vinegar and sickly kids were frequently given pobs which were bits of bread soaked in warm milk and sprinkled with sugar: presumably being the only food the invalid could face.

116

The worst that could happen would be to get toothache and be sent to the local dentist-cum-butcher by the name of Mr Ackers who was feared more than Satan.

In fact to my generation, he was Satan. He hadn't grasped the concept of anaesthetics: restraining you by the dexterous use of his knee in your groin while his pliers attacked your teeth with blood spurting everywhere.

You only have to mention Old Ackers to men and women of a certain age in my home town and their legs buckle under.

At Uncle Walt and Auntie Phyllis's in Northwich. Taken a split second after banging my head on that bloody windowsill. Mam hasn't noticed or perhaps she's just ignoring my fruity swear words.

DENNIS THE MENACE

Geroff an' milk it!

I led a bit of a charmed existence in those days: being known to the blokes at the nearby fire station as Dennis the Menace as they often patched me up and poured Dettol over a wound after being involved in a scrape. It became like a field hospital to me.

This led to being known generally around town as Dennis for a while and some oldsters who remember from those days still refer to me as such. (I've also been known as Sam; Sammy; Dutty; Diddy David and other more scabrous names).

I'd always been a bit of a daredevil. From an early age, I fell out of countless trees; climbed on top of the local factories; walked narrow ledges across a mill "lodge" of steaming water where previous generations of kids had sometimes drowned and I delighted in taking part in tribal pitched street battles with local gangs, chucking stones and lumps of coal at one another. When I was about 5, I went missing on a little three-wheeler bike I had been bought for my birthday.

A policeman found me two miles away pedalling furiously in the middle of traffic on a busy main road in Leigh and returned me safely home.

Shortly after, I was banned from using it outside so I rode out the front door in a tantrum and somersaulted over the handlebars, splitting my chin open and still bearing the scar today: an early manifestation of the genetic Dutton temper.

Me on my Twinky three-wheeler....where to pedal off next? Rhyl perhaps?

One day, while rummaging in the front room cupboard, I found a flattish bottle with a strange flipup cap and stars on the side. My curiosity piqued, I open it and smelled the contents. It was quite pungent but intriguing so I took a drink. It felt very warm and exotic.It was my gran's brandy and from then on, I developed a taste for it. Couldn't have been more than six. She couldn't understand why it kept disappearing and my equally puzzled Mam tentatively offered an explanation...

"It must evaporate or summat, Mother"

I was a bit too inquisitive for my own good. I was lucky to escape with my life when I unscrewed the lightbulb out of my bedside lamp and stupidly poked my fingers into the socket. Not surprisingly, it flung me backwards to the foot of the bed leaving me with burnt digits, shellshock and a lifelong aversion to anything of an electrical nature.

We got up to some stupid tricks in those days. Our gang had staple fights which involved stringing elastic bands between two large wooden clothes pegs and firing sharply-pointed metal staples at each other. (Stick to yer Nintendos kids)

After the fight you ended up covered in little red horseshoe marks where the staples pinged into your bare flesh. My mate Eric got one straight between the eyes above the bridge of his nose and we had to

119

pull it out, leaving him with two punctures as though he'd been bitten on his nose by a kinky vampire. An inch to the left and he would have been blinded.

Indeed, one lad was blinded when a home-made arrow fashioned from a piece of cane with a nail for a point which was hurled from a string slingshot went straight into his eye like 'Arold at 'Astings.

As Bonfire Night approached me and my mate Alan fought battles with roman candles – aiming the blazing multi coloured balls of fire at one another's heads across the street.

We also chucked bangers at each other: big buggers called twopenny cannons. One lad in our gang forgot he was holding one and it exploded in his hand causing his fingers to burst like fried sausages.

When we weren't climbing on top of factories or swinging on ropes over streams, we went on the railway lines and put pennies (the old ones) on the track, then hid in the bushes.

After the steam train went over it only yards away, we rushed to collect them as they were flattened out to twice their normal size.

We must have had more money than sense as we couldn't spend them: only gaze in wonder at them for about two seconds. Then did it again.

I wasn't even safe on roller skates.. We had a greengrocer with a horse and cart who went by the nickname of Billy Milk- an old hunchback bent double like someone out of a Lowry painting who, it was rumoured, was cruelly made to sleep on the stable floor next to his horse by his brother.

The poor animal was nothing more than a bag of bones and it normally plodded through the streets at a very sedate pace. That is until the day I decided to hitch a ride by grabbing the back of the cart.

All was going well until it turned into a cobbled street and the rattle of the roller skates caused it to bolt.

The poor bugger had never moved as fast in its life and I clung on the back yelling "*Help!!!*"as I sailed past my startled Mam who was standing at the front door with her mouth wide open.

We parted ways at the end of the street when the nag turned a corner and I went clattering face first into the factory wall.

For all this, there was nothing to compare with the excitement the Wakes brought to town. That was the local name for the Fair.

This was THE big event.

The caravans with shiny chrome-plated sides lined the streets around the local spare land known as The Brickfield.

Underneath them lay the chained up guard dogs, usually massive alsatians, which leapt out barking ferociously at you should you dare venture too close. The grownups used to tell you scary stories that the alleged gypsies amongst the wakes folk might kidnap you and take you away with them and put spots on your face!

Two of the regular Wakes men were brothers who had suffered horrific burns. It was said they had thrown a match into an oil drum, not realising there was petrol in it and it exploded in their faces. (Strangely enough, I once sat next to a showman's daughter at dinner on a cruise who actually knew them and she told me one of the brothers had died – on a cruise).

Excitement built and we watched in wonderment as the travelling fair gradually took shape... the Waltzer; the Noah's Ark; Chairoplanes, the Dodgems; the Big Wheel; the Whip and all the various side-stalls.

As we walked nearer and nearer, the pop music of the day got louder and louder and the flashing coloured lights of the rides got brighter and the throb of the mighty generators with names like King Kong echoed the throbbing of our own hearts.

The little uns made for the small roundabouts and sat in an open-top Dragon or a small trolley bus or aeroplane and went round and round waving at their Mams and Dads.

The big uns flocked to the Waltzer which spun them round giddily or the Caterpillar, which proved popular with lads and lasses because when the green corrugated cover came over half-way through the ride making it look like a giant caterpillar and hid the people, that was when they had a quick snog

Many a flirtation - and probably a marriage or two - started on the bumpy old Caterpillar ride.

Next to the Penny Slot Arcade was Butterworth's Black Pea Saloon where "musical fruit" (as they were christened by the uncouth) were a specialty.

Maple peas were boiled in a large coke-fired rusty cauldron and served in thick white, often chipped, cups.

They were eaten in their own gravy with a spoon and had a taste of their very own.

121

It may have been the fumes off the coke or the rust from the cauldron that produced a certain je ne sais quoi but try as you may, they never tasted as good when you made them at home.

I gave some to a mate from London once and he thought I was trying to poison him.

We rode our bikes down terrifyingly steep hills; scaled cotton mills; slid down massive slag heaps on corrugated iron sleds and dropped bricks down the capped off mine shaft of the Old Pretoria Pit to hear them splash in the water hundreds of feet below not knowing all those poor souls had died in the explosion down there.

In later years, I learned a local lad called Frederick Stanley Houghton had perished there along with his father and two elder brothers.

He was just 13 and his body was never recovered. Little did we know when we were playing our childhood games that we were dropping bricks on the graves of so many brave men and boys.

I hope young Fred forgave us kids who were not much younger than him for playing on his last resting place.

THE GRAMMAR BUG KID

"If I hear anybody referring to that secondary modern school down the road as The Loony Bin, they'll be in trouble"

…said the wrinkly faced art teacher "Satchmo" before he went off for a crafty smoke, leaving us to sketch a bowl of equally wrinkled fruit on our first day at Grammar School.

Until he had mentioned it, we hadn't even known it was called The Loony Bin, although we subsequently learned they referred to us as "Grammar Bugs".

I became a Grammar Bug by somehow managing to pass the 11 plus exam thanks mainly to an inspirational teacher called Mr Geoff Collier at Howe Bridge School who had prepared us properly for that crucial test by making us do extra lessons at home.

Unfortunately, although she was pleased I'd passed, it meant a great deal more extra expense for Mam who had to kit me out with full school uniform; sportswear and various other equipment.

Because the budget wouldn't stretch to a proper satchel, I had to carry my schoolbooks in an extremely old leather satchel that had belonged to a distant relative.

It looked like the arse end of a mummified horse and I took a fair bit of stick about it but we couldn't afford a brand new one and Mam was of the waste not want not belief.

I was apprehensive on my first day there in September 1958 as I had heard the older pupils baptised the newbies by sticking their heads down a dirty bog and flushing the chain.

Armed with this information, I carefully slid through the school gates and sneaked into the wash block, turned on the taps and covered my head in water: protesting when approached and pointing at my dripping wet hair that I had already been christened.

First day as a Grammar Bug. Oh look - I think my kneecaps are kissing each other…

Leigh Grammar School was modelled on a cut-price public school: with a school song titled "*A school into houses divided*". The teachers wore gowns and the headmaster was a strict disciplinarian called Kenny Bruce.

To be honest, I never cared much for school even though I was never bullied and, being the runt of the class as the youngest, some of the older lads looked out for me.

Some of the teachers, I am convinced, were mad. I mean proper mad. Some of the pupils were even madder. It was a crazy time in my life. I think the "Loony Bin" title went to the wrong school.

The amount of sheer physicality and brutality applied by some of the masters would see them locked up today.

124

There was a Dutch teacher who we called Dirty Lou: a man with a massive cyst behind his ear which he constantly flicked with his fingers in an agitated manner. He had allegedly been a prisoner of the Germans and thanked the British for saving his country and taking him in by battering their offspring.

Misdemeanours were punished by making the offender crouch on all fours while he hit them on the spine with his steel-edged ruler and other similar implements.

There was "Flash Gordon" who battered bottoms with his massive size 12 galosh and a teacher nicknamed Festus who I once saw hit a fellow pupil on the back of the head with such force his face crashed into the desk splattering blood from his nose all over the desk lid.

Another teacher used to hit boys on their bare bottoms (you can be locked up for that now!) and his favourite punishment was to keep you behind and make you hang from the climbing bars in the school gym while members of the sixth form practiced their targeting skills by kicking footballs at you. Sick sod.

So terrified was I of this particular punishment that one day I did my PE in Mabel's knickers.

In my usual last minute rush, I had mistakenly grabbed them off the clothes rack, mistaking Mam's white undergarments for my gym shorts and was horrified when I took them out of my bag in the changing room.

In the hope no-one would notice, I put them on and went into the gym, causing some worried looks off my classmates, one of whom perceptively enquired *"Hey up Dutton. Are them thi mam's knickers?"*

I hurriedly denied the fact, claiming they were just a bit big then shinned up the nearest climbing rope whereupon on sliding down it, my dick popped out to the amusement of all and sundry.

I somehow managed to get away with it by carefully hiding from the PE teacher behind the other lads and never wore my Mam's knickers ever again. Honest.

My mate Yates was hit by one teacher who was partially sighted and failed to see the compasses in the lad's hand which drove the points into his forehead not far from his eyes. (Cue TV advert – *"Have you had an accident that wasn't your fault?"*)

One of the maddest teachers nicknamed "Jem" had been a dispatch rider in the war and I suspect was still suffering from shellshock.

His catchphrase was a loud parrotlike "*Right, right, right, right, right, boys!*" and he was forever lashing out in all directions. He taught French and we once caught him in the local cinema watching mucky foreign films with subtitles which, he claimed, were helping him to brush up his language skills.

The physics teacher earned the soubriquet "Brothel Breath" because of his halitosis, "Arnie Tooth" the metalwork teacher had a wonky tooth and "Belsen" was what we called the woodwork teacher for some inexplicable reason. We used to put stuff in the kettle he made his tea with causing him to yell...

"Here now. Who's put glue balls in my kettle?!"

The cane was liberally applied by Kenny the headmaster although our chief class joker once had a funny turn and shouted "*You're not fucking caning me!*", grabbed the cane off him, broke it over his knee, swung his satchel at him and ran off.

He was referred to a psychiatrist after that incident – the pupil not the headmaster. I'm not surprised really. This lad used to hide behind the curtains for half an hour in geography lessons then run out across rows of desks, banging his chest and doing Tarzan yodel calls.

The English teacher was a Welshman who had been unable to speak a word of English until he was about 15 years old.

We were the first class he ever took and on his debut, his attempt to establish authority by adopting a power stance and rocking backwards and forwards was undermined by the fact his flyhole was wide open. He took exception to the class nutter and on one memorable occasion, for some inexplicable reason he said to him "*Come on boy hit me. Do your best !* " while bobbing and weaving in a most alarming manner - so to the class's delight our lad thumped him in the chest and decked him.

I missed quite a bit of school in the early years after breaking my leg playing football on two separate occasions and had great difficulty catching up again.

The first time I did it playing footy down a back street when I tripped over a sticky-up cobble and went over on it causing my tibia to split in what's colourfully known as a greenstick fracture. There's a salutary tale here. Not long before the fracture, I had been daydreaming, as some imaginative but attention-seeking needy kids do, along the lines of "*If only I had a limp, people would feel sorry for me*".

To this end, I practised walking down the street with a limp just to see how folk reacted.

Shortly after, I got one for real! Talk about be careful what you wish for...

I didn't realise this at the time but I had a spell later in life reading about the power of visualisation. I visualised for a long time about having a lovely house in the country and thankfully, that came to pass.

Not content with that, I also visualised a Jaguar on the driveway and that happened too but unfortunately it was the bloke next door who bought one and put it on our shared driveway! That Universe has some sense of humour.

The second time I fractured my leg was a year later during an impromptu game of footy at a football ground.

 leapt in the air for the ball and landed awkwardly with my leg underneath me.

The "snap!" told me I'd be up to my groin in plaster of paris again although a "helpful" St John Ambulance man didn't believe me and said: "*You sure you've broken it? Try walking on it, son*".

Great diagnostic technique.

I did and collapsed in a heap, whereupon he grudgingly called an ambulance and carried me to it on his shoulders with my leg bouncing about painfully.

I wasn't impressed and have often wondered if the guy had borrowed the uniform off someone for a laugh.

The ambulance turned up and took me to hospital where I was swathed up to my groin in plaster of paris.

I had to keep it on for a few weeks and it doesn't half itch down there when you can't reach it, so I used a knitting needle to push it down a gap inside the plaster to scratch it and ended up making a a hole in my leg.

Stupid boy.

Everybody say Awwww. Well, it's bloody hard riding a scooter with a pot leg.

The mysteries of sines, cosines and tangents and Boyle's Law were boring the arse off me but one really great teacher came to my rescue by helping to further instil the love of literature in me by introducing me to great writers such as HG Wells; Evelyn Waugh; James Thurber; Somerset Maugham; George Bernard Shaw and George Orwell, amongst others. Thank you, Mr Herbert Harrison, aka "Happy Harry", wherever you may be. You made a difference.

We were no angels. There were frequent tossing off competitions on the back row of the class during lessons to see who could, literally, come first (or Fussy Fetch, as the local vernacular had it). How the teachers never spotted the entrants jerking away furiously and competitively in a line at the back of the class, I'll never know. Perhaps they didn't like to mention it out of politeness. Testosterone-fuelled masturbation was rife and on one occasion caused great consternation to our physics teacher who had set up an experiment in a test tube to show how the substance inside would react with litmus paper.

He left the classroom for a few minutes – probably to have a crafty fag – whereupon one bold boy grabbed the test tube and ejaculated into it in front of the class.

When the teacher returned, he dipped the litmus paper in the test-tube with a great flourish announcing *"And now we shall see that the..."*... then scratched his bald head in sheer disbelief, adding *"I can't understand it – it's turned red and it should be blue!"*

I can't help thinking how that poor old sod must have puzzled for ages why the laws of physics had been turned back to front and went to his grave not knowing some dirty sod had tossed off in his test tube.

There was one lad in our class who we called "Fagger" because his fingers were stained creosote-like with the effects of nicotine even from the first form.

He was quite advanced for his years in more ways than one and used to parade up and down the aisle behind one particular teacher waggling his fully developed knob behind his back for a laugh. One day, the teacher spun round and bellowed *"I know what you're doing boy!"*

We all gulped and thought Fagger was for the high jump.

"I'm not doing anything Sir" whined Fagger.

"Yes you are. I'm not stupid - you're throwing ink on my back!"

This was a reasonable assumption as his jacket – a decrepit houndstooth tweed number – was absolutely covered in ink blobs from previous assailants.

Fagger had a thing about displaying his todger and used to beat time with it on the desk in music lessons when the vicar who took the class wasn't looking.

Some lads smoked at the back of the class during lessons and blew it through the window and one gambling mad boy even listened to the horse races on earphones through his portable radio yelling out stuff like *"Get in there!"* and *"Go on my beauty!"*

Fagger used to bait the teachers: in particular, the prissy religious education master to whom he would say things like: *"Is it true the Shittites were a c*nting race, sir?"*

"What was that you said boy?"

"I said is it true the Hittites were a hunting race sir?"

The teacher must have had his suspicions he was having his plonker pulled but couldn't say anything for fear of making himself look a fool.

Boris (after Boris Karloff) was the nickname that was given to a skeletal looking ancient teacher with bad eyesight who, sadly, was the butt of many jokes.

Just before he came into the classroom, we swung all the paintings on the wall and we all swayed sideways together in unison. Boris couldn't believe what his eyes were seeing and probably thought he was hallucinating.

He was a good old soul and I felt guilty when I found out many years later he had served with distinction in the army in the First World War.

If there was one thing I hated more than algebra, it was the cross country run that we were forced to do every week. Luckily some of us found a shortcut through a farm yard and we'd spend 20 minutes or so smoking our Embassy cigs in a barn then catch up with the others when they ran past the other side of the yard.

Some of my classmates had entrepreneurial skills. One lad brought in a constant supply of consumer goods which other lads bought off him for what seemed a bargain.

One classmate proudly showed me a sophisticated camera he had bought at a knock-down price, expressing his delight at the superlative piece of equipment.

He wasn't so delighted when, shortly afterwards, two burly detectives entered the classroom and hawked him away for receiving stolen goods.

It appeared that the other lad had been on the rob and I heard that in subsequent years, he was a frequent guest of Her Majesty.

When you turned 14 you were allowed out of school for dinners so a gang of us walked along the Bridgewater Canal into Leigh and went to the Bluebird cafe for chips and gravy then trooped blithely round the corner into the local Labour Club to drink pints of bitter; stick tanners in the one arm bandits; smoke cigarettes and play snooker. At 14!

We were in school uniform but as we were boosting the club's funds, no questions were asked. The class nutter got so pissed we had to hold him up at the school final assembly.

It was the same one where some bright sparks wired the grand piano up to the electricity mains supply and as the schoolboy pianist lifted the lid and hit the keys for the first chord of the school song, there was a massive explosion, a blinding blue flash and a cloud of thick smoke which enveloped the teachers and headmaster assembled on stage.

The pianist, incidentally, was Roger Smalley who later became a famous composer and musician. Wonder if he ever had flashbacks of that incident?

Our form master "Tippy" Tiplady also taught chemistry and as a special treat during chemistry lessons would do spectacular indoor pyrotechnics that amazed and astounded us.

Tippy was a decent enough teacher but I didn't like it when he took the piss out of me in front of the whole class because I lived in Factory Street (East).

(The name of the street got changed many years later when a group of neighbours got together in the local club and decided a more salubrious name would add value to their houses. They asked me to help because I knew some of the councillors and so it was changed.)

Anyway, back to the chemistry lab. We all preferred pissing about to learning stuff, sometimes rolling mercury round in our mouths and spitting it out into petri dishes – not realising how highly poisonous it is.

"Festus" taught physics but could always be distracted by the slightest mention of bees, which he kept in his back garden. He invited a few of us round once to show off his hives and demonstrated extracting the honey from some converted spin dryer. I couldn't imagine a teacher these days offering home visits to kids to let them watch him make honey, if you see what I mean. Sad, really.

Discipline sometimes broke down on a large scale.

One day there was a pitched battle between all the school prefects and the rest of the school who bombarded them with stones and sods as they made a stand like the Spartans at Thermopylae on a bridge over the canal. It may have been a grammar school but it was a bloody madhouse at times.

In wintertime, we lined the canalside making dozens of snowballs and bombarded passing bargemen who retaliated with colourful vile phrases that some of us had never heard before but which were soon incorporated into our vocabulary.

One day I was invited to audition for a play called Emil and the Detectives, a German play about a gang of kids who apprehend a bank robber.

A few of my friends had also auditioned and when it was my turn, I nervously read the audition piece.

When I came offstage they kindly pointed out how crap I had been and that I had wasted my time – my first real critique, you might say. Mr Boardman, who produced the play, thought otherwise and gave me a good part as one of the child detectives.

I played the newspaper boy – the same part that the great Ray Winstone credited with sparking his interest in becoming an actor when he played it as a 13 years old schoolboy. That's the same age I was but unfortunately the similarity ends there.

I really enjoyed being part of the team and showing off my acting abilities and my Mam sat in the audience beaming proudly.

I wish I had done more drama at school as perhaps my life would have taken me earlier towards that career which I probably always subconsciously wanted but it was my innate shyness and lack of confidence at that time which scuppered me.

I started in the lowest form – 1 beta - and ended up in the lowest form: 5C - mainly because of the time I had missed.

Although we hadn't been taught it in our class, I sat the English literature O-level after studying on my own and passed it.

I was proud of that.

Soon, I ceased to be a grammar bug and became a jobseeker. I was 15 years old.

What the hell was I going to do with my poxy 4 O levels and the rest of my life?

Shocking at sums; comme si comme ça at French; hopeless at History; lost at Geography; Physics and Biology held no charms for me; too scrawny and lacking the skills to play centre forward for Bolton Wanderers: the only thing I was reasonably good at was English.

I have a vague idea I would like to be a reporter but no idea how to become one. Perhaps a careers officer could help.

Let's see...

Climbing the ladder to success? I think not...

CONFESSIONS OF A YOUNG REPORTER

*They're always smoking and drinking and swearing and **worse**...*

"Er, I want to be a reporter, please" I squeak to the rather attractive young lady in the local careers office.

She stares at me with a look of sheer alarm and disbelief.

I might just as well have said I wanted to juggle with babies and catch them on the end of a bayonet.

"A reporter?!" she screeches. *"Oh you **don't** want to be a reporter!"*

Her reaction catches me unawares.

I bloody *do*, I think.

"Why not? "* I tentatively enquire.

"Because reporters are the most awful people imaginable. They're always smoking and drinking and swearing and worse.

I used to work as a secretary in a newspaper office. You're too nice a boy to be a reporter. Oh no. Think of something else".

She is almost in tears.

I sit there nonplussed.

I'm not expecting that.

Although she was as much use as a concrete lifebelt, it didn't put me off. In fact, it sounded to me like it might be a fun way to earn a living.

I also thought that because a reporter met lots and lots of interesting people, that might be the solution to cure me of my shyness and self-consciousness. It would wear it away like sandpaper.

Besides, I simply couldn't think of anything else I wanted to do: I was only 15 and I suppose that on perusing my angelic boyish features, she had had visions of me being corrupted by more hard-nosed cynical persons with a bent towards

more bacchanalian pursuits and she was probably right.

Well, it turned out she *was* partially right but I had been expecting at least a teeny bit of encouragement from her.

Naively, I wrote to the Daily Mirror enquiring about a job as a reporter. I think they call it misplaced optimism.

I don't know how many letters they got from snotty nosed kids who fancied themselves as reporters but I was dealt with kindly.

I got a lovely letter back from the Northern News Editor, as follows...

Telephone : DEAnsgate 3444 Ext.
Telegrams : Mirror Manchester 4

Daily Mirror

Mark Lane Corporation Street
Manchester 4

MW/MK/R

David Rutton,
9, Factory Street East,
ATHERTON, Lancs.

April 26, 1963

Dear David,

Thank you for your letter.

I'm sorry but there are no suitable vacancies on the Daily Mirror staff, as all our reporters must have a good deal of experience before they join us.

By far the best thing you can do is to write to the Editor of a local paper in your area, asking for a job as a junior reporter. If your first attempt fails - try again. And again. Keep on trying and you are bound to succeed.

Weekly paper experience is the best possible training ground for a young journalist. For your information nearly every member of our staff started his career in this way.

I should tell you, too, that journalism involves a good deal of hard work and long hours, but there is a good deal of satisfaction in the work.

I would like to take this opportunity of wishing you every success, and if in a few years' time you still want to join the Mirror, try again!

Good luck!

Yours sincerely,

M. WIGGLESWORTH

Northern News Editor

Got me name wrong but what a gentleman. Thank you Mr. Wigglesworth.

At that time, Mam was earning some extra money for us by working nights in the A1 Chippy in town and one of the regular customers was a local freelance reporter called Clive Cook.

Cooky looked like a proper reporter straight out of the films with his trilby and long white trench-coat and fag constantly dangling from the corner of his mouth. He had also worked in aerial reconnaissance in the RAF during the war alongside top comedy writer and tv personality Frank Muir.

By chance, a few days later, he went into the chippy and as she wrapped his fish and chips, Mam leaned towards him: "*Can you help me please? My son wants to be a reporter*".

"*Does he now*?" replied Cooky. "*I think they're looking for a cub reporter at the Leigh Chronicle. I'll have a word with them*".

It was the right thing said at the right time. A real stroke of luck. A few days later, I attended an interview with the News Editor David Short who sent me to see the Editor-in-Chief Charlie Maynard in St. Helens.

"*Why do you want to be a reporter, lad?*" asked Mr Maynard.

I stammered back: "*Well, erm, it's because I enjoy writing because it's like, er, painting a picture in black and white*".

"*I'll let you know*" he muttered, peering quizzically over his spectacles at me.

A few days later, shortly after my 16th birthday, the letter came offering me the job as a junior reporter.

Mam was really proud, as was Mother and on that day in September 1963, when the Beatles topped the charts with She Loves You; I entered the thrilling world of local newspapers. The wages were £6 10s a week of which I was allowed by Mabel to keep a quid spending money and four bob a day for dinners and bus fares.

My seat was allocated at the large office table, and I was given an old-fashioned Royal typewriter and sheets of pink copy paper on which to hammer out the words which would end up in homes throughout the district. Exciting eh? Well it was to me.

I was really put through my paces on the first day at work. There were only three of us in total to garner the news with which to fill every week's edition.

As well as the editor, David, there was a chief reporter by the name of John who had a reputation of being a ladies' man: in fact there was talk of him having squired a former Miss World which was pretty good going for somebody from a provincial backwater such as ours.

This reputation caused some jealousy among the lads of the opposition paper, the Leigh Journal, who cruelly dubbed him Talcum Knackers as he was always smartly dressed and smelling of expensive aftershave in his pursuit of the ladies.

On my first day, I was sent out to cover over half a dozen stories, one of which spookily entailed interviewing the mother of one of my former teachers at Leigh Grammar who had dropped dead that week in his 40's.

John showed me the ropes and that week we went out walking miles round the area, calling at vicarages; presbyteries; workingmen's clubs; pubs; police and fire stations to see if they had any hot news for us. It's stuff the local papers don't do any more because they seem to pull a lot of what they need off social media.

One local vicar was a little potty. When we asked if there was anything worth reporting in his parish, he'd pick up the cat, put his mouth next to its ear and enquire "*Any cat news Tibby?*" When his church caught fire, the fire brigade flooded it and he paddled a tabletop up the middle of the aisle to rescue a few things. Well he had been an ex submarine commander before his calling to the cloth.

On my first ever round, John and I popped in a pub to ask the landlord if anything newsworthy had happened.

He scratched his head then said: "*Oh aye. Owd Arthur's died. He was a stalwart of the darts and dominoes team and he lived just opposite. His daughter lived with him. Go and have a word*".

We knocked on the door of the little two-up-two-down. The lady answered and we asked if we could speak to her about her recently-deceased father.

She kindly invited us in: John went first and as I turned to close the door, I noticed a bed in the downstairs room. "*That's funny*" I thought. "*The old feller must have been ill*".

Then I saw a nose and two feet sticking up. Then the rest of him: for there on the bed under the window was owd Arthur, as was.

He was dead alright, but what the landlord had neglected to tell us was he'd only just popped his clogs and the undertakers hadn't been round to collect him.

I was horrified as I'd never seen a dead body before. I backheeled the door shut and scrambled quickly into the kitchen where John was

137

asking the dead man's daughter about her late father's achievements in the dizzy stratosphere of the local darts and dominoes leagues. After a couple of minutes, she asked if we would like a cup of tea. We thanked her and off she went to a small pantry to brew up. Dumbstruck, I tapped John on the shoulder and pointed vigorously to the other room, face aquiver.

"*He...he's...*" I couldn't get the words out.

The penny dropped. John's face was a picture. "*Is he in there?*" he gasped, pointing towards the parlour.

I nodded.

"*Bluddy 'ell!*"

It was something about his horrified wide-eyed and slack jawed expression which set me off laughing: a nervous reaction more than anything. I struggled to suppress the laughter but the more I tried to contain it, the more it wanted to erupt. This set John off which made me snort even more.

We sounded like two wood pigeons being strangled.

"*Quick. Shove a hanky in your gob!*" urged John.

So I did. And when the bereaved daughter brought in the tea, she was greeted with the sight of me with my head lowered, shoulders heaving up and down and a handkerchief covering the lower half of my face.

Misreading the signals, she patted me on the shoulder and soothingly cooed: "*I understand luv*" then turning to John, she added sympathetically: "*Poor lad's proper upset*".

This only made me worse and I suddenly leapt out of the chair and out through the back door into an entry at the rear of the house where I gave full rein to my uncontrollable hoots of laughter.

Some minutes later, John emerged and gave me a slight bollocking: "*You silly sod - leaving me to face her*" and we emerged round the corner and into the street clutching one another and still laughing.

I thought to myself, Blimey, I can have some fun doing this job and at least Owd Arthur got his obituary in the next week's edition.

The workload of a junior reporter in those days was quite a hefty one. Apart from walking miles by doing the rounds a couple of days a week, we covered courts, councils, sporting events, public inquiries and inquests.

If there was a fire, we were there shortly after the fire brigade, interviewing neighbours and survivors.

If someone of note died, we had to speak to the bereaved and though it was one aspect of the job I never looked forward to, it never ceased to amaze me how the ones who were left seemed eager to talk about their loved ones and even provide a photograph to put in the newspaper.

I felt it would be some days before it sunk in that they weren't going to see them ever again.

I interviewed people who had lost loved ones in traffic accidents; rail crashes; fires; drownings; murders; through illness; suicides or in the normal course of events. It was part of the job and one we couldn't shirk. The full range of human existence was being unfolded on a daily basis to me.

The biggest tragedies I covered involved children - perhaps the most poignant involved watching three tiny white coffins being carried to the cemetery containing young siblings who had died in a house fire.

I attended courses organized by the National Council for the Training of Journalists, covering all aspects of the job. This lasted three years at the end of which I was amazed to find I had won the prestigiously titled Bert Stone Award for best candidate in the Manchester area and was given a Parker Pen as a reward. It was a much needed boost to the ego.

Proud recipient of the Bert Stone Award while News Ed Hal Dootson (far left) looks on

139

After a while, John left and a new reporter, Big Dave Miller, joined us.

Like me, Dave was an Atherton lad and very down to earth in character. He had come from the opposition: the Leigh Journal. They were our rivals but we always got on very well: even having impromptu games of footy together upstairs over our office, often accidentally smashing a window with the ball and showering parked cars and passers-by with the shards.

One of the Journal gang called Harold was deaf in one ear and, as hard of hearing people sometimes do, he spoke above his weight. When covering court sessions, he frequently did a running commentary on the case in progress with the subject of the charge standing but a few yards away.

"*This bugger's guilty as sin*" he'd boom to the startled look of the accused. "*It's written all over his fuckin' face*".

His hearing-aid used to whistle piercingly in the middle of proceedings, which was very off-putting to a solicitor just getting into full Rumpole of the Bailey mode in defence of a client.

One particular local female reprobate was pleading with the court for mercy and putting on a particularly creditable performance when Harold's voice echoed round the courtroom: "*Three months in Holloway and a fuckin' Oscar!*".

Even the usually severe Clerk of the Court had to force himself to suppress a smile at that one.

He wasn't too chuffed, however, on the many occasions that Harold could be heard frustratedly thumping his defective hearing aid on the Press bench and bawling: "*Fuckin' useless thing!*"

One probation officer was a stout bespectacled elderly lady who had an unnerving habit of sitting facing the reporters' bench with her legs wide open and her ample bloomers on show. Fair made yer eyes water and enough to turn you into a monk.

This caused much mirth among the gentlemen of the Press but what made it more risible was the fact that her name was actually Fanny Bent, leading to scurrilous remarks such as:

"*Is that Fanny Bent?*"
"*No – it's just the way she's sitting*".

Coal picking was a punishable offence in those days. Skint locals pushed old prams to the local slag heaps or colliery spoil tips and picked out choice lumps to burn on their home fires or sell on in the pub for a pint or two. There usually ensued a Keystone Cops chase with the local constabulary chasing folk pushing coal-laden prams all round the pit heaps.

This led to gags such as :

"Nasty accident in Plank Lane. Woman was pushing a pram across a zebra crossing and it got hit by a lorry.
No!
Aye. There were coal everywhere".

There were always moments of comedy and drama in the courts but one of the most dramatic I covered in the late 60's involved a local man accused of the manslaughter of his baby son. He was alleged to have shaken the child to death in a fit of temper and the case went to a Crown Court held in the impressive and imposing neo-classical surroundings of St George's Hall in Liverpool.

It was a long trial and I'm ashamed to say, I scratched my name on the long ancient wooden bench where I sat to cover the proceedings. Over 35 years later, I was collared by an actor who I knew. *"I've just been filming a drama in St. George's Hall and I was sitting at an old bench and saw your name scratched into it. You bloody vandal".*

He also told me John Lennon had scratched his name next to mine but I've never been there to verify it.

Inquests could be another source of drama. They were usually held in a room at the local infirmary and presided over by a rather severe-looking coroner by the name of Colonel R.M. Barlow, ably assisted by a pathologist by the name of Dr. Jacob Schrager who was a diminutive Peter Lorre type with a sinister East European accent which only added to the horror of the grim and gruesome pathology reports he read out in front of grieving relatives of the deceased.

His spiel would be along the lines of:

"I removed ze lungs and zey vere in an advanced state of emphysema. Ze brain was also removed and found, on close inspection, to have be somevat shrunken viz multiple lesions and zere vass also a large tumour on ze liver..." he intoned balefully and in a matter-of-fact manner, peering myopically at his notes.

No gory detail was spared. I often thought it was very cruel that the family had to hear minute details of their loved one's dissection. What was worse was he got paid on the spot by the Coroner counting out the cash.

The shrieks of the bereaved were sometimes horrible to hear. A colleague of mine – the late and much missed Lesley Evans – once had to run out of an inquest shaking with mirth when the coroner heard evidence of one poor old bloke who had died after putting both feet down one trouser leg on the landing causing him to topple over and plunge headlong downstairs. Like cops, reporters often shelter under the umbrella of black humour.

What used to annoy me more than anything though was how the deaths of local miners were more often than not written off as natural causes: thus depriving the widow of an extra pension.

Our news team expanded and we were joined by Les Powell, a tall good-looking lad from Newton-le-Willows; Dave Hodgkinson, an Athertonian of semi-Italian extraction; the aforementioned Lesley Evans who was a former schoolgirls' hurdling champion and several others who joined us for shorter periods of time.

As I said, Dave Miller was a no-nonsense bluff type of guy and when News Editor David Short rushed into the office on the 1st of June, 1965 and announced breathlessly that his wife, Jean, had just given birth to a son, Miller enquired politely as to what they were going to call the child.

"*Nigel*", replied Shorty.

This choice of name did not chime well with Miller's solid working-class roots. His middle name was Herbert.

"*Nigel?!*" he bellowed disbelievingly. "*Nigel?! Jesus Christ! What sort of a fucking name is Nigel?!!*"

Little did we know then that baby Nigel was a little genius who would go on to become chess prodigy Nigel Short MBE: beating his dad at the game at the age of 4; qualifying for the British Men's Final at 11 and winning it at 14; a Chess Grandmaster before the age of 20; three-times British Chess Champion and going on to challenge Garry Kasparov for the World Championship!

Chess is not something we played in our office. We played Contact Darts where the object of the game was to stand by the board with a big stick and try and smack the dart before it actually hit the target. Bit crackers, yes?

Being a small office packed with people, this unsurprisingly led to darts having to be extracted from various spectators' limbs.

This was one of many silly games we used to play: another of which was Penny Plonking which involved balancing a pile of pennies on the elbow and flipping the hand up to catch them in mid air.

There was also the Slappy Eating Championships which I am glad to say I thoroughly dominated. A Slappy is a Leigh\Wigan expression for a barm cake (a sort of large round floury bread roll) which has been sliced and liberally buttered and into which has been slapped a Meat and Potato Pie, then pressed together to form a massive sort of pie sandwich that Desperate Dan would be proud of.

The competition was to see who could then get the Slappy into the gob and down the gullet in as short a time as possible without actually choking to death in the process.

On the shout of "*Go!*" it was forced between the jaws and crammed into cheeks that resembled those of the great jazz trumpeter Dizzy Gillespie at their most distended.

This once nearly caused a fatality, as a seriously asthmatic visiting news editor by the name of Arthur Machin laughed so much at the ludicrous spectacle that he couldn't get his breath and had to be resuscitated.

He was a lovely bloke was Arthur but so badly afflicted with asthma that he could only walk a few steps before using his nebuliser and when he first came to work a shift at the newspaper, a junior reporter burst in crying " *There's an old man dying in the front office!*"

We rushed in and found Arthur, who resembled an ailing Tony Hancock, leaning against the counter gasping like a carp in a smoky taproom and with his trilby askew.

Thankfully, Arthur never witnessed the goings-on at the Thrutching Pole or he would surely have passed over to the other side there and then.

I should explain that the Thrutching Pole was a sort of mini totem pole about 4 feet tall and 8 inches in diameter which was attached to a base to make it more stable.

Thrutching is an old multi-purpose Lancashire dialect word dating back hundreds of years. It generally means to strain, struggle, push against but is also used in a lavatorial sense where someone is constipated and trying to pass a motion.

In our case, it meant straining to break wind because
the Thrutching Pole was the centrepiece of our regular wind-
breaking competitions.
It was covered in rude symbols and photographs of tits and bums and
had a left and a right hand drawn upon it.
These were where the pole had to be gripped tightly by the
participant who, head down, then commenced to thrutch prior to
letting out the loudest fart they could manage.
We took it very seriously, training on baked beans, slappies and
numerous bottles of fizzy Vimto, after which we performed peculiar
aerobic-type bending exercises to enable the mixture to generate
gas.
Her Majesty's Thrutching Pole Inspector –a local landlord called
Norman - enforced the rules and we solemnly marched into the
abandoned printshop behind the office to participate in the
tournament.
The News Editor and the Inspector adjudicated the contests and
marks were awarded according to length and loudness of the fart.
Farts were graded. A Trouser Creeper was the lowest you could
score and the Triple Flutterblast was generally considered to be the
target to which one should aspire. (Following through obviously
meant instant disqualification.)
There was a general air of craziness about the office. I suppose some
of it was excusable when you'd just seen three tiny coffins taken out
of a house after a fire or covered the death of a toddler who had
drowned in the local canal.
We had an eccentric caretaker, old Tommy Evans, who lived round
the corner and came in, ostensibly, to man the boiler and to generally
look after the premises.
I say ostensibly because, it didn't always work out that way. He used
the same mucky mop bucket of water for weeks to "clean" the office
or redistribute the shite as we used to call it.
Mr. Evans was an ancient white-haired Welshman who seriously
claimed his father had been the Jumping Backwards Champion of
Wales as well as being a top bricky who had helped to
build Caernarvon Castle, neither of which assertions rang true to our
ears.

Me. Working. Allegedly.

He always wore a cloth cap and was forever challenging people to *"Try and knock my cap off my head. Go on. See if you can knock it off boyo. I bet you sixpence that you can't".*
It must have been some sort of bizarre rural sport in the Welsh village whence he came.
But we did knock it off: every time. So why he kept going on about it, I'll never know. His battered and twatted flat cap constantly flew off like a frisbee in all directions but we never took his money. Well he was nearly 80 and we were mainly in our teens but, hey, he started it.
Although we were fair to him in this respect, we weren't in others. He used to hang out (ie hide from his wife) in a pokey boiler room underneath our office, supping cups of tea and reading the paper. When we'd been out for a drink, which was often, we went down to the cellar and while one of us (probably Powell) distracted him, some dirty disgusting person (probably me) peed on the smouldering coke in the boiler.
Then as the clouds of steam rose, we skedaddled up the cellar steps leaving poor old Tommy fanning himself with his cap and wondering why his eyes were stinging.

145

Our office was in an old Victorian building and as part of it was the disused printworks, we had whole families of mice running all over the place. It got so bad that we asked Mr Evans to deal with it.
"Leave it to me now boys. I'll put some poison down for them". he said.
Next morning as we sat down to work, it looked like Mouseageddon. There were pathetic little dead Mickeys and Minnies everywhere: in the in-trays and out-trays; under the desks; on the typewriters and in the toilets. It was revolting.
When we pointed out the manifold corpses to Mr Evans he simply muttered: "*I don't know how they got there. They weren't there first thing".*
We never figured how he came to that conclusion because what he had actually done was mop *round* them.
We could tell he'd done this because there were little circles of dried mud like a scene of crime outline on the lino around each corpse from the filthy contents of his old mop bucket.
We decided after that to get an office cat which we christened Herbert after David Herbert Miller. This worked a treat until unfortunately the news editor, Hal Dootson, came in one morning to find "Herbert" had given birth in the envelope drawer. Now we had kittens as well as mice. Our office was beginning to look like a crap menagerie.
Dooty decided to get rid of him\her. Never did find out what happened to the Mousefinder General but I didn't like to ask.
The layout of the reporters' office was strange. It was one room with an old lavatory ensuite. This meant everyone could hear what was going on when you went to perform your ablutions and when someone had a curry the night before,we all suffered from it.
Many's the time the office had to be evacuated as we all fled outside and stood on the pavement waiting for the smell to evaporate.
Hardly like working at the Washington Post.
When it got towards Bonfire Night, the usual procedure was to wait until someone had settled down for a comfortable crap and then throw a lighted jackjumper or banger inside while holding the door firmly shut as the air filled with screams and swear words. You try that these days with yer Health and Safety!
It was a distinctly unprivate privy. The bottom half of the window was covered in curious green paint but the top half of the glass was

clear and sometimes as you were sitting there cogitating and thrutching, the window-cleaner's head bobbed over the top and he waved his shammy leather cheerily at you as you waved back, whipped your kecks up and beat a hasty retreat.

Eventually, another lavatory was installed upstairs at the far end of the building. Even there you weren't safe as the top was open and as you took your ease, someone evil get would creep up and drop burning newspapers on your head from above. If you were only halfway through doing what you were doing, you were forced to bat it out with your bare hands.

Another favourite trick when visitors came was to put red ink in the cistern which when flushed filled the lavatory bowl with what looked like blood, almost giving the poor dupe a heart attack as he or she thought they had some incurable bowel disease. Once, the upstairs light went out so we told Mr Evans we were having difficulty finding the lavatory in the dark.

"Leave it to me boys" he murmured, touching the side of his nose. We did. Next day we went upstairs to find he hadn't replaced the bulb but instead had painted a thick white line up the stairs and across the entire floor to the pitch black lavatory in the corner.

"Just follow the line and it'll save putting a bulb in" he explained.

It wasn't all fun and games though. We did cover some serious stories, including one of mine which, unknown to me for decades, had an important effect on the burgeoning Gay Rights movement in the UK...

Monkeying around on the Leigh Reporter. Me, Les Powell and the late much missed Lesley Evans.

Another quiet day at the office…

You never see the staff at the Sunday Times doing this.

I LIBERATE THE GAYS. SORT OF.

"I thought that your editor had sent along a cub reporter just to wind you up and embarrass you"

Ok. Slight exaggeration there about me liberating the gays although it appears I did have a small but apparently crucial part in the early ongoing movement to liberalise the oppressive laws concerning homosexuality.

Incredibly, I didn't discover this until 40 years later when, as I was flicking aimlessly through the channels on the television one evening I came across a BBC documentary – The Gay Decade - about the struggle of homosexuals to be freed from prosecution under the archaic laws that then existed.

I was absolutely astonished to see my name and the front page lead story of the Leigh Reporter that I had written all those years ago shown in close-up in the documentary.

As the camera floated over the 8-column headline down to my name, I sat transfixed and open-mouthed in amazement.

The programme featured Allan Horsfall, a former local colliery worker, who in a very bold move in February 1965 had printed 10,000 leaflets campaigning for reform of the laws discriminating against homosexuality, which at that time was an inprisonable offence.

He posted one of these leaflets to our editor who then sent me to interview Allan at his small former miners' terraced house in Hindsford on the outskirts of town, actually next door but one to where my grandmother had been born nearly 85 years before.

There was naturally some mickey-taking of the *"don't bend down to pick owt up"* kind about me going to see a man whose sexual leanings were obvious, so with some trepidation and those jibes ringing in my ears, I went to see Allan to discover what the campaign was all about and why he had started it.

The so-called Swinging Sixties had yet to hit our area (if indeed it ever did) and most of the miners and millworkers and other folk in the area would be presumed to be disapprovingly Victorian in outlook on matters of this nature.

Allan was a very pleasant gentleman and he welcomed me with a cup of tea. He explained the aims of the campaign and I went back to the office (and more jests) to write up the story.

It came out on the Thursday as the main lead.

The strap at the top of the paper read: **Call to implement Wolfenden Committee's Report**

The headline said: **HOMOSEXUALS AND THE LAW**

The sub-heading read: *Hindsford man is heading NW Campaign*

The by-line read: *by DAVE DUTTON*

The story began: *Ten thousand leaflets concerning male homosexuality and the law will be distributed throughout the North West in the next few weeks. And the secretary of the committee producing the literature is a Hindsford man.*

A former Nelson Labour councillor Mr. Allan Horsfall, 3, Robert Street, is secretary of the newly-formed North West Homosexual Law Reform Committee whose aims are to make the Wolfenden Committee recommendations law.

It went on to explain that in 1957 the Wolfenden Report had recommended that British law be brought into line with other civilised countries in that homosexual behaviour between consenting adults should no longer be a criminal offence.

What Allan was seeking to do by issuing the leaflets was to test public opinion in the area to see what the reaction would be.

He had feared a serious backlash in such a tightly-knit working-class area and was really concerned for his job as a clerk with the National Coal Board and the intactness of his windows. Therefore, it was a brave move on his part.

What happened after my story appeared in the paper astonished and delighted him.

Because nothing happened.

There was no outcry from the local mainly working class community ; no indignant letters and no bricks through the window.

As he said later:

" I thought all hell was going to break loose. Not a murmur. No letters opposing it, no hostility from neighbours, not much at work".

As he stated in the pamphlet, his aim was to disprove the alleged widespread public hostility to a change in the law as a complete myth and the lack of an angry response to the story I had written went some way to proving his case.

Indeed, the only negative reaction he got was from our own news editor, who in an article in the same edition blasted the aims of the campaign by saying: " *I wonder where it will end if homosexual practices between consenting adults were made lawful.*

Surely it is a fact that most of today's homosexuals became homosexuals through contamination when they were children".

Contamination! Ouch! Strong words from a hard nosed ex Fleet Street man.

Aside from this and thus encouraged, Allan then went on to form the Campaign for Homosexual Equality which played a major role in the legalisation of homosexuality in 1967.

After the programme, I searched the internet and sent Allan an email. He kindly sent me a photo of that Leigh Reporter front page of Thursday the 4th of February, 1965 adding:

"How nice to hear from you. I remember the interview in Hindsford very well. I never expected the front-page spread that your story got; indeed, I looked back in the file and I couldn't see where the Leigh Reporter had used an eight-column headline before.

I am sending the newspaper headline which appeared on TV and in the Guardian and Gay Times and OutNorthWest as well as in the Lesbian and Gay Humanist.

Gay rights was quite controversial at that time in some circles and I thought that your editor had sent along a cub reporter just to wind you up and embarrass you!"

Spot on. He may have had a point but at least it got him the desired result.

Allan died in 2012 and was described in the Oxford Dictionary of National Biography as one of the grandfathers of the gay rights movement and one of the truly great pioneers of LGBT equality in Britain.

The whole episode made me reflect that sometimes, our words and actions have consequences that ripple down through the years and sometimes we don't even realise it.

As the Socialist Worker wrote in his obituary:

"Today, when Pride marches are sponsored by multinationals, it's remarkable to think that key events in the history of the LGBT movement took place in a miner's cottage near Wigan".

The late Allan Horsfall with my page one lead in the Leigh Reporter that was one small step towards helping him change the law of the land...

THE PHANTOM NUDE BATHER STRIKES!

Y-y-you've got no bloody trunks on!

Among the reporters who drifted in, stayed a while and drifted out was a man who changed his name and is now quite big in a certain part of the arts world. I shall keep him nameless because at the time, he was a bit of a lad.

The Lad, as I shall call him, was part of a daft hoax which also found its way into the paper.

He had a friend by the name of John Willy who used to pop into the office now and again to have a chat.

One lunchtime, he came round just as we were all planning to go for a swim at Leigh Public Baths and the conversation went like this:

"Where are you all going?"
"The Baths. We're having a swim"
"Cor. I'd love to join you but I haven't brought me trunks"
"You don't need your trunks today".
"Don't need me trunks?! Why not?"
"It's a men-only session. You can go in the water without them".
"I didn't know that. Can I come with you then?"
"You bet!"

And he did! We never thought he would fall for it but we all changed into our trunks at lightning speed, dove in the water with eager anticipation and waited for him.

The Lad stood at the entrance to the changing rooms, shouted *"Here he comes!"* blew a *"**TA-TA-TA-TARRR!**"* fanfare on an imaginary trumpet and the (aptly named) John Willy came cavorting into full view completely naked with his impressive manhood bouncing in all directions. We nearly choked laughing.

He jumped in the water, swam around a bit, then got out again walking round the baths with his dangling dick, still unaware he was transgressing local council swimming regalia regulations when an eagle-eyed attendant pointed frantically at him and spluttered apoplectically: *"Y-y-you've got no bloody trunks on!"*

To which John Willy innocently rejoindered: *"I don't need any trunks pal. It's men only".*

The attendant went stratospheric: "*Get out! Get out at once you dirty bugger or I'll call the police!*"

We started to panic. Well we didn't want our names in the Police Gazette. We had reputations to uphold. Sort of.

" *Tell him you've lost them in the water* " I hissed.

"*I've lost them in the water*" shouted John Willy.

"*Well bloody well find them and quick!*" responded the incandescent baths attendant.

John Willy made a show of looking for his trunks then crept out sheepishly to dry off and put on his clothes, slowly realising he'd been done.

"*Bloody rotten bastards*" he muttered.

We got back to the office and enterprisingly phoned the Baths.

"*We believe you've had someone swimming without any trunks?*"

"*Aye. Bloody unbelievable what people get up to these days*" said the attendant, confirming the facts.

As it was the day the paper was put to bed, we phoned the story through to the news editor in St Helens where the paper was printed and next day's headlines read: **THE PHANTOM NUDE BATHER OF LEIGH BATHS.**

It was a case of having your own fun and printing it.

Not long after, the Lad's stay with us came to an abrupt halt when, without giving in his notice, he eloped with a local girl and made page one lead of his own paper.

We had some strange regular visitors who interrupted our flow of work, or play as the case may be.

One such man was a local chiropodist who, ironically, had no toes. He had lost them to frostbite while serving in the army.

In he marched singing a filthy version of Colonel Bogey, telling us of a strange vision he had where, at the top of a local slag heap, the ghost of his father had pointed to the town laid out before him telling him that one day, he would represent the constituency in the Houses of Parliament. (He didn't.)

He used to stand in the visitors' gallery at the Town Hall blowing very loud raspberries at the entire council before being frogmarched out by the police. He later ended up being voted in as a councillor where he continued to cause havoc.

As such, he joined that august body of men who were prone to malapropisms, a la Hylda Baker, as former Leigh colleague and BBC presenter Kevin Cosgrove reminded me in a website message. The councillors spoke of things *"being taken for granite"* and on one occasion when someone appeared to be choking, a voice shouted from the council chamber *"give him the Heineken Manoeuvre!"*

Even funnier, I once covered the annual general meeting of a local workingmens' club where the chairman asked us all to stand and give a minute's silence for *"our diseased members"*.

Incidentally, I spotted the aforementioned toeless councillor many years later on breakfast television where, under an assumed name, he claimed to be able to predict people's fortunes by the ancient art of Tibetan Flower Reading! What a character.

Almost as memorable was the local clog dancer who kept coming in to perform for us in his clattering clogs in an effort to get featured in the paper.

You'd be trying to speak on the phone to some local dignitary and struggling to make yourself heard above the racket of his pesky clogs clattering and banging on the office floor.

He got to be such a nuisance that the then news editor, Shorty, had to write and tell him not to bother us ever again. Two days later, he hanged himself.

We kidded Shorty that the police had found him clutching the curtly dismissive letter. He was mortified.

Being a mining town at that time, the Lancashire Miners' Gala was a massive event attended by big-name speakers and was a great day out for the pitmen and their families who travelled from all over the county, proudly parading their colourful banners, accompanied by brass bands. One year it was held in Leigh and the speakers were Tony Benn; TUC leader George Woodcock and the redoubtable stout Liverpool MP Bessie Braddock.

Dave Miller and I were deputed to cover this important gathering and we duly went along with our notebooks at the ready. It was a fine day and we decided to quench our thirsts in the beer tents that were spread all over the gala grounds.

The ale disappeared down our gullets faster than a greyhound after a rabbit as we worked our way from one hostelry to another. For several hours we drank and drank and I vaguely remember listening to Tony Benn's speech and eventually, Miller and I were so pissed,

155

we could hardly stand up, let alone write anything in shorthand, longhand or backhand.

Somehow, we got back to the office and desperately trying to recall what we had seen and heard, we bashed away at our old Royal typewriters for the best part of an hour.

"*What have you written*?" I slurred.

"*Buggered if I know*" replied Miller. "*I'll show you mine if you'll show me yours*".

When we each looked down to see what we'd written, there was nothing there.

We were both so pie-eyed, we'd forgotten to put any paper in the typewriters!

So we started again – this time with typing paper inserted and we bashed away for another half hour.

"*Let's see what you've got*" said Dave.

"*You as well*" I replied.

When we swapped paper, we couldn't read anything because we had thumped the typewriter keys so hard, instead of forming words, we had just hammered hundreds of holes in the paper. The next day, with empty notebooks and thick heads, we scoured the daily papers and wrote our reports from other reporters' efforts. It was either that or a big empty space where the big story should have been.

The careers lady had been correct: the corrupting influence of alcohol featured greatly in our lives and was to do even more so when a mysterious stranger came into our lives.

This guy had worked on some of the biggest-named papers in Fleet Street so we could never figure out what he was doing in our little neck of the woods. He was to some extent an enigma.

We'll call him Fleet Street Tone. He was a charismatic Cornishman with a lovely West Country burr to match and a prodigious capacity for the fags and booze.

We didn't know who or what he was hiding from, if anything, but he told us not to mention he was working on the paper if anyone phoned or came looking for him.

Quickly realising that tits sold papers, he introduced the groundbreaking concept of glamour to the front page in the shape of a gorgeous busty platinum blonde local model called Annette who we regularly featured in various states of undress to boost circulation: thus pre-empting The Sun by a few years.

This was really unheard of in local papers in the mid sixties and when you consider The Sun only launched in 1969 and started putting nude ladies on Page Three, it was a bold imaginative step on his part.

Anyway, PC stood for Police Constable in them days. Or Partly Clothed in this case.

We almost fought one another for the privilege of going to Annette's mother's house to lasciviously rifle through the bulging suitcase of nude pics of her daughter who modelled for the noted London glamour photographer George Harrison Marks, featuring in his best-selling raunchy magazine called Solo. She was also in the 1965 film, The Naked World of Harrison Marks if you want to check that out.

The photographs went down well with our male readers who suddenly took an interest in local news but we had trouble from a little old lady called Millie who lived next door. She used to come in on publication day and slap us all round the head shouting "*Filth! Disgusting Filth!*" and all because we'd put tits on the front page.

As well as general reporting duties, I ran a showbiz and pop column – Dave Dutton's Pop Scene (trendy 60's name eh?)- and got the chance to interview some of the big-name stars who appeared in a local club called The Garrick which had been a garment factory and was run by a great entrepreneurial character called Roy Jackson. Shirley Bassey, Diana Dors, Frankie Howerd, Tommy Cooper, Status Quo, Bob Monkhouse, Frank Ifield, Ken Dodd, Engelbert Humperdinck, PJ Proby, Russ Abbott and the Grumbleweeds all performed there and only three weeks before he died back home in America, Rocker Gene Vincent was paid up by Jacko who called him a rock'n'roll has-been after Vincent labelled him a fat cigar-smoking slob. The spat got so bad that it was featured on the north-west television news.

When Bassey arrived and took at look at the primitive setup (the dressing room was basically a big cupboard), she asked Jacko for a separate lavatory. He came back with a bucket, placed it in front of her and said: "*Here y'are luv – that's the best I can do*".

One of the best live acts I ever saw there was The Killer himself – Jerry Lee Lewis – who mightily upset Jacko by jumping on the very expensive piano he had rented specially at great cost and playing it with the side of his booted foot.

I never managed to interview The Killer because of the close proximity of a bodyguard with a suspicious bulge at the shoulder but got exclusives with stars appearing locally such as The Who, The Hollies and Tom Jones, who I found to be very quiet and polite, and Sandie Shaw who I absolutely adored and who changed into her stage frock in front of me for what was her first ever cabaret performance!

Very good she was too and I might have pulled her (he kidded himself) if it wasn't for the fact that she was accompanied by Paul McCartney's brother, Mike, at the time.

Local lad Georgie Fame also did shows there. He had been born Clive Powell and was brought up in the crackingly named Cotton Street in Leigh. I went to interview him at his old terraced home when his "Yeh Yeh" knocked the Beatles off the top of the charts in January 1965 and we had a game of crown green bowls with his dad at the pub round the corner. His sister told me the story of how his dad used to lock him out after gigs, forcing him to sleep in the outside lavvy. They put a plaque up in the bog when he was famous saying: "*Georgie Fame slept here!*"

About 10 years later, I interviewed him on Piccadilly Radio and he invited me to the nightclub he was appearing at in Manchester.
I was courting my wife-to-be Lynn at the time so declined the offer - which was just as well as the cops raided his dressing-room that very night.Talking of dressing rooms, I once had a very interesting experience in one that was full of nude ladies...

Sorry. Got no nude lady pics, just this sexy man....
Oh I do suit a pipe....

TARBY, SOME BARE NAKED LADIES AND ME

You nearly set my fanny alight!

I was on an assignment. It was sweaty. It was packed. There was booze; gambling; smoking; dirty stag comics and women with no clothes on.

My careers officer was right. What more could a young lad ask for? The club scene in the sixties was thriving. Our most notorious local one was the strangely named Keg o' Kee: a casino and strip club which attracted coachloads of punters from all over the North West intent on seeing a bit of naked flesh and in the process losing most of their week's wages on the gaming tables.

The Keg as it was fondly known was the scene of great embarrassment to me when I went to interview comedian Jimmy Tarbuck there.

Tarby had just come to national prominence through appearing on a major ITV show called Comedy Bandbox the month before in October 1963. He was 22 and had become one of the most talked-about entertainers of the time – after the Beatles.

Indeed, with his moptop hair and his cocky Scouse self-confidence, he was often called The Fifth Beatle.

That he was appearing at a distinctly dodgy small town strip venue made it all the more interesting but the fact was he had already signed the contract and had to honour the booking. There was no way he could get out of it without being sued.

Tarby's misfortune was the Keg's stroke of luck and it was packed to the rafters on the night. Strip Night!

Slightly nervously, I meandered up the stairs and met the manager who took me through the crowded, sweaty, smoky, noisy entertainment room to the dressing room to introduce me to Tarby.

I have to say Jimmy was very amenable and didn't mind being asked questions by a gauche, fresh faced cub reporter. In fact, he probably wondered what I was doing there in the first place. I had not long turned 16 and probably shouldn't have even been allowed in.

Tarby was the comedian\compere for the evening and very soon, we were joined by the strippers themselves.

There were four young ladies: well two were young-ish but the other two had probably entertained the gallant troops at Mafeking.

They had brought their spangly costumes with them and hung them on whatever hooks they could find in that cramped, oxygen-starved box of a dressing room. They greeted Jimmy effusively and regarded me suspiciously as I sat in the corner, pencil gripped tightly, notebook in hand, eagerly waiting to start the interview.

Mr T broke the ice. *"Ladies, say hello to David "*

"Oooh, Hello David " they chorused, pouting and preening.

I nodded and smiled uncertainly back at them and hurriedly began the interview. It started well.

I had just asked Jimmy what it felt like to suddenly become famous when one of the younger women slowly started to peel all her clothes off within my eyeline.

I desperately tried to think of something sensible to ask Tarby who had cottoned on that she was intent on causing maximum discomfiture to the fluffy-bollocked kid she had within easy reach. First the blouse, then the jeans, then the bra, then the knickers were dropped one after the other on the floor.

Bravely, I continued the interview trying to pretend it was nothing out of the ordinary. These things were always happening to us reporters, weren't they?

The room got even hotter and my forehead became clammier as, provocatively and deliberately standing before me, was the first fully naked fully-grown woman I had ever seen outside the stuck-together pages of Health and Efficiency nudist magazine: aka the Wankers' Weekly.

Whereas in that respected publication the tits were on full display but the muff was generally airbrushed out; not half a yard before me in all its sinful eyewatering glory was the embodiment of all things feminine: pendulous boobies; furry fanpiece and when she suddenly spun round, an amply upholstered totally bare lady's bottom. A real one: not some suspiciously-stained photograph of one in a well thumbed periodical.

I could feel stirrings.

Then as she sat on my knee and dangled a pair of golden G strings in front of me and wiggled into my smouldering lap, she purred: *"Now then David. Which one should I wear? This one or that one..?*

It came out in a eunuch-like falsetto: *"Er, that one",* I squeaked, pointing at the nearest scanty item through blurred vision.

"*Good choice, you clever boy*" she murmured in my ear, blowing erotically into it at the same time.

I looked up to see Tarby winking like a wanker back at me and relishing every second of it.

I just wanted to get out of there but she hadn't done with me.

She bent down and picked up her handbag, taking out a packet of cigarettes and a box of Swan Vestas matches.

She offered me a cigarette. I declined. She placed one seductively between her rubied lips and passed me the box of matches. She sat next to me and leaned close.

"*Would you be so kind*?"

Slowly, I took a match out and closed the box. It was then I noticed my hands were in the thrall of what resembled incipient Parkinson's. After several shaky attempts to strike the match, it finally burst into flame and I held it up to the cigarette but I was trembling so much that she was desperately moving her head from side to side like a pair of windscreen wipers in an attempt to light her fag.

The match went out.

"*Sorry*" I squeaked.

I struck another but by this time I was shaking so badly, the match dropped from between my fingers and landed smack in the middle of her densely populated lady forest..

Angrily, she leapt in the air batting her smouldering vegetation.

"*You stupid sod. You nearly set my fanny alight*!" she screamed.

She reminded me of those angry Bargemen we used to bombard with snowballs at school.

"*I think you'd better go*" she snarled. Only she didn't actually say "*go*".

By now, Tarby was rocking backwards and forwards with laughter. He must have thought I'd been through enough as he came over, put his arm around me:" *Have you got sufficient son?*"

I nodded.

"*Well if I can ever do anything else for you, give us a shout*"

Then he made his way onstage to rapturous applause and I shuffled shamefacedly out of a more muted dressing room.

From the grotty Keg o' Kee, Tarby went on to become the compere of Sunday Night at the London Palladium and subsequent fame and fortune.

There is a strange footnote. Little did I expect that nearly 25 years later I would be working alongside Jimmy's daughter Liza Tarbuck in *her* first big break on telly in the hit Granada sitcom Watching. And little did I imagine when I once interviewed the Kinks at our local dance hall that I would end up singing the Ray Davies' hit Days on the telly for a funeral in the BBC's popular drama "Cutting It". Who would have thought it?

Incidentally, the Kinks caused a riot involving the police on that occasion when they turned up late at the gig and came offstage after a couple of songs. It went down in local history.

Interviewing well known folk sometimes threw up stuff you'd rather not see: such as top guitarist Bert "Play in a Day" Weedon at the Keg who was in such a rush to get away, he enthusiastically dried his bollocks in front of me with a towel as we spoke. Every time he came on the telly after that, I had post-traumatic flashbacks of his goolies.

Towards the end of my stay at the Reporter, we had an addition to our staff in the shape of a cherubic, well-mannered, soberly-dressed vicar's son named Philip who was neither a drinker nor a smoker. His main interest in life revolved around a social group called the 18-plus which he had been encouraged to attend by his parents, probably to bring him out of his shell a little.

This organisation seemed rather square and out of kilter with the Swinging Sixties to those in the office more interested in boozing, carousing and getting our ends away, but to a young Christian gentleman it must have seemed the perfect recreation.

Philip was really in the wrong workplace. He was too nice.

He also wasn't really cut out to be a reporter. We discovered this when, in his first week, he was sent to cover the Sports Day at at a local Secondary School.

"What do I do when I get there?" he plaintively enquired.
"Well what do you think? You're not going there to do the sack race. Just bring the effing sports results back", said the exasperated editor.
"Is *that all*?
"Yes!"
So we sent him off for the afternoon and skived off to the pub.
On our return, we had a struggle opening the office doors.

163

Big Dave put his hefty shoulder to the door and proclaimed "*There's summat wedging it*".

Indeed there was. For behind the door were several large wooden boards with the results of all the races pinned upon them.

It took a few seconds to sink in but we slowly realised that instead of simply writing down the results in his notebook, Philip had taken the instruction to "bring back the sports results" literally. He had lifted them off their easels and carted the school blackboards a couple of miles through the packed streets back to the office.

We absolutely wet ourselves laughing.

"*Bloody hell !*" chortled Fleet Street Tone pointing at the boards. "*Are you making a fucking rabbit hutch?*"

I think Philip had realised what he'd done and had tried to hide the boards behind the door before planning to smuggle them back to the school.

After this inauspicious start, to help him fit in more we tried to persuade him to come to the pub with us but his response was always: " *No. I'm going to the 18-plus tonight. My parents will expect me to be there*".

"*He's never going to fuckin' fit in*" muttered Fleet Street Tone. "*We'll have to drag him out for a drink*".

So finally one evening, we absolutely insisted he came out for a drink.

"*Just a small one then*" he announced to our astonishment. "*There's no 18-plus meeting tonight*".

A "small one" was progress as far as we were concerned.

Sad to say, he got a taste for it.

The next few times we went to the pub, Philip came eagerly with us and discovered a new alternative to the 18-plus as he progressed from halves to pints; from a proffered Will's Whiff cigar to fags and in no time at all, he was as bad as us.

He was getting pissed, smoking profusely and swearing with the worst of us. Soon, he was dragging us out to the pub. He blamed it all on Tone who he dubbed: "the Devil's Emissary".

Wonder what became of him? He probably ended up as front man for a thrash metal band.

Nice lad and looking back, I'll concede, yup - that lady careers officer had a point after all.

Hello. Newsdesk. Naked women you say? Hold the front page!

YEAH YEAH YEAH

It's all in the Bible, Mister Booth – Bloody Hell, Shit, Piss – the lot!

I had a Beatle mop top before the Beatles. It's sort of just grew naturally like that in those long off days when I actually had plenty of hair.

When the Fab Four first came into prominence, girls pointed at my head and muttered "*he's copying the Beatles!*" I'm not saying whoever designed their definitive hairstyles once saw me on a bus and decided "*that's the very look we've been searching for!*" but it's a nice thought.

There were still loads of blokes dressed as Fifties teddy boys sporting Brylcreemed quiffs and DA (Duck's Arse) hairstyles. I had fallen for that particular look a few years before and thought I looked pretty natty sporting my long jacket, drainpipe trousers and winklepicker shoes.

Indeed, throughout my formative years I adhered loosely to the fashion of the moment being at various times a mod and later on, a cut price hippy: then progressively wearing stuff such as kipper ties; ultra thin bootlace ties; jackets with slim lapels; jackets with wide lapels; flared trousers; beads and shells round my neck; fancy waistcoats; blue velvet jacket and even, horror of horror, a pink shirt..

I caught up with the latest American music by listening under the bedclothes to Radio Luxembourg, as did most of my contemporaries. It had a horrible habit of fading in and out or making whistling noises so you only heard half of the tune.

Like most kids at that time, we could be found gathered round a jukebox – Happy Days style -in the local cafe: in our case, the colourfully named Zambezi, listening to Duane Eddy's twangy geetar sound or bopping along to my personal faves like Woolly Bully by Sam the Sham; Duke of Earl by Gene Chandler or Nut Rocker by B Bumble and the Stingers. Great tunes; great names.

We smoked. Boy how we smoked. Anything we could lay our hands on from the "coffin nails" working class favourite Woodbines to the unfeasibly long ones called Joysticks which measured about six inches.

Pre-boozing days, we also hung about in the local Temperance Bar raising our dimple glasses and quaffing Hop Stout that looked like the real deal. The off-duty Lancashire United Transport bus drivers used to chortle at us pretending to be proper ale drinkers.

Characters abounded in the "temp"- from Stan with a neck like a giraffe who fascinated us by taking about 30 seconds to draw on a fag which burned halfway down in one go or the legendary Wanking Annie, a lady with a limp who gained her name, it was alleged, by giving hand shandies. There was also a chap named Wanking Ken who hung expectantly about the bogs on the local market with a pulled-down face and stary eyes like something out of a horror film. We never went near him!

There were loads of eccentric characters about in our town in those days. My favourite was an ex Desert Rat and amateur magician called Tommy Roach who used to draw a crowd round him in the main shopping street by appearing to push cigarettes up his nose and pull them out of his ears.

He had a model of Stonehenge in his little front garden and used to plant real lightbulbs just so he could say to passers-by "*the bulbs are coming out early this year*".

To stop burglars entering he tied old metal bedframes on the windows and doors which were then wired to the electrical mains supply and would have electrocuted anyone daft enough to attempt to break in. He would have his own fan club in the Daily Mail these days.

There was also the Mad Major – who walked round town in an old army uniform shouldering what looked like a fishing rod in place of a rifle, saluting people and attending the parade on Remembrance Day – despite him never having been in the army in the first place. Mabel used to tell me about a much feared local character called the Galoshe Man who terrorised females when she was a lass. If you didn't know, galoshes then were a sort of rubber-soled tennis pump and this fellow used to appear as if out of nowhere to run silently up behind young ladies, briefly molest them and then run off again just as stealthily. It's a hobby for some, I suppose.

Regarding the pop music of the day, I always preferred the Rolling Stones over the Beatles; was a big fan of Acker Bilk(!) and had a thing about Helen Shapiro and the super sexy Sandie Shaw.

R and B was another influence with groups like the Animals and the Yardbirds to the fore. A few schoolmates and I started a group called the $quid$ (what a cracking name!) and we played a few weddings doing songs like Ain't Gonna Work on Maggie's Farm No More; Big Boss Man; You Can't Tell A Book By Looking at the Cover and Too Much Monkey Business.

You can tell how bad we were by the fact that I was the lead singer. I had a wanky little amplifier plus a battered old Spanish guitar that had belonged to my Uncle Syd but I got thrown out by my so called mates for not being able to afford better gear.

Shortly before, we had been chucked out of our rehearsal room – the local Independent Methodist Hall – by the church leader and lay preacher who heard us swearing onstage.

"*Your language disgusts me and you will never be allowed to come back here again*" he ranted.

Up piped our mate Brian Marshall: a Southern lad, who informed him: "*Swearing? Nothing new. It's all in the Bible, Mister Booth – Bloody Hell, Shit, Piss – the lot!*"

He looked mortified and his little legs were a blur as he pedalled furiously off on his bike.

I've looked in the Bible a few times and I'm not sure Brian was correct in his assertion but, Hell Fire, it still makes me laugh when I think about it.

(Fast forward about 35 years. It's my mam's funeral. As we walk in with the coffin, who's playing the organ? Mr Booth - who I thought had popped his clogs long before. I allowed myself another little smile.)

I suppose I should tell you a little bit about my love life. Not much to report at this stage!

The nearest we got was usually copping a feel in the lovers' seats on the back row of the Savoy Cinema (double seat with no armrest between and tailormade for the job) but that was usually as far as it was allowed to go and by the end of the night, your throbbing testes were ready to explode.

You could tell the lads who'd been halfway to paradise by their pained expressions and the way they walked home like arthritic chimps.

I "courted" many a local girl from an early age and very lovely they were too. I heard that if you took dancing classes, you were in with a better chance of scoring but it worked in the opposite way for me because I was so bad at dancing that if they saw me walking towards them to invite them to do the cha cha cha or whatever, they skedaddled off.

This meant I was mostly confined to the periphery when me and my mates went on Saturday night to the Bolton Palais dance hall, trying to look cool with a Benson and Hedges dangling from my lips.

I count myself lucky I started boozing when proper pubs were around: the type with tap rooms where we played dominoes and learned stuff from old men who had seen a lot of life.

My favourite was "Mick's" taproom (now sadly housing my accountants) which was a men only room. The only woman allowed in was Ethel who served us the lethal Magees IPA and Best Bitter. What a mix of proper men.

There were refugees from the Ukraine, Poland and Romania who worked in local mines and mills and spoke with a curious mix of their own country's accent and a thick Lancashire one.

"Why a you play dat bluddy domino and not de bluddy dubble nine you bluddy piss stone player!"

I found out later a lot of them had shady pasts which they kept quiet about - more or less having been forced to serve with SS Units in the war but to me they were brilliant blokes, full of character, who liked nothing better than to argue over a game of dominoes.

Some cried like babies when they spoke about their families back home who they hadn't seen since the war and were unlikely to ever see again.

There was also the local bookie and the undertaker and his assistant and fellers who could play the harmonica and the spoons and we'd all join in with the "free and easy" singsong.

One very old gent who we called Owd Harry had been a miner and had helped pull dead bodies out when the Pretoria Pit Disaster happened.

I always felt sorry for the cockle man who sold seafood out of a basket and to whom Joe Bunting always enquired: *"Have you got any crabs, feyther?"* When told he had, Joe's response was to scratch his balls and say: *"So have I – they're a fuckin' nuisance aren't they?"* Somehow, it always failed to get a laugh from the beleaguered cockle man.

169

Cool. As.

BANG! – YOU'RE (NEARLY) DEAD

Watch out for the Bits!

I nearly didn't make it through the Not So Swinging Sixties after being sent to report on a job involving a nutter called Blaster Bates – a well known explosives expert and demolition man. He later became famous as an after dinner speaker and released some very funny records.

I didn't think it was funny at the time though when he started throwing stuff at me and the photographer I was with and yelling "*Catch!*"

It turned out they were sticks of gelignite!

Blaster was blowing up the chimney of a local disused factory and he placed us in a position where he assured us we would be safe. Yeah. Right.

The photographer gave me a spare camera as a backup saying "*focus on the chimney and in the unlikely event I miss getting it falling, you'll snap it*".

Eager spectators were set back about 50 yards behind us and there was general excitement as Blaster, dressed in desert camouflage like one of Rommel's finest, lit the fuse, blew his whistle and scooted away from the foot of the factory chimney. I was peering through the viewfinder, concentrating intensely on the chimney, when there was an almighty explosion.

All I could see were little black specks that were suddenly getting bigger and bigger as they came towards me. I was briefly puzzled – until I realised that dozens of bricks from the chimney which were whizzing inches past my head, and almost reaching the spectators far behind me.

I had visions of being killed stone dead with the imprint "Accrington Brick" stamped backwards on my forehead.

No wonder he called one of his LP's "Watch Out For The Bits!"

What made it even worse was the explosion had made me jump and press the camera button instantaneously and all I got on film was the upright chimney before it fell over.

All in a day's work for a local newspaper reporter.

Another close brush came round about the same time when a mate and I went on holiday to Austria.

It was the first time either of us had been abroad and we flew from Manchester airport where amongst all the shining new craft, our particular plane was a poxy DC-4 that seemed to limp onto the runway. As Les Dawson might have said: "*The plane was so old, it had a thatched roof and the pilot's name was Pontius*".

They crammed us in and after a shaky takeoff sucking our barley sugars to stop our ears from popping (do they still do that?) sometime later we reach the coast of France whereupon the plane's alarm system set off with flashing red lights and loud buzzers causing the stewardesses to run panic-stricken up and down the aisles.

We learned from the pilot that we were to make an emergency landing at Lympne in Kent. An emergency landing! Just my luck. My first flight! Should have stuck to me Auntie Nelly's caravan.

The rickety plane did a sharp U-turn and we landed back in dear old Blighty. They never told us what the emergency was and a few hours later we set off for another scary flight to Luxembourg, skirting some trees as we landed. After spending the night there we were shoved into a coach for the long drive to Mayrhofen in Austria, via Munich and were alarmed to see the coach drivers changing shift by means of one man standing up as the other driver slid underneath him to take over the steering wheel while travelling at great speed on the autobahn.

The holiday was a complete disaster. It was the year England won the World Cup over Germany and I am convinced my beer was spiked by some angry Germans who objected to us chanting various songs of victory.

I fell into a deep fever being absolutely drenched in sweat and with my heart pounding like crazy in my chest.

An unsympathetic German doctor administered an injection while I rolled feverishly about the bed as he snidely remarked in an almost cinematic accent "*I thought you British vere supposed to be brave*". Apparently, my blood pressure was so high that only my skin was saving me from being a fountain. He told me I would have to go into hospital in Munich. I told him I wasn't prepared to do that.

It was decided to fly me home and the following day I was hurtled through mountain passes in a speeding Mercedes to catch a plane from Munich to London.

Having survived that particular horror I was given a seat on a Vickers Viscount plane next to the wing where, just before takeoff, I noticed flames coming out of the engine! (Google accidents relating to this aircraft)

Somehow, we got to London and I then had to catch a flight to Manchester sitting next to a woman who was praying all the way and was so jittery she threw gin and tonic all over herself.

I've never flown again.

Happy Days at the Leigh Reporter. L-R: Adman Brian Unwin; me as the Fifth Beatle; lovely Lesley Evans and Dave Hodgkinson who looks like he's kindly removing wax.

MOVING SWIFTLY ON

Now then David what did you really think of me?
To be honest Fred...

Although I enjoyed working on the local paper immensely, after a few years it was time to move on and I applied for and got a reporting job on the West Lancashire Evening Gazette in Blackpool. I moved out of number nine for the first time and into a poky Blackpool bedsit that seemed to constantly stink of boiled cabbage and cost £2 7s 6d a week.

It was a bit like 10, Rillington Place but without the charm. Sometimes, I imagined the pong was dead bodies hidden under the floorboards by a previous tenant.

It wasn't really a fit place to bring girls back to but that didn't stop me. The landlady expressly forbade it and it was a work of art with two people creeping up the stairs trying not to make them creak.

I didn't stay in Blackpool long because the news editor was a bit of an obnoxious git: so much so in fact, that after a drunken leaving do, one disenchanted reporter opened the drawer of the guy's desk and shat in it because he had ordered him to cut short his attendance at his mother's funeral to report on a rugby match.

We called him The Penguin because he had a nasal whine just like the Batman character and the last I heard of him he had met an unlikely demise when he dropped dead disco dancing in a nightclub in New York.

During my brief stay in Blackpool, it was the first time I ever saw Ken Dodd in the flesh so to speak. He was out shopping and being a massive fan at that time, I was quite excited to see him.

Later that day I watched his masterful performance from up in the Gods at the Blackpool Grand Theatre where he gave the audience their usual several hours' worth.

Little did I know that within a few years, I would be writing gags and sketches for him and working on his radio and television programmes. In subsequent years, I saw his act so often I could have done it off by heart – but not as well.

There was also a midnight matinee where stars performing in the town gave their services free for charity. I remember chatting to

Engelbert Humperdinck; the legendary Irish tenor Joseph Locke and Ted Rogers of 321 fame. My Mam was jealous as she adored the first two and we had all of Mr Locke's old 78 records at home. I was brought up on music like that.

But for The Git I would love to have stayed longer in my job at Blackpool as there were some cracking shows, lovely ladies and great bars around at the time and it hadn't degenerated into the bit of a mess it is in today.

I covered the magistrates court in Blackpool during the traditional Glasgow week when Glaswegians came down in droves and virtually took over the resort.

All the courts were very busy that week and I wrote the copy by hand on pieces of paper as the cases were unfolding, with a "runner" dashing backwards and forwards between the court and the newspaper clutching my bits of paper.

This caused me to make a faux pas when I later went for my interview at the Manchester Evening News where the news editor, gruff, chainsmoking, mustachioed Jimmy Ross, quizzed me about my time at the Gazette and I made some remark about the "*bloody Glaswegians making the place hell*" when they took over Blackpool. "*Thanks very much*" he muttered sarcastically out of the corner of his mouth for I had stupidly failed to spot that he himself was a Glaswegian.

Despite that cockup, Jimmy gave me the job and I spent the next two years commuting between my Mam's house and the office that the Evening News shared with the Guardian in Manchester.

Recognised by the police. (Shut it!)

There was a bronze bust of the legendary Guardian founder C P Scott (*"Comment is free but facts are sacred"*) in the foyer that was treated with something less than reverence by us Evening News reporters who frequently left a smouldering fag or cheroot between his august lips.

Although mainly restricted to general reporting duties I really wanted to be a feature writer and took every opportunity to be one. I was particularly proud of a short series of character sketches I wrote about some of the residents of a salvation army hostel who had fallen on hard times, through no fault of their own.

One old guy had been part of a successful acrobatic troupe that had toured Europe but after an accident where he slipped off a trapeze and landed on his head he became stone deaf and couldn't earn his living. The News Editor didn't see it that way though and put a stop to the series saying they were *"just bums"*. Well not really mate – they were human beings with interesting stories to tell.

I also did a feature on a lady medium who ran the local psychical research society.

At the start of the proceedings she solemnly stressed to me the subject was to be written about in all seriousness without a hint of humour.

This was all going swimmingly until Big Stan who was a bluff Mancunian photographer turned up and said to her *"Now then Missis. Can we all go down to the cemetery and I'll take a picture of you bobbing up from behind a gravestone with your arms up, pretending to be frightened by a spook?"*

I was mortified but strangely enough, she went along with it and the "being spooked" photo appeared in the paper.

One of the deputy news editors, Fred Bannister, announced he was leaving to take up a new position at some outpost of the organisation. At his boozy farewell do he sidled up to me and murmured *"Now then David what did you really think of me?"*

A bit drunk, I replied: *"To be honest Fred, I always thought you were a bit of a c*nt"*.

Very shortly afterwards, he left the job he'd gone to, returned to the newsdesk and made sure I knew he hadn't forgotten what my stated opinion of him was and became even more of a c*nt!

George Best was playing for United then and I interviewed him a couple of times. (My wife Lynn would have loved that chance as she became a Man United supporter because she fancied Bestie - as did several million other young ladies of the time.)

On talking to him, it seemed to me he was just a very shy young lad from the back streets of Northern Ireland whose prodigious talent and good looks had propelled him into the glare of the spotlight too soon and left him unable to cope without the aid of the alcohol which finally claimed his life.

I once attended a dinner at Old Trafford where, for some reason, I was plonked on the top table between Bobby Charlton and Sir Alex Ferguson and found them both really good company.

Some people would pay a fortune for that although, to be honest, it was a bigger thrill for me as a Bolton supporter to shake hands with the legendary Lion of Vienna - Nat Lofthouse - when he presented me and the missus with the prize of a luxury weekend in a posh hotel that I won on a Wanderers scratch card.

Sadly, I wasn't getting anywhere with my attempts to be a regular feature writer and after a hectic time at work when I was brought in to cover hectic Salford council meetings I found it all a massive strain and came down with shingles.

That was the turning point. To everyone's astonishment, I handed in my notice and walked out on what was at the time a very well-paid job paying around £50 a week - 50% more than the average national wage.

DUTTON LEAVES MEN

DAVID DUTTON, 22, who won the Bert Stone Memorial Award as the best junior in the Manchester area in 1967, has left his £45-a-week job at the *Manchester Evening News* and is seeking work as a feature writer.

Mr. Dutton worked on the *Leigh Reporter* and the *West Lancashire Evening Gazette*, Blackpool, before joining *MEN*.

They could have phrased it better!

I was 22 and thought there would soon be another equally well-paid writing job along shortly.

I thought wrongly.

I signed on every week at the local Labour Exchange which I hoped was a temporary measure. I was wrong again.

Over 18 months, I sent scores of job applications to newspapers and public relations companies and various other organisations without success.

In a strange way though, I think the hiatus was very beneficial.

Having been unable to afford to go to university, I educated myself at the local library by reading everything I could get my hands on including plays by Tennessee Williams; Arnold Wesker; George Bernard Shaw and Harold Pinter.

Being unemployed for any length of time is dispiriting but in this case, I only had myself to blame.

Strange thoughts entered my head. I was torn between drinking myself to death (but didn't have the cash) or joining the Hari Krishna movement in London! Well, they seemed to have a jolly time dancing up and down the streets and not much work involved.

I attempted a play writing course and although the tutor said my dialogue was excellent and different, I didn't see it through to the end.

I even fancied myself as a stand-up comedian and entered various talent competitions but found the going tough.

In desperation, I borrowed 40 quid off my Mam, went to an Asian wholesaler in Manchester and bought some watches and cigarette lighters which I attempted to flog round the local pubs. The merchandise wasn't very good so that venture fizzled out as well.

I also tried selling vitamins but the rewards weren't as great as promised and it turned out to be a bit of a pyramid scheme.

Jack of all trades and master of bugger all is what I was turning out to be.

Then one day I had another bright idea. I would become a comedy scriptwriter. Deluded or what?

COMIC CUTS – THE DODDY YEARS

I would describe myself as a sincere hypocrite

A comedy scriptwriter is basically a comedian's labourer.
The writer bakes the bricks, carries them up the ladder – and
sometimes it can seem like a bloody long ladder – then the comedian
at the top looks at the bricks, throws the defective ones into a heap
and expertly lays the best ones in a line one after another until a
perfect wall is constructed.
The wall in this case is the wall of laughter that greets the efforts of
both the "labourer" and the "brickie".
Then after the laughter dies down, the writer climbs back down the
ladder, bangs his head against the wall a few hundred times and goes
off to make more bricks.
Sometimes the wall falls down and the bricks land in a heap on top
of the scriptwriter, closely followed by the irate comedian\bricklayer.

This is called a wall of silence.
I hope all this brick analogy is making sense!
Not everybody can be a comedy writer. You have to have a certain
skewed way of looking at things.
It's like being able to play snooker. I think top snooker players are
born grasping a tiny cue – metaphorically speaking.
The best ones still have to practice but they have that innate ability
which makes them champions. I used to play for hours at a time
when I was a teenager and if I got a three-break, I was highly
delighted.
It's the same with comedy writers: the good ones are born with a
certain way of thinking which makes them head and shoulders above
the others. I'm thinking of people like Stan Laurel; Eddie Braben;
Eric Sykes; Spike Milligan; Johnny Speight; the Pythons; Woody
Allen; Larry David; the late Victoria Wood…
Then there are middling snooker players who earn a decent living
and the ones below them who scratch about to keep body and soul
together. As a comedy writer, I ranked probably somewhere between
the latter two.

A lot of people think they can write comedy. You only have to look at some of the so-called funny offerings on the box today to prove a lot of people can't (said an old grump).

It's the same with professional comedians.

I know lots of folks who can have their mates in stitches in a pub but put them on a stage in a room packed with a few hundred strangers and it would be a different matter. It's all to do with technique, stagecraft, confidence, timing, balls and that little bit of magic funny dust that some get sprinkled with when they're born.

Kenneth Arthur Dodd was liberally peppered with that funny dust when he emerged into Knotty Ash on November 8, 1927.

From an early age, he had the urge to perform and the comedy brain and face to go with it. Let's face it, you'd have to be *some* sort of comedy genius to make grown men rock backwards and forwards and cry with laughter at jokes like:

"There's a cow in the garden".
"What's it doing?"
"It's mooing the lawn".
Or even worse:
"What do you think of current affairs?"
"I don't know: I've never had an affair with a currant"
I saw it happen. Many times. There'd be people on the verge of suffocation with all the air sucked out of their bodies after howling at jokes like:
"I'm tickled by all this goodwill.
Have you ever been tickled by goodwill missis?
Good old Willy!"
God how they laughed.

If you wrote a lot of his jokes down on paper, you'd probably hardly crack a smile. It was how he used them that was magic.

From the moment he stepped onstage in his long fur coat supposedly made out of cat fur yelling :"*Ah hairy coms*!" to the "*Tattybye*!!!" at the end of the show some hours in the distant future, the audience certainly had a thorough working out of the chuckle muscle as Doddy used to call it.

He always gave value for money and as a laughter maker extraordinaire, there were few to beat him both in terms of show business longevity and the uncanny hold he had over an audience.

He was a fizzing power pack of comedic energy.

Power.

Interesting word that. Power has many meanings. It can mean having the ability or capacity to perform or act effectively. As a comedian, Doddy had that in spades.

But it has a darker connotation. When someone has power over you that means you are under their control.

And to my mind, that's where Doddy definitely liked to be. In control.

He admitted as much to me one night when I asked: "*What do you enjoy most about doing the job that you do?*"

I was expecting him to say something like "*The joy of making people laugh*" or even "*The money I get for it* " but to my amazement, his reply was:

"*The power it gives me over people*".

To put it mildly, I was taken aback. It seemed to me the mask had slipped a little but at least it was an honest reply.

Many years later in February 2013, I read an interview he gave to Lancashire Life Magazine which was entitled "*I'm a bit of a control freak*".

He was 85 at the time, so little had altered.

I also once asked him "*How would you describe yourself?*" and that answer too was revealing.

His response was:

"*I would describe myself as a sincere hypocrite*".

In a way, I wasn't amazed at the answer but again at the frankness of Doddy's reply.

I don't think we shall ever totally know the real Ken Dodd. Perhaps his legacy of laughter is enough.

He was certainly a very intelligent and complicated person who loved to study psychology: the science of the human mind. Perhaps that is what gave him the edge over people.

But this is my story and, although we had our difficulties, Doddy played a big part in my life in my mid 20's to early 30's so I'm going to report what happened between us. (I was a reporter at one time, remember.)

I can only write from my own personal experiences of the performer – and the man.

Meanwhile, here's a picture of me and some elephants.

And a stuffed Green Parrot

HOW TICKLED WAS I?

Why do you want to look at me? I haven't got two heads...

It's the old saying: "*Never meet your heroes*", only in my case, they might have added "*and never bloody work for them either...*"
My comic hero as a kid had always been Ken Dodd who was already a major star and household name when I was still at school.
I loved his brilliant surreal sense of humour and his ability to paint funny pictures in your mind. He was a comic genius.
In July 1972, I'd been out of work for the best part of 18 months and was getting desperate.
Mam was trying to keep us both on the £10-50p a week she received from working at the mill.
Although I kept sending out job applications on a regular basis, I realised the longer you're unemployed, the harder it is to get back into it so I decided to have a go at comedy scriptwriting.
I had recently shelled out four shillings for a book called Who's Who On Television which was compiled by the staff of TV Times. It contained pictures of a couple of hundred stars of the time with a short writeup about each and trivia such as their hobbies, star signs, shows they'd appeared in and date of birth.
What I found unusual was although most of them gave their agent's details as a point of contact, Ken Dodd had given his own address in Thomas Lane, Knotty Ash near Liverpool (Hobbies: golf; watching racing and football, though as he said to me later "*You could hardly put drinking and shagging!*")
I thought it was very peculiar for a major television star to give out his own personal address for all to see. (No wonder he got stalked later on.)
He also put his address in the variety artistes' bible The Stage Directory, so that any lucrative work could come directly to him, thus cutting out an agent's fee. I suppose in Doddy's case expediency trumped privacy.
Several weeks previously, I'd been for an interview at Granada television for a job in the news department. When I got there, a panel of four fired questions at me and afterwards, I felt I'd failed miserably and was totally out of my depth.

I went for a consoling stiff drink in a nearby pub afterwards and was totally blanked by one of the interviewers which didn't make me feel any better.

A few days later, I wrote a florid letter to the Director of Programmes, Mike Scott, who had been present at the interview and I remember including some overblown idiotic phrase which, as I recall, went: "*I apologise for my demeanour which was like an aspen tree shaking before the four great winds...*"

I must admit now, it does sound a bit Les Dawson-ish.

He must have either thought I was a nutter or trying to be funny and he wrote back: "*Sorry you didn't get the job. Have you thought of writing comedy?*"

At that stage, I hadn't but I recalled that several years previously when I worked on the Reporter, I'd written a series on Famous Leigh Folk. One such person was Ronnie Taylor – a comedy writer who had been born in the town and successfully worked for a number of major UK stars. I can remember sending him a letter afterwards expressing the hope that he had enjoyed reading the article and cunningly adding a PS enquiring about becoming a comedy scriptwriter.

He never responded, so that particular career possibility was put on a back burner.

Mike Scott's remarks, however, must have flicked a switch in the Dutton subconscious, so that day, I bought a pad of foolscap paper, picked up a pen and started writing jokes. I have been living on my wits ever since.

Doddy was on the radio at that time in a very popular daft half hour show called, unsurprisingly, Doddy's Daft Half Hour.

As I said, I'd always loved the guy -even as a teenager, I used to quote his radio show catchphrases to such an annoying extent some of my mates called me Doddy Dutton. It was indeed daft humour – and I've always been a fan of daft.

I must have had a spark of comic inventiveness waiting to burst out for I wrote 12 pages of jokes in almost no time at all.

I'm not saying they were woofers or boffo gags (as we pros call the ones that get the biggest guffaws) but they couldn't have been totally crap because the following week, I was writing for Doddy's radio show and some of the gags were actually used on air. It all seemed totally surreal to me.

I wish I could remember those gags. On second thoughts, I'm probably glad I don't.

I had bunged the 12 pages in a large envelope and sent them off to Thomas Lane. A couple of days later, a letter arrived from Doddy asking me to give him a ring. Well he couldn't ring me because we couldn't afford a phone.

I couldn't believe it! My comic hero Ken Dodd wanted me to ring him. Can you imagine? This big star wanted to speak to little old me. Excitedly, I grabbed some pennies and headed for the nearest public telephone box. I dialled the 051 number with my heart leaping like a demented frog. The phone rang and a voice at the other end mumbled something indistinguishable.

"Could I speak to Mr Dodd please"

"Speaking"

"You wanted me to ring you"

"What?"

"I'm Dave Dutton".

"Who?"

"I sent you some jokes and you sent a letter asking me to ring"

"You want Ken. Just a minute"

It was his dad, Arthur. Some moments later, I heard a clearing of the throat at the other end of the line.

"Hello. Ken Dodd speaking"

I gulped.

"Oh hello. My name's Dave Dutton. I sent you some jokes and you wanted me to ring you" I gabbled.

" Ah, young man. You are a young man I take it"

"Er, yes. Last time I looked"

"I was impressed with the material and I'd like you to come and see me so I can have a look at you"

"Why do you want to look at me? I haven't got two heads" I stupidly stammered, instantly wishing I could have bitten off my tongue. It's the short of defensive retort that shy people do all the time.

"Two heads would be an advantage to a comedy writer" he rightly quipped.

He gave me an appointed time he wanted to see me at his Knotty Ash home and I said I'd be there.

How was I to get there? At that time, I couldn't drive because I couldn't afford a car. I could hardly even afford the bus fare. And where the hell was Knotty Ash anyway? I'd always assumed it was a made-up name.

Luckily as I came out of the phone box I met a bloke called Stan who I knew from the pub and told him of my predicament and he very kindly agreed to run me there in his car.

I rushed back home and changed; left a note for Mam for when she came home from the factory and headed westwards up the East Lancs. Road towards the land of the Diddymen and the Jam Butty Mines.

Stan waited in the car as I walked up Thomas Lane, nervously hesitated, took a deep breath and then knocked on the great man's front door. After a few moments, an oldish bloke opened the door in his vest (Old joke alert: *Funny place to have a door…*)

He muttered something and I told him the reason for my visit then he grunted something else, slammed the door and vanished.

I waited on the doorstep, wondering if I had come to the wrong house.

A few minutes later, the door opened and there he was – the man I had listened to and admired on the radio and the telly for all those years…

Kenneth Arthur Dodd himself – all sticky-out teeth and copious hair! Doddy extended his hand in greeting and cried "*Ah young man! It is a young man*".

My young man's thought processes raced and I pondered to myself "*Why is he so interested in me being a young man?*" and I must admit the thought crossed my naïve mind fleetingly that he might be bent as I'd heard a lot of showbusiness people were.

Obviously he wasn't and as I later learned, it was merely one of his stock greetings to people, irrespective of their age.

He waved me into the house and what a house it was. It was hardly the abode of a rich and famous person. In fact it was rather ramshackle. There were scripts, books, props and old clothes everywhere. Everything looked a bit threadbare: from the carpets and the curtains to the furniture.

I subsequently found out the vest-clad old bloke who had gruntingly greeted me at the front door was his father, Arthur, a former coalman who had bad emphysema.

I used to subsequently dread him answering the phone because I could never make out what he was saying.

We sat in a little front room (on all my subsequent visits, I never got any further into the house). He went to bring me a cup of tea and I was left with two quite old dogs for company – a somewhat smelly ancient drooling boxer dog and an overly large poodle which kept trying disconcertingly to stick its nose between my legs to smell my nadgers.

Doddy came back with the tea and he sat down and reiterated he was pleased with the jokes I had sent adding that he thought I had a talent for the job.

He then asked if I would like to write more material for his current radio series. I could hardly believe my ears. This is what I had been hoping for but hardly thought possible.

Then I spotted over Doddy's right shoulder a painted wooden motivational sign which bore the following words:

"A journey of a thousand miles begins with but a single step..."

And here was I: on the first step of a journey I fondly imagined might take me to fame and fortune – preferably fortune.

Hadn't the brilliant Eddie Braben worked for Doddy for 14 years and then gone on to stellar success with Morecambe and Wise? I knew I was no Eddie Braben at that stage and probably never would be but perhaps the sign was in itself a portent of what might be achieved?

"Well young man?" said Doddy, rousing me from my reverie.

"Would you like to write jokes and scripts for me?"

"I would". I said eagerly.

"In that case I shall put you on a weekly retainer and as we're using some of your jokes in next week's show, I'll give you a cheque now".

And in saying that, he reached grandly for his chequebook and started to write in it.

My mind raced. He was going to give me money! I'd hit the jackpot. I'd hit the big time. I was quids in!

Well, fifteen quids in as it happened. I thought it might have been a bit more as it was a top rated radio show but at least it was a start.

I was even more discomknockerated (to use a Doddy expression) when I found out the size of the workload I was expected to shoulder.

Doddy got through jokes like a fat person gets through Pringles and M and Ms.. He gave me a subject to which I had to adhere – it might be on the subject of food one week or history or holidays the next and I was expected to churn out hundreds of gags around the particular theme.

I rang him daily and he had a weird quirk of answering the phone talking like a cowboy by saying: "*Well hello Big D....or Howdy Big D...*". in a strange cod American drawl.

I used to think was unique to me but found out he also addressed other writers by their initials likewise.

I must admit, I found the joke-writing process almost like going into a trance. One minute you were sitting looking at a blank sheet of paper – the next, you were still sitting looking at a blank sheet of paper. Or if you were lucky, a page full of gags. Then another page and another... it was a bit like working on a production line at a joke factory.

Most times, I didn't even remember what I had written until I read it back. It's a strange process.

It's also a bit like panning for gold. There was a lot of dross but one or two nuggets in there. I must have provided the requisite amount of nuggets because the gags were used on the radio show and I got my name mentioned in the credits. Now that was a thrill. For years I had been an aficionado of all sorts of comedy on the wireless: from Al Read to the Goons; Jimmy Clitheroe to Hancock's Half Hour and the Billy Cotton Band Show – and of course Doddy's own shows when I was at school.

To hear my name coming out of our plastic Bush wireless (still got it somewhere and it still works!) gave me unimaginable pleasure. I taped it and kept playing it back.

When you've been labelled a Mr Nobody as a kid, it's an incentive to become a Mr Somebody and hearing some posh BBC announcer say my name over the airwaves was a confidence-boosting step along the thousand-mile highway.

Mam was thrilled to bits: especially when people stopped her at work and up the high street and said: " *We heard your David's name on the wireless!*" I was glad to make her proud of me.

The worst part for both of us was everybody thought I was making a fortune yet I was only on £15 a week and it stayed that way for a long time.

Doddy was cleverly always hinting there would be more money on the table when his television shows came along. He was shrewd that way. Well, he'd studied human nature hadn't he? I remember him once going into great detail about something he knew a great deal about called Gestalt psychology. I hadn't a clue what he was talking about.

I looked it up recently on the internet and it said:

"The key properties of Gestalt systems are emergence, reification, multistability, and invariance".

I still have no idea what he was talking about. It meant jam tomorrow as far as this scriptwriter in the early 70's was concerned. I turned into a sort of human sausage machine: churning out the jokes and then sketches.

My equipment consisted of a battered old yellow portable typewriter I had bought for a few quid second hand. It was customary to type one's name in the top right hand corner of each script. I then passed them over to Ken who vetted them and sent them on to a script editor.

One day, a lot later on, I was amazed when a script editor confided in me that these scripts had the names cut out of them by Doddy. I later discovered that the reason was he was being paid the script fees by the BBC and then giving the writers less pro rata than he was getting in total and keeping the balance for himself. Naughty Kenneth!

The names were presumably cut off so no one knew which scriptwriters had written what and what he himself had supposedly contributed.

This also had repercussions many years later after I had stopped writing for him. I'll go into it further down the line.

Recently, another comedy writer suggested we should write a book about our experiences with Doddy and call it *"How Tickled We Weren't!"*

Soon I was invited down to London to watch the shows being recorded and meet the cast.

Sometimes I travelled down in Doddy's blue Jag which was driven by a sort of chauffeur/minder and on one of these journeys we had the first of our many arguments as it was during the 1972 miners strike and being the grandson of a miner with many pitmen in my family, I supported them but Doddy being an out and out Tory took the opposite view. Bit much considering his dad had been a coal merchant who wouldn't have had a business but for the brave collier lads!

190

It was also well known in show business and something of a standing joke that Doddy was known to be "careful" with his money. When my mother's employers at the cotton mill opened a factory outlet, they sold "seconds" – shirts with slight but almost unnoticeable flaws with the labels cut out. She bought some for me to wear and look presentable.

When Doddy found out about this he asked if my Mam would buy some of these shirts for him. They only cost about five shillings (25p) each and he gave her the money when he came round.

I remember seeing him being interviewed on television several times wearing one of these distinctive cheap shirts! To be honest *that* tickled me.

This was a guy who must've been a millionaire or possibly a multi millionaire by then with the money he had made from his shows and major hit records.

At his infamous tax fraud court case in 1989 it was reported he had £336,000 in cash scattered about in wardrobes and cupboards at his home; had £777,000 in 20 offshore bank accounts yet he was buying shirts off Mabel at 5 bob a throw!

It was claimed in court that over 40 years, his entire expenditure was only £23,000. Plus he never even paid the stage school kids who performed onstage as his Diddy Men.

I suppose that's how you get to accumulate such riches. Looking back, I was lucky to get that fifteen quid!

He also persuaded Mabel to sell his plastic Diddy Men dolls to her workmates and friends paying her sixpence commission (2.5 pence) on each one.

(When we cleared out my Mam's house after she died, I found one of these dolls with its eyes burnt out with a cigarette like some strange Lancashire voodoo retribution: my Mam's revenge for how she thought I had been treated by Doddy.)

He was a regular visitor to our house: coming to pick up the scripts I had written that week and was very affable to any of my family who may have been in the house at the time -including my uncle Ned who poked him in the famously insured teeth that time to see if they were real.

Sometimes a crowd of children gathered in the street, unable to believe the bloke they had seen on television was actually there in the flesh.

As the years progressed, I became his chief scriptwriter but still the money wasn't all that good. The retainer only went up by 10 or 15 quid but I earned a bit of extra money from the BBC by being commissioned to write sketches for his various television shows. Doddy's control freakery went a step too far when he appointed himself the vetter of my girlfriends. (He didn't like me having a beard either – saying that bearded blokes were untrustworthy.)

One beautiful girl, some years younger than me, who I took to one of his shows, didn't meet with his approval for some reason and the next time I met him, he took me to one side and said "*She'll be so fat in a few years' time that you wouldn't piss on her*".

Another one who smoked was dismissed by him as "*a croaky old hack*".

One who did meet his approval and that of his fiancée Anita was my wife-to-be Lynn who they both pronounced as "*a good un*". They were right there. It was 1974 and Lynn was a neighbour of my best mate Johnny Davis. We got chatting one night in a nearby pub. She was only 17 years old and I was nine years older but that didn't stop me from asking her out. Her long blonde hair and lovely big eyes had something to do with that.

Shortly after we met. Her dog's name was Brandy. It was a great day for hanging the washing out too.

In my Mam's belongings, I found a diary note she had written regarding a conversation with Doddy:

192

"Phone rang and I picked it up and a voice said 'Hello Mabel. Is Diddy David there?'.
I said 'no Bob' as I thought he was the landlord of David's local as he was always saying that.
But it was Doddy. He had to convince me who it was before I believed him. He said he would ring again in the morning and I told him that David wouldn't be long as he was out courting.
He asked if I approved of her and I told him yes but if George Best saw her, David had no chance as she was his type and he was hers. Doddy laughed at that. I said she was lovely with long blonde hair and he jokingly asked me if I'd seen her back teeth then. I said no – but what I saw, I liked. She is the one for him".

She was right. We hit it off from the beginning and got married the following year with Doddy turning up (late as usual) at our wedding reception with a present of six wine glasses that gradually over the years got knocked over and broken.

We got spliced in a local Unitarian Chapel and the Minister in charge was a bit of an old dodderer. It was his first marriage service and he was more nervous than us to the extent that when I placed the wedding ring on the Bible, he was shaking so much, it bounced up and down like a pingpong ball on a fountain.

After we had signed the register, Lynn tried to walk with me back into the chapel. She found herself unable to move at which point my usher, my old workmate Les Powell, piped up: *"Excuse me Reverend but you're standing on her train!"*

We often wonder in view of the fact the Minister didn't seem to know what he was doing if we were really married after all!

The reception didn't pass without incident either. A disgruntled bloke who was thrown out the pub took his revenge by chucking a full house brick through the window, narrowly missing some of the wedding guests.

Mabel had threatened not to come to the wedding because I didn't want my father's name on the wedding certificate. She said the fact I wanted to leave it blank made her look like she'd been with lots of men and didn't know who my father was. I agreed to put his name on and she turned up looking resplendent in a big hat.

We had planned to honeymoon in London but a comic who I had provided some gags for reneged on payment at the last moment so we couldn't afford to go. Instead, we spent it in the house - an old terraced property with a manky settee; lino in the living room; a lean-to for a kitchen and mites in the cupboard. Not perfect but all we could afford on the little I was earning at the time. The old lady we bought it off was found dead sitting up in a chair with the radio still on. Come to think of it, we bought that chair off her family afterwards and it had a few stains on it!

1974 was also the year the IRA bombed two pubs in Birmingham and I remember passing through on the bus down to Shepherd's Bush to watch another of Doddy's television shows being recorded.

The BBC were on heightened alert. I use that term loosely because I breezed past "security" waving a feather off a dancer's skirt accompanied by the brilliant "One Foot in the Grave" writer David Renwick who deftly proffered his Sketchley Dry Cleaners' Discount Card in front of their unseeing eyes.

I was also responsible for a security scare when I left my green duffle bag full of cheese butties, crisps and cans of cider on my seat in the studio and went to the loo.

Someone noticed the unattended bag and reported it to the authorities who were on the verge of stopping the show and evacuating the place when I returned to get me butties. They weren't best pleased.

It was an exhausting time for me. I was burning the candle at both ends as I was expected to travel down to see the shows then go back home and start writing for the next one. To be honest it was a bit of a treadmill and I was churning out one-liners and sketches which sometimes wouldn't even see the light of day.

Another complication was Doddy used to come round to our little terraced house to pick up the scripts but he annoyingly got progressively later and later: sometimes keeping us up till 2 am and after. Whenever I rang him, he always claimed he was on his way. This would happen several times in a night.

Doddy was notorious for his lack of punctuality (he once famously kept Prime Minister Harold Wilson waiting for ages) but this was taking the piss. He obviously didn't subscribe to the old adage about it being the politeness of kings.

The weird thing was that sometimes, he sat outside in his car for an hour or so before knocking on the door.

Lynn was working full time as we couldn't subsist on the money Doddy was paying me and his late arrivals disturbed her sleep. This sowed the seeds of discontent and when he eventually turned up on the doorstep in the wee small hours I told him I wasn't prepared to carry on in that manner and he could get someone else to write for him.

He responded that he would make sure I wouldn't work in television again. I said that was fine by me and slammed the door in his face, feeling a great sense of relief.

I told Lynn what I had done and she fully supported me even though we didn't know where the next penny was coming from.

The next morning Doddy rang me saying that we both needed each other but although I carried on writing my heart wasn't really in it.

Doddy and I had had many a discussion during those late nights/early mornings and sometimes, he revealed his thoughts to me about his fellow entertainers.

These were often less than flattering and quite shocking but when any of them died and he came on television to pay tribute to them, I fully realised what he had meant by deeming himself a "sincere hypocrite".

He was a complicated man and I have no idea why he felt that way.

A strange quirk I noticed was that for some reason, after travelling from his house to ours, he would always go and relieve himself down the back of the houses opposite ours. I thought of having a blue plaque put up saying *"Ken Dodd peed here"*.

I worked for Ken as his main writer for about seven years and it wasn't all doom and gloom. I met his first fiancée Anita, a wonderful lady who looked after his props and did his sound effects from the side of the stage. He had been engaged to her for many years until her tragic death from cancer. I also met many times with his second fiancee, Anne, another lovely lady (who he married two days before he died) who took over setting out his props when Anita died. She had a good singing voice and often did a spot on Ken's stage variety show.

She too made many visits to my mother's house with Ken and Mabel always got the best china cups out for her.

During one visit, Doddy's eye alighted on an unusual set of books that I had just bought off an antique stall on our local market. They were miniature versions of Shakespeare's plays – each in its own tiny book in a small bookcase, like something out of a doll's house.

He made it clear that he wanted it and started offering me cash. I shook my head until it got to something more than he was paying me per week when I decided that it would go towards paying the bills. I couldn't afford to say no. What Kenneth wanted, Kenneth got.

I had ambitions to be a comedian myself during that time and Doddy gave me one or two hints and lessons at his house, which I still have on tape somewhere. One line he gave me which he said I should open the act with was: *"I suppose you're all wondering why I sent for you tonight..."*

I tried it and not surprisingly, it got me off to a flying stop!

I even opened the show on gigs for him on several occasions but I can't recall making much of an impression on his fans.

My mate Johnny Davis and I used to travel to pubs in the Manchester area where I entered some talent competitions (unsuccessfully). I think my material was a bit too way out (*"My granddad drank so much he had a plimsoll line on his waistcoat"*) and I recall one occasion in a rough Salford pub saying to the audience *"You'll always have money as long as you remember these three little words: Stick Em Up!"* then pulling out and firing an imitation pistol.

One rough looking Salfordian came up to me after and said "*I fucking shit myself when you pulled that gun out. What the fuck were you thinking about?*"

Salford is definitely not the place to try anything like that.

One day, Doddy asked me if I wanted to do some walk-on work on his show for a bit of extra cash from the Beeb so I jumped at the chance. It was being filmed in Skegness where he was appearing in summer season.

My first part was as General Amin's legs! Probably regarded as a non-PC thing to do these days but the makeup girls blacked my legs up and in the sketch, Doddy was seen crawling towards me out of the desert (Skegness beach) thinking he'd found a rescuer who turned out to be the aforementioned vicious African dictator.

I also played various other parts including a caveman; a Red Indian; and Harold Wilson as King Canute sitting in a deckchair trying to hold back the tide in his gannex mac and pipe in mouth and eventually getting washed out to sea.

As we were filming, we didn't notice the tide creeping up behind us and Doddy and I, along with the whole television crew and cast were in danger of being swept into the freezing North Sea and had to be rescued by an amphibious vehicle which turned up in the nick of time and carried us back to safety.

Two incidents stand out in the memory from that summer in Skegness. In Doddy's show there was a young ventriloquist called Larry who was just starting out and he was a little unsure of himself. Every night, Doddy heckled him loudly from the wings at the start of his act which made the audience laugh but threw him somewhat and members of the cast didn't think this was right.

They asked me to provide Larry with some heckler stoppers to throw back at Doddy (*Last time I saw a mouth like that, it had a hook in it etc*) and after the show a furious Ken came charging round and gave us all a bollocking saying it had destroyed the comedy value. He didn't refer to me specifically but I knew that he knew where the gags had come from.

There was also a curious event where during Ken's performance a moth kept interrupting his act by flying around his head- much to the amusement of the audience. I was standing in the wings of the theatre and he turned to me and said desperately "*Quick! Give me a line!*"

197

I threw back a couple of crap quips saying something like *"tell them it thinks it's a betting shop and it's coming in for a little flutter"* or *"it's lost and looking for its moth-er"* which he used. When the moth persisted in interrupting his act I threw a football onto the stage and hissed *"Say it's a mothball"*.

He thanked me afterwards but I found it a little strange that an experienced comedian like Ken couldn't think of an adlib on the spot - which was most unlike him.

The audience were in hysterics at the antics of the moth and it turned out to be a very funny part of the show.

I always enjoyed watching Ken do his act. He was a consummate craftsman who had perfected his art from working the back room of pubs, to clubs and theatres and all the way to a record breaking run at the London Palladium. The word legend is much overused these days but it's true to say he deserved that title.

Towards the end of my time working for him, my old News Editor, Hal Dootson, came up with an idea for a book -"*The Ken Dodd Butty Book*". It was a mixture of sandwich ideas and jokes which eventually got published, amazingly enough under the prestigious MacMillan publishing label. As we neared the completion of the book after working on it for some time, Doddy suddenly announced he wanted a bigger share of the royalties. Obviously, we couldn't do anything about it as his name was on the front of the book!

By the time it came out, I had actually finished writing for him because the pay wasn't really getting any better and the workload was proving stressful.

Like most people, I had a mortgage to pay and a house to run. He was always promising more money but it never seemed to materialise. Working for Ken just wasn't putting the jam in my butties.

So it was embarrassingly uncomfortable at the launch party of the book to find myself sitting near him at the same table. For some reason, the talk turned to the advantages and disadvantages of self-employment and Dodd looked towards me with a strange expression and said pointedly *"Everybody should have a boss, shouldn't they Dave?"*

As our relationship gradually fizzled, I began to try my hand at writing for other comedians.

Years later, he did a series for Thames Television and I noticed he had resuscitated some of my BBC sketches without crediting me for them or even paying me.

I got in touch with the Scripts Coordinator at Thames and pointed out they were using my material without my permission and her reply, after contacting producer Denis Kirkland and light entertainment director Philip Jones was "*All that material has been written by Mr Dodd. We have paid him a great deal of money*".

At the time I was writing for Doddy, he was in the habit of saying that he had lost the originals of sketches and kept asking me to send the copies.

As luck would have it, I had copies of most of the sketches that Thames were using and the original notebooks they were written in. I contacted my literary agent at the time- a big London agency called Curtis Brown - who sent the evidence off to Thames who then admitted they were in breach of my copyright and they had to pay me. They were furious with Doddy and said he would never do another series with them. Whether it was coincidence or not, he never did, although his brilliant Audience With Ken Dodd resuscitated his career somewhat and introduced him to a new audience.

During our relationship, Doddy had told me I was a better comedy writer than Eddie Braben. I wasn't even flattered by this because I knew I wasn't. I was a jobbing writer and Eddie was a master of the art as far as I was concerned.

When Doddy was having his "bit of trouble" with the taxman in 1989, I was approached several times by a Sunday newspaper to do an interview about him.

I turned them down but the persistent reporter made an offer…

"*It doesn't have to be too controversial and I'll come round myself and give you a grand in cash*"

That would have been very handy money for me at the time and I must admit I considered it.

So what did I do?

I took an unorthodox approach to resolve the matter by taking a Bible from the bookshelf and with my eyes closed, opened it at random and touched a part of the page.

It's an old Northern method of divination: something I had seen my superstitious Mam do in the distant past, so I thought I would give it a go to gain a bit of advice from a higher power, if you like.

It was a half-hearted thing really but I was curious to see the result. I slowly opened my eyes to look where my finger had landed and to my shock, the following words jumped out at me:

"What will ye give me, and I will deliver him unto to you? And they covenanted with him for thirty pieces of silver".

My jaw dropped; I stood dazed for a few seconds then slammed the Bible shut.

A higher authority **had** spoken so next time the newspaper guy rang I politely declined the offer.

Doddy was found not guilty of all charges - no doubt disappointing the inmates at Walton jail who had strung a banner outside their cells with *"KEN DODD. APPEARING HERE SHORTLY!"*emblazoned on it.

Twenty years after I stopped working for him, he came to perform at a village hall near me. I decided to bite the bullet and take my son Gareth to see him in action because he was still a fabulous comedian.

I was persuaded by the organiser, an old magician friend of his, to have a word with Ken before the show so I took Gareth round to meet him. We had a little chat about the past and Anne kindly asked about my mother - remembering those posh china cups she used to serve her the tea in.

There was a very funny unscripted comedy moment when his big poodle dog tried to shag the long red thick furry coat he always wore at the start of his act and Doddy jumped up and swung the coat round the dressing room trying to dislodge the enthusiastic canine humper, shouting " *Get off!* "

I made my excuses and left, as they say and that was the last time I ever spoke to him.

In 2013, the curious incident of the dog on the coat came to mind after I read a revealing interview Doddy did with BBC reporter Ian Youngs.

It was rather sad.

He told Ian: *"There are all different kinds of love. Parents must love their children. I don't know. I suppose I would. I love my dog. I love him very much and all the dogs I've ever had, I've always loved them.*

So I must have the capacity to do it. "

How strange.

He was 85 and still wondering if he would have had the capacity to love the children he never had as much as his dogs.

I'm glad he got his knighthood. He certainly deserved it. Comedy is rarely recognised in the honours list.

Having known him in his ebullient prime, I was deeply saddened to see him in decline in his final weeks in hospital.

Doddy was a complex character whose sole raison d'être seemed to be to perform his comedy onstage where, of course, he loved to be (and I think where he would have wanted to have died) and where he was in complete control of himself - and more importantly, in control of his adoring audience.

But, as he discovered, there's one thing even he couldn't control.

That final curtain.

None of us can…

DAVE'S TOP TIPS FOR ASPIRING COMEDY WRITERS…

1. *Write to the comedian's style.*
2. *Prepare to sweat blood.*
3. *Prepare to lose your sense of humour*
4. *Keep copies of everything.*
5. *Get another job.*

Doddy working the camera while most of us look like something awful has just walked through the door of the pub. I'm pretty sure that this isn't when the brick came flying through the window but it's a long time ago.

Left to Right – Front: Bridesmaids Julie and Tracy. Back. Ma in law Marjorie; Mabel's head; Johnny Davis (Best Man); Kenneth Arthur Dodd (comedian); Lovely Lynn; Dashing Dave and Lynn's brother Ian. Dig my sidies and the double breasted jacket. I must have been a bit nervous on the morning of the ceremony as I tried to wear Johnny's suit. Well it does look seventies similar. Pic taken by my late colleague John Holland, ex photographer on the Manchester Evening News. He very kindly did our wedding album.

LIFE AFTER DODDY – OR, BEYOND OUR KEN

I'm going to put the bubble in

When you are forced to live off your wits, it can be very character building. It can also make you very skint.

Things got so bad at one stage that all I could afford to drive was a clapped out Austin Allegro which drank so much oil on a drive down to Dawlish, we had to stop at every other major motorway service station to top it up again.

At one stage, we couldn't even afford a car. To pay the bills, we had to sell our jalopy and Lynn and I trudged home for miles through fields clutching the pittance we had got for it from the used car salesman.

We dreaded getting bills through the post. As soon as one was paid another seemed to land on the doormat.

One day, when I was still working for Doddy, I received a letter out of the blue from Ronnie Corbett asking me if I would like to contribute some material to his very popular armchair monologue in the Two Ronnies.

Would I?!

I kept looking at the letter. It was a bit of a shock to be honest and I later discovered a top BBC producer called Michael Hurll had recommended me to little Ronnie.

I told Doddy but he wasn't best pleased! In fact he was furious with Hurll, saying: "*I'm going to put the bubble in*" which I took to mean he'd give him a mouthful although I haven't a clue what he did about it, if anything.

I was commissioned to do some work and although some of it got used – in fact Ronnie kindly told me how pleased he was - it was in no way comparable to the work of the legendary Spike Mullins who wrote the original monologues and who I later came to know.

However, this led to me writing some of the opening news items and closing gags for the Two Ronnies show for which I'm still getting royalties that, if clumped together, might one day buy a bag of cheese and onion crisps.

I was invited to a party for the writers (including top guys such as Barry Cryer and David Renwick) at the Mayfair Hotel in London during which Ronnie Barker and Ronnie Corbett went round pouring

drinks for us, serving us snacks and were the epitome of charm
It was just like being in one of their sketches. Spike Mullins was there but was one of the first to leave claiming *"I'd better get back to Slough before it shuts"*.

Spike was a great bloke. The measure of the man is in the fact that many years later, when I'd got a good part in the TV comedy "Watching", he took the trouble to find out my telephone number; ring me and tell me how much he and his wife were enjoying the show. He said *"I tell everybody – I know him* (me)" Small kindnesses are always remembered.

After I left Doddy I was still doing bits and pieces for shows like the Two Ronnies.

I also managed to get some work seen on the very popular Dick Emery show although I was warned by the producer not to put too much "business" in the sketches as Dick had problems handling that side of things apparently.

It was very strange for a lad from my background to find himself standing at the BBC bar talking to top men like Ian McNaughton, who produced most of the Python shows and rubbing shoulders with the legendary Dennis Main Wilson, who was responsible for the top comedy shows of the time.

I continued to contribute bits and pieces for other programmes such as the Basil Brush Show, Three of a Kind with Lenny Henry, Tracey Ullman and David Copperfield and also for the very popular Little and Large show and one-liners for variety shows involving Cliff Richard and the ex footballer and comedian Charlie Williams.

I had first met the legendary Tommy Cooper when I was writing for Doddy after he turned up at a television recording.

It was like a collision of zanies: Doddy with his buck teeth and wild hair and Tommy with his massive frame, splayed feet and soulful fried egg eyes.

There were several of us in the dressing room and Tommy regaled us with an inconsequential story about his frustrated manager trying to locate him one day in London. I can't remember the details. It was about nothing really but all I remember is here was this giant of a man telling a story which, told by anyone else, would have been a run of the mill tale but Tommy's unique deadpan interpretation had us all clutching our sides and falling about.

I'm not sure we even knew what we were laughing at. Even after watching reruns of Tommy's cabaret act on television, it's still clear he had some once in a lifetime magic formula that induced laughter in millions who hadn't a clue what was making them laugh.

Anyway, spying an opportunity to work with Tommy, I got his phone number and address and sent him a few ideas for scripts for a television sketch programme he was working on at the time.

He invited me to meet him at some club up north which bizarrely had a Viking longboat as a bar. I sat in the audience and watched people rolling about helplessly as his voice boomed out while he pretended to be locked in his dressing room. He'd got the audience in the palm of his hand before he had even set his massive feet on the stage.

Later as we talked in his dressing room after his performance, he gave me an outline of some of the sketches he was using on the television show.

One I recall was him miming a man in a pith helmet cursing and ostensibly strenuously hacking his way out of the jungle: but when the camera pulled back, it would show he was only in his overgrown greenhouse. Not many people have had a Tommy Cooper sketch performed personally for them!

He was wearing a large white dressing gown which revealed legs the size of tree trunks adorned in thick varicose veins. It's well documented Tommy was a prodigious drinker and the copious bottles of spirits on his dressing room table that he stipulated had to be provided by the establishment were scooped into a big cardboard box and taken back by him to his hotel room later.

The only other experience I remember about my dealings with Tommy was that he got a bit ratty when I made several follow-up phone calls enquiring about the material I had provided for him. When, for some reason, I informed him I used to be a reporter he replied: "*Yes I thought you must have been*" - which I took to mean a reference to my persistence or the fact I was making a nuisance of myself.

As we didn't have a phone at home, I had to ring from the one outside the local post office and keep shoving money in it. His wife, Dove, was lovely about it and said: "*Don't worry. There was a time when we couldn't afford a phone too*".

205

Sadly, nothing much came of my efforts and he continued to be just as much of a massive success without me!

I also met the equally legendary Les Dawson a couple of times. The first occasion was fairly early on in his television career when he lived in a small bungalow at a place called Unsworth near Bury. What stands out in my mind is that the dwelling was called Igls, which seemed a little strange but I later learned it was a place in Austria where Les and his wife had spent their honeymoon.

I had sent him a few scripts which he liked and he encouragingly wrote me an appreciative letter which included the line "*I think you have captured my style. It escaped some years ago under the name of Jeyes Fluid*" - a typical Dawson quip.

The landlord of my local, Bob Ellis, drove me to his house and Les came to the front door with his shirt open and took the scripts off me. We weren't invited inside and all I can remember is Les commenting in his typical laconic style about the noisy street activity "*we have kids round here like other places have mice*".

One or two of my ideas were used in the telly show but it wasn't really a happy experience because one sketch was used which I recognised as mine - although I was not even credited with it. Another sketch was lifted, rewritten and used in a later series and I never got paid. I'm not blaming Les but it's one of the perils of being a struggling scriptwriter as many have found. Not naming names but I recently read that the guy who did it was complaining about the same thing being done to him on another show! Karma eh?

I met Les again some years later when he was at the height of his success and me and a friend were invited to his very posh large detached house in Lytham to discuss an idea we had for a book to be fronted by Les.

This time I got invited inside and we spent a couple of hours talking over the project. We were treated in his study to an impromptu couple of Les's amazing rambling flowery comedy monologues for some reason, which certainly made the trip worthwhile.

He came to wave us off on his driveway and I remember him laughing at the GOB registration numberplate of my car: the frequent butt of finger-pointing by gleeful kids.

I should have met Les a third time when I came up with an idea for a comedy record based on the 12 days of Christmas. I travelled with a top record producer all the way to Bridlington where Les was appearing in summer season.

He failed to turn up at the appointed hour and we chased him all over Bridlington without success. The runaround pissed the producer off and he didn't want anything more to do with Les. That idea came to nought as well but subsequently became a chart success for a comedy actor although again I couldn't prove anything.

Les was a down to earth Northerner and a true comedy great: distilling the best of top old variety acts such as Frank Randle, Robb Wilton and Norman Evans and adding his own flavour and style. He died far too young.

THE SEX PISTOLS ESCAPE A MAULING

Sid would love this doll..

Because I hadn't been able to subsist on the money Doddy was paying me, I was forced to look for other earning opportunities. When Piccadilly Radio opened up in Manchester in 1974, I dropped them a line offering my services. Luckily, I got an interview with the gaffer, Colin Walters, who on the strength of my background as a reporter, offered me some freelance work which I eagerly accepted. It was the city's first independent local radio station and it was very exciting to be in at the beginning of it all. Stars such as Chris Evans and Timmy Mallett first made their names on the station which was a vibrant contribution to the culture of the city.

They gave me use of a white van with Piccadilly Radio 261 emblazoned on the side and a recording device called a Uher. Wherever you turned up in the van, you'd be surrounded by hordes of kids all chanting the "Piccadilly 261" jingle.

Soon I was doing vox pop interviews in the street; talking to studio guests; taking part in phone-ins and when we were quiet, making up stories such as Percy the incredible talking budgerigar who did impressions of famous people. I was the voice of Percy, pretending to be Benny Hill and other stars of the era.

I interviewed Sid the farting traffic warden who was in fact a mate of mine who had made a mechanical contraption consisting of a piece of metal with a rubber band and a washer which he tucked under his arse to manufacture disgusting noises while sitting next to unsuspecting folk in the pub.

We doctored tapes sent from America which made it sound like Raquel Welch was going on a picnic club outing with a load of Lancashire boozers and people thought it was real.

One of my comedy heroes, Spike Milligan, popped into the studio one day to plug his latest book. Unfortunately, I just missed him as I had been doing an outside broadcast but he typically brought mayhem to the station by doing clucking hen noises during the news and bursting into the managing director's office yelling "capitalist swine!"

Maggie Thatcher turned up one day and my co-presenter Roger Finnegan asked her how much she thought a tin of baked beans was.

She hadn't a clue and tried to bluster her way out of it but it showed how out of touch she was with ordinary folk.

I did a series on comedians and interviewed the infamous Bernard Manning several times including one occasion at his mother's house where I watched as he was forced by her to eat a gigantic plateful of the local delicacy known as "tater hash" (a working class dish made with corned beef, onions potatoes and carrots) just like a little schoolboy.

Working in radio was very enjoyable but an incident on January 27, 1975 could have cut short my broadcasting career, as well as me.

I had just interviewed pop star Wayne Fontana who had been big in the 60's and as we were going in the same direction home, we left the station together. We decided to take a shortcut through the basement of Lewis's store and very shortly after we passed through – BOOM! - an IRA bomb exploded, injuring 19 people: one very seriously.

To think I could have died with Wayne Fontana is mindbending. (That's a pisspoor joke by the way - his backing group were called the Mindbenders.)

There was another near miss in March 1993 when Lynn, Mabel and I went shopping at Warrington Ikea. We were planning to go into the town itself but for some reason changed our minds at the last minute. It was the day the IRA planted a bomb which tragically killed two young boys in the centre of Warrington. It's the roll of the dice I suppose: like the time during a gale in Manchester when a strong gust of wind blew a huge coping stone off the top of a shop, crashing down on the pavement two feet in front of me.

Working at Piccadilly Radio was a lot of fun. It was the height of the punk era and on December 9, 1976 we interviewed the biggest name in punk: the Sex Pistols.

This was a week after the infamous television live interview with Bill Grundy when their foulmouthed behaviour scandalised the nation. The first single, Anarchy in the UK, allegedly encouraged violence against the government.

They came to our studio with their manager Malcolm McLaren to publicise their Manchester gig and we decided beforehand to set up a madcap stunt involving them but without their knowledge.

One of our regular contributors was a burly local wrestler by the name of Abe Ginsberg who sat in on the interview with them.

209

At a key moment, one of us was going to casually ask the Pistols "*so you advocate violence then?*", which was to be a signal for Abe to don his wrestling helmet and start duffing up them up shouting "*How do you like it?!*"

It was a tense moment which turned into an almighty letdown when at the crucial moment, Abe just sat there looking sweet as apple pie as we all nodded to cue him in.

We remonstrated with him after but he confessed *"I hadn't the heart to beat 'em up. I realised it was all an act like I'm doing with me wrestling"*.

Fair point. Anyway, we weren't going to argue with Abe as he was a champion grappler.

When I tried to engage Johnny Rotten in conversation afterwards by naively asking him if he didn't think there was already too much violence in the world, I didn't get past his starey, scary eyes as he totally blanked me and studiously looked up the frock of a doll left underneath the Piccadilly Radio Christmas tree, commenting "*Sid would like this*" - Sid being the Mr Vicious of that name who joined the group shortly after.

I'm quite pleased the stunt didn't come off as I really like John Lydon, as he is now. It would have been a rotten thing to do to him anyway... Geddit?

I could've been big in the radio business. If only I'd known how to work the desk...

LANKY SPOKEN HERE

Dost yar mi?

"Why don't you write a dirty book – there's money in that " – that was a frequent call of my Mam's. I found that a bit surprising as she was easily embarrassed and so would I have been at the thought of her reading any porn literature that I might have concocted.
I quite fancied the idea of being an author so I thought along other lines...
I'm what you might call trilingual. I speak passable English; halting French and Lancashire dialect expertly.
"Lanky" is in my blood. Growing up in a South West Lancs industrial town surrounded by relatives, neighbours and friends who spoke broad dialect, it comes as naturally to me as breathing.
I can put on a posh telephone or acting voice as and when necessary but I much prefer the comfy slippers feel of the old Lancashire lingo.
My Gran was a major influence. It was never cold it was "*cowd*". It was never you it was "*thee*". She never said "do you hear me?" It was " *Dost yar mi*?"
Starlings were "*Sheppies*". Moths were "*Buzzerts*". Mice were "*Moggies*". (You heard that right: a cat was **never** a moggy in our neck of the woods.)
Though not as prevalent, the dialect still persists in a great many parts of our wonderful county and my heart always warms when I hear it spoken.
Put two Lancashire dialect speakers together and I can assure you that the conversation would be as impenetrable to outsiders as Serbo-Croat or Swahili.
With this in mind, I decided in 1978 to write a language guide: a tongue in cheek one admittedly but one, I am glad to say, seems to have stood the test of time.
I called it Lanky Spoken Here. With the help of my Mam, Mabel, I put down as many Lancashire phrases and words as I could think of, then added "translations".
I sent it to the top London literary agents Curtis Brown who must have wondered what the hell it was all about but to my surprise they found me a publisher almost immediately.

We got the brilliant cartoonist Bill Tidy to illustrate and pretty soon it went from hardback to paperback in several editions.

I got letters from all over the country and different parts of the world from Lancastrians thanking me for reawakening their memories of the dialect.

Again on the off chance, I sent a copy of the book to someone at EMI records and to my astonishment they decided to make an LP of it.

We recorded it in Leigh. I wrote some songs with my friend Bernard Wrigley, and the dialect translations were read by top BBC newsreader Robert Dougall; presenter Sheila Tracey and veteran actor Tony Melody.

Bernard and I were on the record along with a host of others including Fivepenny Piece; Bob Williamson and Gary and Vera Aspey.

From the first posh translation the invited audience were in fits of laughter and we knew we had a success on our hands. You can still get the record online as EMI reissued it 25 years later..

Mabel was in the audience and it's very moving for me when I listen to the record to hear her distinctive gleeful laughter preserved for posterity.

We even took the show on the road, doing such major venues as the Free Trade Hall in Manchester where I extracted "*awwws*" from the audience with my heartfelt song "*I'm in Love With Angela Rippon*". I followed the book up with "Lanky Panky" and "Completely Lanky". All three are still available today in some form or other on Kindle and Amazon etc.

Since the Lanky books, I have written over a dozen more including a couple about great eccentrics (Oddballs and The Book of famous Oddballs); ghostwritten books for such as Jim Davidson and Noel Edmonds; a book of gruesome facts called "Horrors!"; a couple of insult books; the best selling "How to be a Crafty Cruiser" which gives tips, tricks and time and money saving ideas for cruising holidays. Search on Amazon, buy a few and make an old chuffer happy.

I even ventured into the highly competitive world of writing children's books. I invented a doggy detective called Sherlock McSporran who appeared first in "Who Ate The Zookeeper?!" I also penned a couple of vegetarian cookbooks, including "The Green Revolution Cookbook".

I became a veggie in 1973 on moral grounds as well as the fact that as I mentioned before, for some reason, from being a child I had an aversion to eating animal flesh. I also remember as a reporter interviewing a very healthy octogenarian by the name of Mr Turtle who always had a stockpot of vegetable soup on the go and still looked fit and healthy into his 90s. I thought that'll do for me.

My wife Lynn turned vegetarian when she married me in 1975 and we brought up our son Gareth as a vegetarian. He is a good advert for the way of life, being a powerfully built black belt in tae kwon do and a strapping 6ft 2 inches tall.

He shares my daft sense of humour but is a lot more laid back than me. Just like I walked out of my job at the Manchester Evening News all those years before to pursue other things, so Gareth walked out on his HR job at Hounslow Council to follow his dream of becoming a professional photographer: a dream which became reality. Top companies and magazines now employ him and put his considerable photographic skills to good use. Well done son!

Then.

Now. Nearly as cool as his dad.

WALK ON, WALK ON...WITH HOPE...

Get in the back of that police van

In the early 1980's, having made a bit of a name for myself with my Lanky books and record, I was invited as a guest panellist on a quiz on Radio Manchester called "*The Name Game*" and one day, the quizmaster Alec Greenhalgh's wife Muriel came in to have a drink with us.

She had recently had a small part in Coronation Street and she asked me if I had an agent or whether I'd ever done any extra work.

I told her I had had a bit of fun filming stuff at Skegness with Doddy but that was the extent of it.

"*You should give it a go*" she said and kindly gave me the name of her agent in Leeds, suggesting I arrange a meeting. So I did.

It's the small events in life that seem to determine our destiny and it fascinates me to think that if that lady hadn't turned up on that day with that suggestion, I probably would not have had a television career. Secretly, I had always fancied being an actor but had very little clue of how to go about it. This was my chance and I took it.

A couple of days later I turned up at the office of ATS in Leeds which was part of the old City Varieties Theatre. I say "office" but it looked more like a large cupboard and when I was admitted, I was astonished to find there were four people working inside.

There were the bosses: brothers Stanley and Michael Joseph and their employees, Barbara Peasland and Sue Jackson who did most of the acting agency work.

I got on well with them and was pleased to be immediately offered some extra work as a policeman in a then current BBC TV crime series called Juliet Bravo.

A couple of days later I duly reported to the meeting point which was a pub in Burnley and I was fitted out as a policeman.

There was one rather camp actor there who after donning his police uniform in the wardrobe department exclaimed delightedly "*Oooh the frock fits!*" which made me chuckle.

Once changed, we all sat around awaiting the call to be ferried to the film location on the hills outside Burnley: my excitement mounting as we waited... and waited... and waited... We waited so long that people were running out of "humorous" anecdotes relating to their sparkling careers as extras or should I say walk on artistes.

After what seemed like an eternity, we got the call to action and were taken a few miles away up into the hills, where we waited... and waited...and waited once more.

I was beginning to get the impression this acting lark wasn't as glamorous as people made it out to be and was further vindicated in my opinion when an assistant director grabbed hold of a few of us and barked "*You lot are wanted immediately!* "

Ready when you are, Mr DeMille I thought. My big moment had arrived.

He then pushed us towards a large police van and shoved us in the back of it saying "*The director wants you as ballast to make the van look like it's full*".

Me. Bloody ballast!

That was how my glorious acting career developed: graduating from being used as a double for General Amin's legs to being treated as a bit of unseen ballast.

Still, it was a start and I soon learned that extra work was mainly 90% sitting around doing bugger all.

It was fascinating though to talk with some of the other extras who were a lot older than me and had had good careers on the old variety circuit including one elderly lady who had enjoyed success as a tap dancing paper tearer and a guy who had worked as an assistant to a mind reader who swore the man could actually read people's minds.

If he could have read my mind over the next couple of years during my time as a television extra, he would have discerned one pissed off and bored person who didn't take kindly to being barked at by some little jumped up twit of a floor manager fresh from graduating in media studies.

Pretty soon I found myself driving my faithful ancient blue Morris Minor over the tops on the M62 through a howling blizzard at 4 am heading towards the set of All Creatures Great and Small, risking life and limb for not much money and asking for directions from unsympathetic Yorkies on my CB radio.

I think you got paid around £30 a day at that time but should you be fortunate enough to need a haircut for the part, you got an extra £4.60p (and a free haircut of course).

You could also an extra few quid through "*special skills*" such as riding a bike or driving a car and if you took instructions off Mr Director, that boosted your status even further as did being given a line such as "thank you" or "goodbye".

It annoys me to see non-speaking walk on artistes nodding and gurning like idiots in obvious situations such as being customers in a shop, just so the rich television company can save a measly few quid in upscaled fees. It also looks unnatural.

I did all sorts as an extra: taxi drivers; postmen; policemen; man with typhoid; man in field; man in the street; man in the house; man in court; man in Rovers' Return. You name it, I was up for it. Not brilliant money but the pot needed to be kept boiling and there was always the faint hope of being spotted.

If you fancy a bit of extra work, I have to warn you that sometimes it's like this:

1. *Get up **very** early. Crack of sparrowfart as we say in Lancashire.*
2. *Drive to studio: possibly a long way away.*
3. *Sit for a while with a load of others in a little room somewhere. Make small talk for couple of hours. Then grab a bit of brekky from the butty wagon or canteen. (After main cast have had first dibs.)*
4. *Go to wardrobe to be dressed as a Victorian policeman or a country bumpkin or whatever.*
5. *Go to makeup to be, er, made up, with fake blood, massive sideburns or caked with mud or whatever.*
6. *Go back to little room and sit with your fellow extras again for a few hours, awaiting the call.*
7. *Run out of telling and listening to interesting anecdotes and funny stories.*
8. *Break for lunch. (Get served after main cast, of course.)*
9. *Come back and have another sit in for what seems like an eternity but probably only five or six hours.*
10. *Await entrance of flustered 3rd Assistant Director (little more than a child) who says "Sorry guys. Few technical holdups. See you tomorrow early". Or "Sorry guys. Your scene's been cut. Thanks for coming".*
11. *Drive home.*

12. Crawl to bed vowing to ring agent in morning asking to be taken off the sodding books as there must be better ways of earning a few bob.

You also have to remember to wash off the fake blood and pancake makeup too as on more than one occasion I had some very funny looks off petrol station attendants.

It's not all sitting around though. That's why people who do it are called walk-ons.

It's also a nice thrill to see yourself on the telly the first time you do it.

Doing extra work can also mean you find yourself in close proximity (though not in conversation with) famous actors. I found myself next to Anthony Perkins of Psycho fame on one film shoot in Leeds. Inevitably, the crew made gags about not taking a shower when he was in the hotel.

If there isn't too much pressure, sometimes the main actors will have deign to have a chat with the lower orders as did the late and wonderful Jeremy Brett who played Sherlock Holmes in the Granada television 1980s series. The Eton educated son of a Cadbury heir, he took the time and trouble to talk and include you in the conversation, referring to your proper name.

His politeness and kindness made an impression on me which I have tried to carry through in my treatment of other people throughout my career.

I also came within touching distance of that Master of Misery and Sarcasm, the late Kenneth Williams who was walking back to his dressing room after a recording of Countdown.

One of my fellow extras nudged me and said in too loud a voice: *"Bloody hell – it's Kenneth Williams!"*

Williams, who was dressed in a pale blue suit, turned round and gave us a withering scowl that stopped us dead in our tracks then rushed off haughtily to his dressing room.

I read in his excellent diary books many years later: *"there is always the moron's nudge and the cretin's wink to make me hasten away"* (although he loved it when builders shouted and wolf whistled at him for some reason).

Walk ons are always dreaming of better things in the constant hope that on some day, they will be given proper parts. Gradually, I went from performing nods to saying "thank you's" then on to longer lines and eventually great speaking parts. I was one of the lucky ones and I am thankful for being given the chance.

It's a strange thing that from being such a shy lad, appearing in front of television cameras has never bothered me – my only concern is to get it right and not let the other cast members and crew down. Amongst the slog of extra work, were the golden nuggets of relatively better paid television commercials.

I was once the poster boy for Boddington's beer: appearing on massive billboards all over the North West looking lasciviously at a freshly pulled pint of Boddies' bitter.

I also did a commercial for Websters Yorkshire beer and a memorable one for Guinness (see a theme developing there?) The Guinness ad was shot in an old aircraft hangar down south somewhere and I appeared at the start of it for a split second. During the shoot I managed to persuade the actor behind the bar to keep pumping pints of free Guinness for me and I drank so much the director sent over his assistant who warned "*Mr Dutton. If your face goes any more purple, we are going to have to take you off the commercial*".

I eased off and appeared in the final cut although the company weren't for paying me repeats because I was only on for a very brief time.

I phoned Equity who contacted them and got back to me within minutes telling me they had secured the repeat fees of £1500 which brought Lynn and me great joy at a time when money was exceedingly tight.

It's always a delight to land a commercial: especially when the repeats are good. I once did one for Maltesers where I played a granddad playing his son at table football, using the babies as strikers by holding them over the table while they kicked Maltesers into goals like tiny footballs!

I had to nick the Maltesers and stuff them in my mouth and eat them so by the end of the day's shoot I felt pretty sick I can tell you.

The most remunerative telly commercial I did was for Gala Bingo's "Night to Remember" ad where I played a husband who was left minding the baby while the ladies of the house went out to play bingo.

It was recorded one morning in Watford and ran for ages: netting me a jackpot of well over £14,000. HOUSE!!! Not bad for a morning's work. I wish more mornings like that would come my way.

Being chosen to do a commercial can be a long process sometimes involving a recall, often a couple of hundred miles away. I once did five different sets of improvisation with five different women for a washing powder advert after a recall and didn't get the job. The bloke who got it never even spoke at all in the advert.

I also did a Volkswagen commercial where we were messed about for days and finally filmed it but didn't end up in the on-screen version although I could be heard humming and whistling the Beach Boys' "God only knows". However, despite that, my clever agent Debs managed to get me the very lucrative full amount.

So my advice is get a good agent and join Equity.

The maddest one I ever did was a commercial for Hovis which turned into a three day boot camp type ordeal in the wilds of the Peak District.

There were about a dozen of us so-called "Heroes" which is what the advertising industry laughingly call the main protagonists in their productions.

Personally, I find this term to be an insult to the real heroes who put their lives down on the line for us in the face of enemy fire, like my granddad who took a couple of bullets for his country.

As well as us "heroes" there were 50 or 60 extras to join in the "fun" of pretending to be real farmers taking part in a hazardous cross country race.

We were summoned from our beds in Buxton while it was still dark to be ferried by a bloke whose breath smelled suspiciously of alcohol driving at breakneck speed to a farm in the middle of nowhere where we changed into our farmers' gear.

I was given a flat cap, a pair of corduroy trousers and massive leather boots three sizes too big despite me having specified I was a delicate size 7.

There was intimation of what was to come when in the first scene the director had all 60 or 70 of us cattle\actors charging down a steep hill towards a tiny gap in a dry stone wall, ordering us to jostle each other for position. Shepherds' sticks, elbows and knees caused quite a few bruises on that first charge and even more on the subsequent half-dozen retakes.

Then they filmed us running like madmen up a hill across open soggy fields towards a grandstand made out of straw bales where the supposed finishing line lay. They made us do this time after time after time and the distance was around 250 yards – sometimes moving us back even further.

We had hardly time to pause for breath when some jumped up cockney minion bawled at us to get back to the start and do it again and again.

I was 64 and instead of being physically and mental abused in such a manner (where is the Royal Society for the Protection of Knackered Old Chuffers when you need them?) I should have been playing cribbage or a gentle game of crown green bowls somewhere.

My legs felt like I'd been stretched on the rack. I was beginning to feel pangs of sorrow for Guy Fawkes.

I was not helped at all by the oversized boots which were dragging at my tendons. One of our number – an elderly comic from Yorkshire – collapsed and had to be given first aid. Another "hero" had to continually throw himself down face first in a puddle of mud as we ran past him.

This torture went on for a few hours while the director lined up different shots to his satisfaction. They didn't seem to care that many of the participants were suffering badly.

Over subsequent days, we were required to crawl under barbed wire fences; run across rocky brooks; over cattle grids; hurdle over straw bales; chase tractors and career dangerously downhill through a perilously steep wooded area – which an ex SAS veteran turned stuntman had to be brought in to do alongside some of the main actors.

This went on for three long days by the end of which there were real injuries and one of our number displayed his bruises which went from his ankles up to his buttocks. Painkillers were being swallowed like sweets. I had more or less given up after the first day through a ricked tendon but managed to complete the other two days by missing out some of the more arduous events.

On the last day, we had to run through the farmyard scooping up drinks at a table and scattering hens. We thought that was that but then came one final twist. The director had half a dozen of us ferried about 3 miles away while, in fading light, we ran through a ploughed field full of stones as he artily filmed us in silhouette. By then, after doing it half a dozen more times we were dead on our feet. And in our souls.

When he shouted "that's a wrap" it was like all our birthdays and Christmas Day had come at once. I have never been as glad to leave a job in my life. It took my legs several weeks to recover.

A lot of the actors have remained friends to this day and I can imagine it was like squaddies felt when they had been put through their square bashing in their national service.

When the final advert was shown, I was on it at the start for a brief second or two. All that pain just for that. My reward was about 1500 quid which I think was the hardest money I had ever earned in my life.

Now, every time I see a Hovis loaf, it makes my legs ache. Plus they can shove it where the sun don't shine!

That's what it's like as an actor: you'll have a go at most things because if you don't someone else will. The best part of the job is the variety of work you, hopefully, get offered and the chance that the next phone call could be the one that changes your life forever.

I have even been auditioned by Ken Loach on a few occasions (including once for an ad for Caramac chocolate believe it or not) but never made it into one of his amazing, gritty films. One day, perhaps...

Talking of famous directors, I once travelled all the way to London to audition for a McCain frozen chip commercial and should have been auditioned by the legendary Ken Russell.

I say should because the old bugger never showed up, after deciding to extend his no doubt liquid lunch by several hours.

Still, I suppose being asked to direct an advert for oven chips was a bit of a comedown for him after masterminding *"The Devils,"* *"Women in Love"* and *"Tommy"*.

I think in his position I would probably have stayed away and got pissed as well.

Start of the Hovis Farmer's Race. Take 202....That's me wearing 55 next to famous actor Pete Dunwell wearing 65. Should have been reported to the RSPCA (Royal Society for the Prevention of Cruelty to Actors).

A proper Charlie

How times change. My mate Bernard Wrigley and I once had a
piddle in the middle of Downing Street one dark night.
We were down in London in 1980 to make a record and after visiting
a few pubs we were wobbling along the famous thoroughfare when
the urge to urinate suddenly came upon us.
The Downing Street bobby must have nipped for a pee as well.
There was nobody about but us. Or perhaps Maggie Thatcher
peeping out through the curtains muttering "*Dirty Northern
bastards*".
Nowadays, they have cops with machine guns to stop people doing
stuff like that.
Bernard and I were there to do a song we had written called "*The
Martians have landed in Wigan*". We recorded it at Eel Pie studios
owned by Pete Townshend of The Who. Also in this stellar lineup
were Dixie Dean and Hughie Flint from the McGuinness Flint Band
and Pete's brother Simon Townshend. We even persuaded the old
telly astronomer Patrick Moore to introduce it. It's a cracking funny
song but for some strange reason it never got into the charts. No
accounting for taste.
From Downing Street we went on to the House of Commons to
witness a debate but were disappointed to find out we almost
outnumbered the MPs.
You could just more or less walk into the place at that time. Not now
though.

We could have got into the cast of Hair! The legend who is The Bolton Bullfrog and me leaning on a lamppost at the corner of the street. We've written lots of songs and done lots of shows together including Christmas specials all over the North West with top Northern favourites, the Houghton Weavers.

It brought back memories of six years earlier, when I had stood in front of the door of number 10 with a friend of mine, John Cooke, a national newspaper reporter who I knew previously from the local papers. The then Prime Minister, Edward Heath, was clinging onto power by the tips of his fingers and everyone wanted him to leave office.

Cookie motioned:"*Here – take my notebook and pen. I've got to go somewhere to file copy. If Edward Heath comes out, have a word with him*".

Then he buggered off quickly leaving me crapping myself somewhat.

It was a critical moment in the history of the political life of this country and I was expected to record Mr Heath's valedictions. Thankfully, old Ted kept holed up in his den..

While I am at it, I may as well tell you about the time I got within spitting distance of Prince Charles.

He had come to officially open a little restored cottage in Kirkby Lonsdale overlooking the banks of the River Lune and the locals gathered in the churchyard to welcome him: me included.

I had my old-fashioned film camera with me and started taking pictures of him from a few feet away thinking how surprisingly handsome he was in the flesh. No, really.

It was the time he had just split from Diana and one cheeky Cumbrian wag bawled *"Where's the wife then Charlie*?" which he obviously regally ignored.

I congratulated myself on getting some astounding close-up pictures of Chas but alas, on checking how many shots I had left I discovered I had failed to put a film in the camera.

Rushing off to the shop to buy a new one, I was dismayed to see his fancy car departing with him in it when I got back to the scene.

The following week, there was a massive photograph on the front page of the Morecambe Visitor including a close-up of me ostensibly taking a close-up of HRH.

I phoned the newspaper to order a photograph and told them it was me with the camera in the paper. The lady said "*Ooh I bet you've got some good photos*".

I stupidly told her I had no film in the camera. A reporter rang me shortly after enquiring about the incident and I urged him not to put anything in the paper about it.

Being a former reporter, I suspected he would though - and indeed he did with the screaming headline: "**ROYAL SNAPPER WAS A PROPER CHARLIE**!". Thanks brother.

At the time, I was playing a photographer in Coronation Street which was very unfortunate. It attracted quite a few "funny" remarks from people who had seen the newspaper piece such as "*Hope you remembered to put a film in the camera in Corrie*". But when you think about it, the irony was I didn't need a film in the camera in Corrie as it's all codology!

The year 1983 was an important one in my life. After auditioning in Liverpool, I got my first proper speaking part – as a window cleaner in Brookside where I had a row over not cleaning the windows properly with one of the Close's posh residents then gave him two fingers and mouthed "*piss off*" at him. Hardly Chekhov, granted, but I was immensely chuffed.

Around the same time, I got my first lines in Coronation Street when I played a delivery man and couldn't believe I had the chance to actually speak in my favourite programme.

Even better than those two career defining events was the birth that year of my son Gareth.

We brought our little bundle home from the maternity unit on a snowy February day little suspecting he would turn into a massive bloke with an appetite to match.

I worried, having had no father, how I would fare myself as a dad as a consequence of not having a template to follow.

Somehow, I muddled through and I am more than pleased with the result. We have a great relationship and we are on the same comedy wavelength. Whenever we are together, we always end up bouncing comic surrealisms off one another and fall about laughing.

From an early age, when not playing with his Ghostbusters, Mutant Ninja Turtles or He-man figures, he showed a precocious aptitude for computer and video games which he hasn't managed to shake off up to this present day.

That's not to say he is a couch potato: achieving a black belt in tae kwon do and being a regular visitor to the gym balances it out nicely. Plus, you can't be a couch potato with two kids.

He seems to be able to adapt to any situation. I put it down to the fact that he went from a packed primary school in town to a little fellside country school and thence to senior school with hundreds of pupils before ending up at University in Manchester where he met his lovely wife Frances who is an English teacher in a big London senior school.

After I played the first Brookside window cleaner I hit upon what I thought was a brilliant idea. I wrote to the production office outlining where I thought the character could go: suggesting he could be a bit of a scally with a line in scams and an eye for the ladies.

They took up my suggestion but gave the part, which they now called Sinbad, to another actor – Michael Starke – who in all fairness did the character justice and remained in the show for 16 years. Good on him. The money would have been very handy though!

Sometimes, it doesn't take much to change your luck. A phone call from an old pal proved very lucky for me...

Les Powell, an old workmate of mine on the Leigh Reporter, called me from down south and during the conversation mentioned a piece he'd seen in a newspaper. An actress called Barbara Kelly, an old tv celeb from the 50's, had started an agency providing after dinner speakers for functions all over the country and was doing well with it.

This sparked me off. I had recently done some extra work for Emmerdale in Leeds and I discovered most of my fellow walk-ons had a second string to their bow such as a market stall or antiques business because they couldn't survive on the bits and pieces they were doing for telly.

The speaker agency idea sounded a good one and I discovered there were at that time only two or three agencies providing that service. Cheekily, I wrote to Kelly's outfit to obtain a list of speakers to see what was on offer.

I put some feelers out and got in touch with a former motorcycle cop by the name of Goldie Goldsmith who was pretty big on the speaker circuit.

Goldie kindly gave me some phone numbers of good speakers he had worked with and it snowballed from there.

Working from a spare room and on a shoestring budget, I started to provide speakers for service organisations such as Rotary and Round Table and for business events, presentations and personal appearances.

It was a lifesaver to me and my family and for the first time since leaving what you might call a proper job I was making enough money to relax when the bills plopped on the mat.

A friend who worked on the national newspapers gave me a list of personal numbers for some very famous people who I was able to ring and ask if they wished to join the agency which I had called Now You're Talking.

Soon, people were ringing me to ask if they could come on the books and the business steadily got bigger and bigger.

Lynn helped me in the office, juggling her time between looking after Gareth and answering calls when I was out on acting work.

I say "office". To be honest, it was our back bedroom. I made a tape recording of typewriters clacking, phones ringing and general murmuring which I switched on when anybody rang to enquire about a speaker, to make it sound like a proper busy place of work.

A big bonus of being able to work from home meant I was able to watch Gareth progress and grow up. If I had had a 9 to 5 job I would have missed out on so much.

I worked hard to build up the list of speakers, including, I must admit, some unusual characters including a mountaineer with no legs; white witches; an ex prison governor; a blind explorer; a professional farter and one guy called the Vulgar Vicar: an actual priest who did very rude after dinner speeches.

At one dinner, when he was asked what he thought should be the position of women in the church, he replied "*On their backs with their legs in the air!*"

Unsurprisingly, this upset a table full of Christians who stood up, walked out then came back and threw 30 pieces of silver (ish) coins at him before storming out again.

One speaker was a well known boxer who was a recent convert to Christianity. He shocked the room when he zealously declared: "*Anyone who does not believe in the Lord Jesus Christ Our Saviour is a c**t!*".

(I once also upset some Christians by putting on a psychic evening upstairs at a pub in Leigh which was picketed by religious types chanting and holding candles. Ironically, the speaker who was allegedly a spiritualist, failed to materialise anyone from "the other side" and I thought we were going to get lynched.

Strangely, a big burly bloke stood up and defended the so-called psychic by saying the stage lights had been shining in his eyes and putting him off. To my surprise, I recognised him as the aforementioned Mr Baskeyfield: the bobby who had collared me and my mate for setting fire to the field in Atherton all those years before. He hardly looked any different- perhaps *he* was a ghost!)

Gradually, I built up the business to include hundreds of speakers including such famous names as Sir Ranulph Fiennes: Eddie the Eagle; Chris Bonington: Fred Trueman; Tommy Docherty; Ian St. John; Gordon Banks; Jack Charlton and many more.

The extra money meant that eventually we were able to move to a house near Kirkby Lonsdale: a place in a beautiful unspoiled area that we had come to love through having a little second hand touring caravan overlooking Morecambe Bay which I had bought from the fees of doing some Corrie episodes. (The caravan not the Bay.)

There was a great deal of guilt attached to this move as I don't think my Mam wanted us to go even though it was only just over an hour away.

We had to do it though because we wanted Gareth to have a chance to be brought up in the countryside where he had an idyllic childhood, playing in the fresh air and helping out on the local farms at haymaking time.

The money also enabled us to go on cruises (I don't like flying, remember?) and Gareth was able to see places he wouldn't normally have seen which, I hope, expanded his horizons.

One day, I was asked by a PR agency to provide a big name speaker for a conference in Ireland. I put forward a few suggestions of people I didn't even have on the books and they chose Denis Healey, the former Chancellor of the Exchequer. I managed to get his phone number, rang him and he agreed to do the job.

The following year, they came back asking for an even bigger name with some connection to Europe so I threw a few suggestions in the hat and they plumped for Herr Willy Brandt, the former German Chancellor. Fine. My next problem was how the hell did I get hold of him?!

By ringing the German embassy, I obtained a telephone number for his secretary in Germany and after several calls he agreed to do the booking. The client was delighted with the news but less so when

232

Herr Brandt had to pull out on the last minute over some personal crisis.

Dennis stepped in again if I remember correctly. I once even persuaded Healey to dress up as Father Christmas to promote Christmas cards! Our relationship ended sourly though when after I had asked his availability for a couple of events that didn't come off, the next time I rang he said sourly:"*You're that chappy from Bolton who keeps ringing and wasting my bloody time, aren't you?*" before slamming the phone down on me. The ungrateful pipsqueak.

Although working from home had its benefits, it could also be intrusive with people ringing at all hours: including one irate very famous cricket commentator who, obviously the worse for wear, phoned one Sunday afternoon after lunch demanding to know why I wasn't getting him more work. I tried to placate him but his tipsy response was "*how dare you talk to me in that rather supercilious manner*". I like to think that's the last thing I am. To be fair, he phoned the next day to apologise for his attitude.

Some dinners could be riotous affairs especially when Round Tablers were involved. They had a habit of soaking knotted napkins in red wine and lobbing them at each other. Rugby commentator Ian Robertson reported back to me about one such rowdy dinner in a Scottish castle where, upset by the Tablers' behaviour, the stressed out chef took his gear off and jumped out through the window, leaving the Tablers to cook their own meal.

The Vulgar Vicar once found himself at a Round Table dinner where the guest of honour was a duck that walked up and down the dining table, quacking loudly during his speech.

" *I didn't mind that so much but when it shat in my dinner I was forced to complain*" he reported.

I even tried my hand at after dinner speaking myself but after one mismanaged drunken Round Table event where I got up to speak near midnight and couldn't get order, I signed off with:

"*What's the difference between a proctologist and an after dinner speaker at a Round Table dinner?*"

"*Tell us*" slurred the Tablers.

"*A proctologist only has to look at one arsehole at a time*".

Didn't go down well. At all. Thank you and goodnight.

Frequently, although they put bums on seats, it wasn't always the well-known speakers who were the best at the job. A former bank manager; submariner; air traffic controller; policeman; failed goalkeeper and an ex Coldstream Guardsman were amongst the most in demand.

Top motivational speakers and faces off the telly can command five and sometimes six figure sums for up to an hour of their time. If companies are willing to pay that, good luck to them.

If there is a lesson to be learned, it's this. Always listen to people closely because if I hadn't listened to my mate Les on that day, I wouldn't have picked up on the idea of the agency and life would've been a lot different.

My old workmate Les Powell. Still two rum buggers together. Looks like Buckingham Palace in the background but it's Wetherspoons Liverpool Street Station.

INCLOGNITO

Heckled by a pissed up Vicar...

For 10 years I enjoyed being the front man for the Lancashire comedy/folk group Inclognito which originally comprised Bram Taylor, Eric White and myself.

I learned to plonk a few chords on the ukulele although not being much of a musician it was left to me to do most of the gags but I also wrote a lot of songs for the act. We recorded a song I wrote called "Nasty Allan Beswick"about a controversial local radio phone-in presenter.

We played most of the major theatres in the north-west as well as folk festivals, clubs and PTAs.

It was at one of the latter when we had an incident involving the local vicar who we christened Dick the Vic.

Due to the generosity of his parishioners who were buying him drinks all night and plying him with home-made dandelion wine, it was evident he was getting more and more steadily pissed.

To their dismay he started to heckle us and then jumped onstage in the middle of one of our numbers to sing a song he had picked up in the West Country called "The Blackbird".

We indulged him in this then suggested it might be a good idea for him to resume his seat, which he reluctantly agreed to do.

The last we saw of him he was being dragged out of the room by the elbows in a semi-comatose condition by two burly parishioners. It's not often you get heckled by a pissed up vicar, thank goodness.

At another PTA in Warrington, a lady came up and revealed that when we had appeared there 12 months before, she had laughed so much at one of my funny poems she had fractured a rib.

I told it was very brave of her to risk doing it again. I was secretly proud of making someone laugh so much they had bust a rib.

Very wrong but very satisfying.

Probably one of the worst gigs we ever did was at a major police headquarters during the miners' strike. The audience consisted of knackered bobbies; hardfaced policewomen and humourless traffic wardens.

We were just about to go into our usual routine when I hissed "*For fuck's sake don't do The Miners Wife's Lament tonight*!" Needless to say we died on our arses that evening.

We did a bit better when we warmed the crowd up one Bonfire Plot Night on the Russell Harty Show, despite the legendary darts commentator Sid Waddell trying to get us pissed at the bar causing us to nearly miss our spot. I made a song up about Russell and afterwards he gave me a limp handshake and said: "*I believe you were very good*". He hadn't even listened.

We did a few radio shows – including The Stuart Hall Show on Radio 2 – performing live in front of him like three kids before a headmaster.(Perhaps I shouldn't mention kids.)

After a few years Eric left the group and we were joined by a great all-round female singer and musician by the name of Jackie Finney. Bram reminded me of the time I had been caught short just before we were due to take the stage. Apparently I desperately relieved myself into a pint pot, almost filling it in the process and during a break he came off stage to find somebody whisking it away with the words "*Waste not, want not* ".

"*It had a head on it!*" laughed Bram.

In Inclognito. Jackie Finney; Moi and Bram Taylor, making 'em 'ave it.

COUNTRY MATTERS

Most places dad goes, he retains the nickname "Stripper"

The income that came in from the speaker agency enabled us to
move to a cottage in the countryside in 1992 – a beautiful stone built
semi detached barn conversion with an upstairs living room that
gave us magnificent views of the surrounding lush, green fells and
the majestic mountain of Ingleborough in the background
It was situated in a timeless little hamlet at the tip of Lancashire
called Ireby – which means Town of the Irish Vikings – that had
fewer than 80 residents and a little babbling beck (Norse for stream)
running in front of it, across which lay an ancient clapper bridge.
The place is so old it features in the Domesday book.
The Brontes – Charlotte, Maria, Elizabeth and Emily – went to a
school for Clergymen's Daughters just down the road and Conan
Doyle's Mam had once shacked up with a doctor in the next village.
Doyle himself got married in a local church.
Another famous resident lived a short walk away – Mark Owen of
Take That. A fellow named Jesus knocked on our door one Sunday
afternoon asking if we knew where Mark resided. He'd driven all the
way from Southern Spain with his daughter and her friends because
they were mad keen fans who wanted to meet him.
Mark knocked on our door shortly before one New Year's Eve
asking if we knew of anywhere in the village his friends could stay
because he always threw a massive party at that time.
He also used to play for the local footy team in Kirkby Lonsdale
where he was subjected to opposition footballers kicking his legs
from under him and yelling: *"Take that!"*. He apparently always took
it in good part.
Anyway, fairly interesting but I digress….
On moving into the hamlet, we followed the furniture van down the
winding country lanes with me driving, Gareth in the back and Lynn
sat next to me cradling our pet goldfish in a bowl on her lap and our
beloved Cavalier King Charles Spaniel Thomas crouching in front of
her.
Although we were delighted to be lucky enough to move to such a
beautiful area, the switch from our home town was a wrench on two
counts. Gareth went from an urban school with lots of children to a

tiny stone built Victorian one on the fells in which he was the only pupil in his year. The entire junior school had only 26 children in it. I also felt guilty at moving away from Mabel but I phoned her every night and we visited her almost every weekend.

It was a sheep farming area and had been probably since Viking times. The dairy cows went past our front door twice a day for milking and it was an amazing sight to see hundreds of sheep brought down from the fells for shearing.

We were in close proximity to the Yorkshire Dales and there were kingfishers, dippers, wagtails, buzzards, woodpeckers siskins, goldfinches, curlew, cuckoos, skylarks, barn owls —an endless variety of ornithological wonders. We were there for 22 years and although high on the fells, we were never snowed in once – apart from one glorious day when the drifts piled up so high that the children were excitedly throwing themselves into them and disappearing.

At times, it was like living on the set of Emmerdale. Frequently, I'd scoot round the hamlet frantically waving a walking stick while trying to round up sheep that had escaped from neighbouring fields. I once freed a cow that had its head stuck between the gate and a post. Everything was at a slower pace – even Roger the postman sometimes only delivered the mail at 5 o'clock in the afternoon because he'd either been picking mushrooms on the way round or stopping at all the farm houses for cups of tea and home made scones.

There was plenty of thinking time. When I read in a local paper that a Rotary club was having difficulty in sending Christmas presents to Romanian orphans because of the cost and the fact they might not get there in time, I contacted them and suggested asking people to fill jiffy bags with small toys and useful stuff such as toothbrushes and combs and send them first class. I called it "Romania in a Jiffy" and it was a resounding success.

Hundreds of jiffy bags made it in time for Christmas because it was quicker and cheaper to send them than parcels. The scheme continued for several years and I even got a visit from a Romanian Pastor who had organised the distribution at the other end. He told me how delighted the children had been with the cards and presents and he thanked me for coming up with the idea. It was a bit of lateral thinking I was immensely proud of.

As a bird lover, I hated it when men came into our village fields shooting crows. After one session which seemed to go on all afternoon, I approached one brave camouflaged sportsman.

I asked him what pleasure he got from slaughtering defenceless creatures and he went ballistic.

He swore at me before slowly lifting his shotgun towards me then aiming it over my head and pulling the trigger.

He blasted a crow behind me then ran and picked it up, waving it round above his head like someone demented.

Deciding I couldn't argue with an armed lunatic, I slowly turned round and walked gingerly back to the cottage.

When I went out later, I saw dead birds everywhere and a solitary quivering crow sitting on a branch looking traumatised. It was one of the saddest things I've ever seen. That was until a few years later when I saw a local boy walk past the window dragging a beautiful brown hare he'd just shot on the fells.

I remonstrated with him and got upbraided by his mother for my trouble.

I know I'm at risk of being labelled a townie for my views but this side of rural life did not sit easily with me.

Our garden was round the back of the house and basically it was just an overgrown piece of the fell filled with rubbish until over the years I transformed it into flower and vegetable beds and even a pond which I stocked with frogs and toads to do my bit for wildlife conservation.

We had lovely neighbours, especially our friends Lesley and John who threw wonderful parties for everyone's birthdays, as well as Christmas and Halloween when half the village turned up in fancy dress.

The place had its fair share of eccentrics, including one guy who used to dress up in a penguin costume and stand in a chicken and duck enclosure waving at astonished passers-by – just for a laugh.

It was a wonderful place to bring up Gareth who made friends with James the local farmer's boy and they shared many adventures - climbing up trees, wading in the beck and helping make haystacks together.

Being a town boy, he initially had a little bit of difficulty fitting in with the rural kids in the junior school but his gregarious nature soon won them round and he even starred in the Christmas play as Papa

Panov who treats a visitor with kindness only to discover he is none other than Jesus.

It was great to see him in the starring role.

He learned tae kwon do in a remarkable youth club built by the locals and subsequently gained his black belt which gave him loads of confidence and I think helped him enormously through his teen years.

After a couple of years, he went to the local senior school – Queen Elizabeth in Kirkby Lonsdale – which had a brilliant reputation and was taken there and back in a little school bus along with other children from the village.

Recently, while going through old papers, Lynn found an essay he had done where he had been set the task of writing about his most embarrassing moments. Sad to say, I star in it.

The essay is more embarrassing to me, to say the least.

Nevertheless, being the good sport that I am, here it is word for word as he presented it to his teacher.

(Excuse me while I hide behind the sofa with my eyes shut and buttocks clenched.)

"My most embarrassing moments" "Dad Drunk at Party" and "The Runner"

It was a fairly ordinary day; nothing special; nothing new; nothing embarrassing (not yet).. The phone rang. After dad answered and some muffled conversation behind closed doors, we were off to a party.

The horror began at The Sun, a pub in our local area. This is where he started to drink. It all looked casual now but things were to become much worse. After a medium drinking session, everyone was invited back to the party at a nice chap called Graham's house. Plenty of beer and lager were on offer here.

Everything looked fine until He started dancing to the dance music, controlled by the cocktail of alcohol and rhythmic beat.

Before I knew it, he and an equally intoxicated friend called Graham Brentville were spreading garlic dip over each other.

Other bad points included being naked except for underpants and spitting beer in each others faces.

Graham Brentville always keeps the same slightly droopy expression. If you picture this face in your head and then cover it in garlic dip, you begin to get an idea of how comical it looked.

They eventually ended up taking a shower together helped to stand on their own two feet by Graham's son and I who had to use a hosepipe on them to get rid of the garlic dip.

After this, all the stereotypical things about a drunk occurred: being sick; falling asleep (and over) and being walked home. Your typical episode of You've Been Framed, in fact.

Most places dad goes, he retains the nickname "Stripper" and many a garlic dip joke has spawned from his antics.

"The Runner" is when our family is in a restaurant and the food has taken too long to be served. We then run off without telling the staff. This particular Runner was in a pizza restaurant in Skipton. We had ordered a lot of food and were really quite hungry as we hadn't had much for breakfast that morning.

My mouth was salivating at the thought of a deep pan pizza: the very words making me hungrier every time they were thought about.

About 20 minutes since we ordered now no sign of the food. Dad is getting frustrated, uttering curses under his breath. He asks the waitress that served us where the food is. She replies "It will be right with you" – the famous last words that triggered an infamous "Runner".

Dad stood up after another 15 minutes of waiting, saying "Shall we scarper?" To which Mam reluctantly agreed.

By the time I had stood up they were both out the door.

I walked out too. It felt like (and looked like) everyone was staring at me. Apart from extreme embarrassment at this point, I also felt very guilty.

Halfway down the road, guess what? I'd left my coat behind! I make a desperate sprint to get it – too late. As I grab my coat, out walks the waitress with all our food on a tray. I give a nervous smile and a little wave of acknowledgement to the poor woman who is completely nonplussed and almost dazed and I fly out the door.

That has got to be our most infamous Runner ever, an incredibly close shave as the wave and smile just confused her for long enough for me to escape, a bit like a S.W.A.T team manoeuvre really.

So there you have it, either two times of embarrassment or two examples of life with my Dad.

(Has it stopped? Can I come out from behind the sofa and unclench my buttocks now?)

Bloody hell! I wonder what his teachers made of that? I bet they pissed themselves laughing in the staff room.

I won't hold it against him though as all that good schooling paid off and he studied at Manchester Metropolitan University where he gained a BSc and met Frances his future wife and the lovely mother of our grandchildren.

My garlic dip buddy – Brenters in typical pose. A great guy.

The two decades we spent in that beautiful area seemed to pass in a flash but as time went by, we were constantly up and down the motorway as our parents succumbed to sickness and infirmity.Gareth and Frankie had been living in Mam's old house but they moved down to London so we eventually moved back to our home town (and the old family house) to be nearer to them and our lovely and funny granddaughter Sam Daisy who was born in 2011.

Just over four years later, her sister was born– our wonderful Georgia Florence who I christened the Beautiful Battler. Her story is amazing and very moving. I will tell it later.

The clapper bridge over the beck in lovely Ireby.

The view from my bedroom window. Better than the one I painted at junior school.

THE INCREDIBLE MR. MURPHY

I laughed when Bobby Kennedy ripped his britches arse

Picture this guy. He's just over five feet tall. Stocky but quite chubby. Baggy trousers. Softly spoken with a thickish homely Lancashire accent tinged with a slight hint of American. In his 70's. No airs and graces. Wouldn't look out of place in Wetherspoons. Quite ordinary, you might think. But you'd be wrong.

To look at him, you wouldn't think he had once tipped a bucket of dirty water over Joan Crawford or babysat the Kennedys and rubbed shoulders with some of the biggest names of the 20th century. Stan Laurel absolutely adored him.

Allow me to introduce Mr Jimmy Murphy – probably the most interesting man I've ever met.

I'd like to devote a chapter to him because he's worth it. I think you will find him fascinating too.

He mixed with monarchs; presidents; film stars; gangsters and the rich and powerful yet still retained that lovely Lancashire accent of his humble upbringing.

Jimmy was born in the small industrial Lancashire town of Newton - le-Willows on Valentine's Day, 1909.

His dad walked out on the family and his mother died giving birth to another child just 10 months after he was born, leaving him to be brought up by an aunt.

Of Irish extraction, Jimmy had done a number of jobs in his early life – as a foundry worker, pitman and undertaker's assistant. He also tended the gardens of the rich folk of the town and mixed with their children. Thus began his association with well-to-do people which was to last a lifetime. His own home life was less glamorous: his bath consisted of a beer barrel cut in half.

The local undertaker, whose motto was "*you can roam the whole world over but I'll nail you in the end* " took Jimmy to theatre shows-initiating his long association with show business.

The area he lived in had a volatile mix of Welsh, Scottish and Irish inhabitants who, along with the English, provided Jimmy with endless opportunities to practice the fisticuffs which were to stand him in good stead in later life.

I first met Jimmy in the early 1980s when along with another writer, the late Graham Nown, we flew him over from New York intending to write his life story. Unfortunately, despite many days and endless hours taping interviews with Jimmy the book never materialised because we couldn't find a publisher.

(I am glad to say an American gentleman called Joseph Hyatt has since published a book all about Jimmy which I recommend heartily.)

Among the local "aristocracy" Jimmy knew as a lad were the Harrison family – owners of the local Hippodrome – a silent picture palace which also showed live music hall. He laughingly told us the cinema pianist, Maud, had to wear wellingtons because kids peed with excitement on the sloping cinema floor down which rolled a tsunami of urine that hit the heating pipes at the bottom, causing rising clouds of steam that made her eyes sting.

Jimmy did the sound effects for the films and also ran errands for visiting early Hollywood celebrities such as Pearl White and the Gish sisters who were on promotional tours of the provinces.

It was also here he struck up a lifelong friendship with a young hopeful nervously waiting to make his stage debut: the young George Formby (then known as George Hoy) who was making his first attempt to follow in his late father's footsteps.

Jimmy's fortune changed completely however when he was taken to a restaurant where he found an expensive diamond ring belonging to a famous American black showbusiness star who had been dining there. Being an honest Lancashire gentleman, he handed it in at the stage door of the Liverpool Empire where she was appearing.

The star was Nina Mae McKinney – otherwise known as the "Black Garbo" - who immediately took a shine to Jimmy. She booked him into a room at her hotel and they became lovers. This relationship and Nina Mae's contacts subsequently established him in top show business circles and resulted in a job as a valet for the then famous Irish American tenor and film star Morton Downey who was appearing at some of London's top night spots.

Jimmy quickly adapted to the social life of the capital and among the many friends he made was the then undergraduate Donald Campbell, the famous daredevil who was to die in a speedboat record attempt many years later in the Lake District.

They picked up "nippies" – waitresses from Lyon's Corner House and took them in Campbell's sports car into the countryside for a tumble in the hay.

After a spell as Morton's valet Jimmy began work for Madame Rose – one of London's most celebrated society madams with a stable of call girls who entertained a steady stream of aristocrats at her luxury apartment.

"I took £1,500 a week to the bank. It were a lot of money in them days"

In the intervening years, Jimmy worked as a valet with a succession of visiting American variety stars including the legendary cowboy Tom Mix and the bill topping phenomenal one-legged tap dancer (I kid you not) Peg Leg Bates who was one of the highest paid stars of the era.

Jimmy was somewhat accident prone and on one of the tours Jimmy somehow managed to lose all his boss's different coloured artificial legs and had to have some urgently specially made.

In 1937, he rejoined Morton who was appearing at the Cafe De Paris and it was here Jimmy widened his circle of society contacts when he met the Duke of Windsor in Morton's dressing room. He was later to meet the Duke many times in America.

Jimmy was infamous for getting into various scrapes and had at this time a hilarious and unscheduled introduction to the German ambassador Von Ribbentrop.

He accidentally locked himself out on a hotel balcony in his underpants and was forced to rattle at the French windows of the Nazi's private apartment. A startled von Ribbentrop called his man to let Jimmy in and thawed him out with a cup of tea.

Ironically, at this time, Jimmy made friends with Paddy Hitler (I kid you not again!) - the Scouse nephew of von Ribbentrop's boss Adolf Hitler who was working as a waiter in a nearby cafe. (Paddy, not Adolf).

Jimmy's inherent clumsiness later caused him to tip a New York socialite called Sweeney out of his coffin after praying by the side of it and using the side to pull himself up! He almost did the same again to a former employer - a famous American comic by the name of Burt Wheeler.

In 1938, Jimmy set sail for America and toured the states with Morton and the Tommy Dorsey band, also landing a job at the

World's Fair in New York the following year where he worked for Johnny "Tarzan" Weissmuller who was part of a choreographed dancing and swimming extravaganza.

Johnny had a partiality for alcohol and one day got so drunk he jumped off the diving board naked and Jimmy had to rush round with his dressing gown to cover him up. Jimmy told us Bing Crosby, who also like to drink, jumped off the same diving board with a yachting cap jammed on his head and his pipe still lit in his mouth.

When they were in London, Morton had introduced Jimmy to his old friend Joseph P Kennedy, the American Ambassador and Jimmy, Morton, and the Kennedy family all worshipped together as Catholics.

Morton asked Jimmy to show the younger Kennedys round the World's Fair so he took the Kennedy kids – Bobby, Teddy, Pat, Rosemary and Eunice on the rides and bought them ice cream.

He told me he remembered Bobby Kennedy as "*a bit of a snotty kid*" who slipped and split his trousers – much to Jimmy's amusement.

"*I laughed when Bobby Kennedy ripped his britches arse*" chuckled Jimmy.

No-one could have foreseen then that the child with the torn trousers would grow up to become American attorney general and be assassinated in 1968.

Shortly after, Jimmy landed a plum job when, on Morton's recommendation, he became valet to Stan Laurel.

As they were both Lancashire born (Stan was from Ulverston) the two of them hit it off straight away.

Despite Laurel urging Jimmy to call him Stan, he always respectfully referred to him as Mr Laurel. They sang Lancashire songs together and Jimmy said one of Stan's favourite words was the very Northern "*champion*" to describe something as being better than good.

Jimmy revealed to Graham and me that Stan told him he was called Stanley by his parents as a tribute to the Victorian explorer Henry Morton Stanley and he had decided on the surname Laurel after Laurel Canyon in the Hollywood Hills.

This was probably the happiest time of Jimmy's life as he was treated by Stan and Ollie as an equal and frequently went to dinners at Hardy's house where the big man himself prepared all the meals, tasting the food and pronouncing it "*perfect*".

Corn on the cob was usually on the menu as was chicken – the bird frequently being dispatched by Ollie himself.

"He made me feel like a king. They got together every couple of weeks and had a few drinks and worked out ideas for shows and films
I felt a bit uncomfortable watching Ollie constantly blowing kisses to his wife Lucille over the dinner table though. I felt like a gooseberry".

Hardy was an old-fashioned Southerner, set in his ways and when Jimmy told him he had slept with the coloured singer, Nina Mae McKinney, he said *"You would have been slaughtered in the South for doing that".*
He also once saw him throw bandleader Louis Prima bodily out of a theatre they were appearing at together for bringing a black girl in on his arm.
Stan was a prankster and Jamie was witness to his many wind-ups. No-one was safe from his mischief. His ranch was booby-trapped with toilets that sank into the floor and on the walls hung painted portraits with the eyes cut out that Stan used to peer through and wink at unsuspecting visitors.
He even had the film company's prop men set up a snow machine outside his window and when he had guests to dinner in the middle of a boiling hot summer they stared in open mouthed amazement at the spontaneous blizzard that appeared to be raging outside.

"He'd even fill a hot water bottle with potato salad, carrots and peas and hide it under his shirt. Then he'd make like he was throwing up off a fishbone stuck in his throat. One of his favourite daft tricks was to slip an Alka Seltzer under his tongue, then stumble down the stairs and pretend to have a fit " chuckled Jimmy, shaking his head.

The two Lancastrians got on like brothers and Stan placed a lot of trust in the little feller.
Once, when Stan and Ollie were on tour, and Stan was in between wives, Jimmy accompanied him to a mob-run brothel in the township of Cicero near Chicago.

"Stan went in with his trilby over his eyes and his camel coat collar turned up. He picked two tall girls at a cost of two or three hundred dollars".

While the pair of them were amorously engaged, they had most of their clothes and valuables stolen and in a scene like something from a Laurel and Hardy film were forced to leap through the French windows and return to the hotel wearing nothing but their overcoats and boots.

A Chicago mob contact later retrieved the stolen possessions. Graham and I spoke to Jimmy over many sessions and were kept spellbound by his fascinating life story. One of Jimmy's best friends in Hollywood was Sabu the Elephant Boy who was a massive star at the time.

They seemed to get in a lots of scrapes together but by far the most serious was an incident in which Jimmy was to lose most of his teeth after a prank backfired in a Hollywood nightclub – the Clover Club – which was owned by Bugsy Siegel, a psychotic member of the Jewish Italian organised-crime conglomerate known as The Syndicate and at one stage part of Murder Incorporated.

After an actor friend of Jimmy's daringly gave Bugsy the "hotfoot" (a prank involving a lighted match stuck into the bottom of a person's shoe) Jimmy started to laugh at the mobster.

Incensed by this, Siegel smashed Jimmy's teeth out with the butt of a pistol. Jimmy fearlessly retaliated by grabbing Siegel's nuts and giving him the Lancashire Shuffle - a double headbutt in the face. The enraged crime boss then sank his teeth into Jim's ear and bit a piece off. Jimmy and Sabu escaped in a hail of ricocheting bullets pursued by Siegel and his henchmen as well as a posse of star Hollywood tough guys including Victor Mature and John Garfield. Garfield intervened to save his life and the pair escaped in the Elephant Boy's little MGB sports car.

The following day Stan and Ollie took him to their dentist and treated him to a set of false teeth engraved *"property of Laurel and Hardy"* which, they kidded him, had to be handed in if ever he left their employ.

By this time Jimmy was an American citizen and was conscripted into the US Army in the Second World War. After a tearful farewell with Stan he found himself cleaning out the regimental latrines with suave screen heartthrob Melvyn Douglas who had only just made a film with Joan Crawford (who was to play a major part in Jimmy's life in the 50s.)

It was in the army camp that Jimmy met his lifelong friend Cary Grant who was on a morale boosting tour of US bases and on his first appearance with Cary, his famous Laurel and Hardy teeth shot from his mouth during a sketch involving a trampoline, to the delight of the soldier audience and the amazement of the star.

Jimmy seemed to have major problems with his teeth. When Graham and I took him into a pub in Southport, the first thing he did when we got to the bar was to sneeze heavily causing his false teeth to shoot out and land ten feet away on the pub floor, snapping at someone's ankles.

I could tell many more stories about this fascinating man but I've just remembered it's supposed to be my life story so I will wind up by talking about the time he worked for the boss of Pepsi-Cola – Al Steele – who married diva actress Joan Crawford.

Although most people in Hollywood loved Jimmy, Joan Crawford seemed to have a love-hate relationship with him. Jimmy was devoted to Al and put up with the petty restrictions she tried to impose on him.

She was an alcoholic and drank up to a quart of vodka every day. Jimmy had to smuggle her personal stock of preferred booze through customs when they went abroad.

He joined the household in 1955 and this was the beginning for Jimmy of four mind-boggling years in the Crawford madhouse – "one big unhappy family" as Jimmy called it.

He had many rows with Crawford punctuated by periods of a strange intimacy when she sensed a bond between them in their mutually poor working class upbringing.

Then she knitted jumpers for him, cooked his breakfast and chatted about her day-to-day problems in a way which no one else quite shared.

This didn't stop him rebelling against her tyrannical nature when ordered by her to do what he thought to be unreasonable duties.

One night, Jimmy had been given tickets for a sell-out Joe Louis title fight and was eagerly looking forward to his night off but Crawford imperiously ordered him to stay in and look after her beloved poodles which had the run of the house and were always shitting in her bed.

"We had a blazing row and I tipped a bucket of dirty mopping up water over the top of her brand new picture hat, soaking her expensive gown as well. I thought I'd had my chips but she didn't bother".

He thought she would fire him but strangely, she gave him a small part in her latest film – "Autumn Leaves" in which Jimmy played a flower seller in a theatre foyer but held up production because he couldn't remember the names of the flowers he was supposed to be selling. He kept saying "*Buy my camellias*" and a frustrated Crawford kept yelling "**Carnations** *Jimmy.* **Carnations***!*"
Al Steele was sacked by Pepsi due to his extravagant lifestyle with Crawford and shortly after was found dead in bed in 1959.
On Crawford's instructions, Jimmy had to swiftly clear up the vomit and blood and he intimated to us he thought there were suspicious circumstances. A few hours previously, Crawford had given Al some home-made meatloaf she had made (which Jimmy had refused).
Sadly, Jimmy's downfall came when he upset a very powerful Jewish agent at a party by singing an old music hall song called Abie My Boy which the agent misconstrued as racist. Suddenly Jimmy was taboo and unemployable.
There were no more Hollywood jobs for Jimmy after this and he joined a road gang digging holes for a gas company on the same New York avenues which he had strolled along with the rich and famous.
Indeed, one day Joan Crawford was walking by and spotted Jimmy in his grime and dropped a 10 dollar bill into the hole in which he was working, with the words:" *I hope you are well James*" to the amazement of his dumbfounded workmates.
This is only a small part of Jimmy's incredible story. I wish we could have got it published for him while he was still alive.
He died in 1985 and had met everyone from Lucky Luciano to Ronald Reagan; Gracie Fields to General Westmoreland who employed him as his valet in the Army and was friends with many stars including Frank Sinatra, Errol Flynn and Maureen O'Hara.

He was even on nickname terms with the Archbishop of New York - Cardinal Cooke, who he called Cookey! He saw everyone as no better and no worse than himself.

He was feted later in life by the Sons of the Desert Laurel and Hardy aficionados who loved to hear his stories of the famous duo.

When Graham and I took Jimmy down to London to meet a publisher's go-between we were walking through the streets when Jimmy encountered some men digging a hole in the road.

Having done that himself in America he enquired of the man with a shovel "*What are you digging that hole for?*"

The worker looked up and replied: " *So people can have a shit in it*".

Jimmy was very disgusted and I have no doubt that had this happened forty years earlier he would've flattened the bloke.

Jimmy had his own unique way of talking and, like a lot of elderly Lancastrians, was prone to using malapropisms.

These are some wonderful "Murphyisms" as heard first hand by me...

"He was a venquilotrist"
"She was an extortionist" (contortionist)
"My friend Gary Grant"
"He was crenemated" (cremated)
"A lot of the acts went on the roof and sunburned" (sunbathed)
"It was a Moppoly" (monopoly)
"He drank Yardley's Bristol Cream"
"They were Mohawks" (Mormons)
" It was a subsidence" (subsidiary)
"They were a moffadite" (A hermaphrodite)

That was Jimmy Murphy. As Stan Laurel and he used to sign off :"*God bless*".

Jimmy, I will never forget you.

WATCHING

I'll bring 'em over

After I left ATS Casting, I was agentless for a few years and contacted the telly casting directors myself. I sometimes took an unconventional approach.

I can remember writing to the Casting Department of Granada TV with the usual "*anything available?*" letter and including the lines "*don't let the fact that I am the nephew of David Plowright influence your decision in any way*". (David Plowright was at the time the Chairman of Granada Television).

I don't know whether this amused them or confused them but it frequently seemed to work. I cringe a bit thinking about it now.

By taking what is now known as a proactive approach and by sending out letters, I managed to get more and more small parts on the telly.

I was by turns a taxi driver; hospital patient; butcher (ironic for a veggie); a tramp; a security man; a prison officer; policeman; taxi driver; market stall holder; deliveryman: you name it. And I had lines to deliver!

Ironically, I was probably making less money doing small parts than I would have made had I continued as an extra: because extras, especially ones posing,say, as Rovers' regulars in something long running like Coronation Street got frequent work: indeed, one guy called Chris Canavan was in it for 50 years – mainly milling around in the Rovers – until he died aged 84.

Then in 1987, Granada Television commissioned the pilot for a sitcom which had originally been written by Jim Hitchmough as a sketch for the Everyman Theatre in Liverpool. The name of the programme was "Watching". It featured a naive birdwatching enthusiast and a street savvy, sassy Scouse girl who somehow despite their opposite personalities began to form an attraction for each other.

I was asked to play the part of a cafe owner and I had only one line to deliver which was "*I'll bring 'em over*" - referring to the cups of tea the young couple had ordered at the counter.

Being a big fan of deadpan comedy, that's how I delivered the line: flat, broad Northern and expressionless.

The main protagonists in the comedy were Paul Bown who played Malcolm the birdwatcher; an actress fresh out of drama school by the name of Emma Wray who played his sassy Scouse girlfriend, Brenda and Jimmy Tarbuck's daughter Liza who played Brenda's sister Pamela – giving both actresses their first big break in television. I gave Liza a laugh relating the tale about her dad and me with the strippers.

We met up in our rehearsal room at Granada Television and half way through proceedings, I was dismayed to see a couple of the production crew frowning and shaking their heads as if to say *"this show has no chance"*.

Little did they or anyone else present suspect that "Watching" would go on to major success: stretching to seven series and four specials, pulling in audiences of up to 17 million viewers.

It was produced originally by David Liddiment who went on to be head of programming for ITV and was directed by the very experienced Les Chatfield, a quietly-spoken bearded man who got great performances out of the actors.

When the pilot was viewed by the powers that be, they commissioned the first series and as the team had liked the way I delivered the line, I was booked to do more episodes. I popped in and out the first few series and did 11 shows in all.

It was very confidence-building to realise my delivery of that one line had resulted in being given more and more to do in the series with *"I'll bring 'em over "* becoming somewhat of a catchphrase. Watching was a big turning point in my career and it was very heartening to be given a bigger part as the series progressed.

The character was even given a name – Oswald – and eventually, Brenda came to work for Oswald and being the character she was, started to boss him around.

His trademark was a filthy apron and a fag dangling from the corner of his mouth as he prepared the stew for that day's menu, not caring whether the fag ash dropped in it or not.

Round about this time I was contacted by my old News Editor, David Short (Nigel's dad) who had moved on to PR work. He asked if I'd like to earn a bit of extra cash taking part in a supermarket promotion stunt. It seemed a good idea at the time.

It was on St Valentine's Day and the idea was that the prices in the shops had been massacred - in a reference to the famous bloodbath orchestrated by Al Capone. So to be clear, we were basing the sales project on the fact of seven blokes being ruthlessly slaughtered by being simultaneously shot with sub-machine guns just half a century before.

Three of us dressed like Twenties hoodlums with striped three piece suits and fedora hats while an attractive young lady was attired as a gangster's moll in basque and fishnet stockings.

A suitably menacing large car of the era transported us from store to store and as we approached, we rode the running board on the side and here's the thing, we then jumped off and ran in the outlets yelling "*It's a massacre!* " while waving big black fake tommy guns and pretending to shoot the startled customers.

Petrified shoppers pressed themselves against the walls and I'm sure I detected trickles of wee from one or two old dears. As we yelled "*Bargains to be had*" or whatever, they gradually realised it was some shit, half-arsed advertising event.

Not the subtlest of promotions and can you even imagine attempting a stunt like that these days?!

One elderly lady was relieved to clock me as the dickhead off Watching and we had a good long chat about the show.

Other people started to recognise me in the street and use the "bring 'em over" catchphrase. I was always amazed to be spotted or complimented on the part. This was still happening long after the programme finished: in fact 30 years after, I was sitting in the Victorian buffet bar at Stalybridge station when a man turned round to me and said "*You were the café guy in Watching weren't you?*" I obviously haven't changed much – must be the moisturiser.

Watching was shot partly on location but mainly in the studio at Granada television in front of a live audience. (Well, dead ones don't laugh.)

There was a bit of a cockup in one episode when I dropped a lightbulb which then exploded and shot bits of glass in my face. It got a laugh so they kept it in!

It was great hearing the instant feedback from them as we spoke the very funny lines which had been brilliantly penned by Jim and it was a sad loss to comedy when he died in 1997, four years after the series finally ended. He would have gone on to write many more top shows.

All the episodes are now available on DVD and there is still a big fan base for the programme including a very keen and loyal Facebook group – the Meols Mackerels -who even visit the locations and sometimes dress up as my character, complete with mucky apron.

A former university professor also wrote a tribute book which was published in 2013. Unfortunately, the book states I was "born into poverty", which isn't exactly true!

Emma, whose real name is Gillian, went on to achieve success in other major television productions but after a few more years, she decided she'd had enough of show business.

In a complete change of tack, she travelled all over the world, became a children's nanny and looked after orphans in different parts of the world including Vietnam. That's what I call making a difference.

Almost 25 years after I last spoke to her on the set, she sprang up out of the blue and we met in Manchester to have a delightful day out and relive old memories. After that, she disappeared again and I haven't seen her since!

The cast and crew of top Granada tv sitcom Watching. I'm on the left next to little Billy Moores who is posing as a Salvation Army man. Lots of famous faces from other telly productions in there.

I'll bring 'em over - Oswald –replacing the cherries on top of the cakes after spitting on them and polishing them on his filthy pinny.. That's probably a Nil on the Hygiene Rating Scheme then?

I'M ABDUCTED BY ALIENS

It's called acting, love

Even a vegetarian actor such as me likes to get his teeth into a meaty part and fortunately a few came my way after Watching.

One of the weirdest characters I played on telly was Mr Skip: an eccentric bespectacled UFO spotter who suddenly turned up from nowhere in the middle of Emmerdale.

He rambled around the village in the dark gazing up at the heavens clutching his night vision binoculars in the hope of spotting flying saucers but was mistaken for a flasher and stalker after he bumped into the busty barmaid making her way home.

When her boyfriend found out about it, he nearly battered him in the Woolpack. (Not a nice place to be battered. Wahaaay!)

I did several episodes ending one night when Skip was due to give a talk to a local society but he failed to show up. He vanished just as quickly as he had arrived, mysteriously leaving one shoe behind in his room. The implication was he had been abducted by the very aliens he had sought.

The very odd Mr. Skip

Looking back on it, I wonder if that's what happened to my granddad when he disappeared in 1903?

It was great to catch up again with Steve Halliwell (Zak Dingle) who I had worked with previously when we both played Victorian engineers for a schools' programme, looking resplendent in our mutton chop whiskers and top hats.

Steve and some of the other "Dingles" kindly took me out for a night on the town in Leeds to some great music venues which resulted in me getting back at 3 am. Not good when you have to be up four hours later to film your scenes, but great fun.

It was another late nighter when I played the part of postman Fred Leeder in Heartbeat.

Fred was a kindly soul who came across a stash of cash from a bank robbery but instead of handing it to the police, he played Robin Hood and gave it to deserving causes around the village.

The day before filming, most of the cast and crew met up for a bit of a do in the local pub which went on till 2 am and featured a dog playing on the bongos (don't ask); the cast doing party pieces and me dancing with the lovely Tricia Penrose. Derek Fowler brilliantly sang "Sweet Caroline" a couple of times and I sang my filthy version of Delilah which seemed to go down well.

First class male....Fred Leeder...

I didn't feel great five hours later when, green at the gills, I was driven up and down in a vintage police car on the Yorkshire moors facing interrogation over the robbery.

The props man, Arthur, was a bit of a character who was always playing practical jokes. The cast told me that when Gary Barlow had played a hitchhiker in Heartbeat, Arthur had surreptitiously filled his rucksack with bricks and when it came to "action!" Gary scooped up the bag and nearly yanked his arm off.

Heartbeat was a joy to do and I got a further role as a ticket inspector on a train where the late Geoffrey Hughes turned up making his escape from the taxman dressed as a woman, braving the wolf whistles of the crew.

It's always great to be asked to do a part in a soap as there is always that feeling at the back of your mind that the character you play could become a regular. I'm willing to bet nearly every actor feels the same way. I've been lucky enough to have had five different parts in Emmerdale – Skip, a postman; delivery man; greengrocer and prison officer.

It always amazes me though when people confuse actors with the person they are playing. After a spell in Emmerdale, a woman said to me *"You know that Sam Dingle? Is he like that in real life?"* - referring to the actor James Hooton who plays the nice but dim Dingle. After I stopped laughing I explained *"It's called acting, love"* although I found it incredible I had to say that. I wonder if they think Bruce Willis goes around shooting people for fun in real life too?

When you're filming stuff, more often than not it runs like clockwork. It has to because of the sums involved but shortly after the millennium, a minor calamity occurred during filming of a children's educational series I did for Channel 4 called "*Looking after the Penneys*".

I played Pete Clulow who was the head of a family that needed to be taught a few financial lessons: hence the name of the programme. We filmed it over a few weeks in and around Manchester and on the very last day of filming we went on location to the main house we had been using only to find a scene of devastation.

As we drove up, water was gushing out in a stream from under the front door onto the garden path and it was evident it wasn't going to be a wrap that day.

Something had jammed in the water tank in the attic causing it to overflow during the night bringing down all the ceilings in the house and wrecking almost every room and all of the furniture.

The family whose house it was had gone on holiday in order to enable us to film the scenes and we could only imagine the horror on their faces when they got back to find the interior of their house absolutely destroyed.

The director, Jamie Goold held his head in his hands and wailed "*What are we going to do*?" I suggested we bugger off smartish and leave them a note saying "*Sorry about the mess*".

We had to postpone everything until we found another nearby house in which we reshot all the interior scenes we had filmed in the weeks previously.

The young lad who played my grandson, Jonathan Howard, has gone on to achieve success in Dream Team and Thor: The Dark World. We later met up by chance in a London pub.

I was lucky enough to get more good speaking parts, ranging from several episodes as cancer patient Neville Tweedy in the BBC's Cutting It to a sinister paedo called Sidney Rawton in The Royal Today. You'll be glad to know, Sydney ended up getting shot and operated on by Paul Nicholas.

Cancer patient Neville Tweedy in Cutting It.

Singing Puff the Magic Dragon at a funeral in a wig.

I was a prison officer in the hospital series Always and Everyone where I chained a Scouse prisoner to a hospital radiator.
Although I am grateful for any part that comes my way, I love it especially when there is comic potential to be had.
I was up for the part of a newspaper sub editor in a sitcom called *"Dead Man Weds"* written by Lancashire actor/comedian Dave Spikey who I had known for some years.
After being auditioned in Manchester, I was recalled for another interview down in London. This was shortly before Lynn and I were due to go on a cruise we had booked some weeks previously.

I really wanted this part but the decision making process seemed to go on forever which preyed on my mind all through the cruise.
You meet all sorts of interesting people on cruises and this one, which was round the Med, was no exception. The actor/comedian/writer Stephen Merchant who co-wrote The Office and Extras with Ricky Gervais was on the ship enjoying a holiday with his parents. We got talking and he provided some interesting insights into the inspiration behind his and Ricky's love of comedy which, he told me, owed a great deal to Laurel and Hardy. You can see elements of Hardy in the way Ricky fiddles with his tie and looks to camera a lot in The Office and his other sitcoms.
We met up a few times and chucked a couple of quid away on the roulette wheel but what stands out in the memory was what happened on one hot afternoon as we were sunbathing at the back of the ship.
Stephen was reclining on his sun lounger scribbling furiously and compiling a sheaf of episode plot outlines and gags for his latest project which was at that time the soon to be highly successful "Extras" comedy in which he starred as Ricky's agent.
Suddenly a gust of wind came from out of nowhere, ripped the precious notes from out of his hands and blew them like confetti over the back of the ship!
I stared wide eyed and exclaimed "*Bloody Hell*!" but his only comment was the very stoic: "*Ah well, start again*" in that lovely Bristol burr of his. I was greatly in awe of the phlegmatic way he took the fact that his best ideas had gone into the Mediterranean.
On the final day of the cruise I learned I hadn't got the part but luckily I was given great cameo spot as Arthur Digweed, a grower of gigantic radioactive vegetables (*it's not a leek – it's a spring onion*!) giving me the chance to work with the one-off comedy genius Johnny Vegas who was terrified by the giant potato lurking in my shed whose eyes seemed to follow him everywhere.

Johnny Vegas about to venture into my Shed of Doom…

Talking of cruises….

CRUISING

We are in beeg trouble now

As I've said, I don't like flying but love travelling and we were able to afford our first cruise due to a very kind Silver Wedding Anniversary donation from my late father-in-law George. It opened up the possibility of seeing new places.

Since that first cruise round the Canaries, Lynn and I have become hooked and have travelled to places as far apart as the Caribbean, Newfoundland, Iceland, The Faroes and Africa.

There is no other way to travel; seeing a different country almost every day and being fed the finest food in relaxed surroundings is my idea of heaven.

Although it has given us some of the best moments of our life, it also gave us the worst few hours we have ever spent on this planet.

It was on a Midnight Sun cruise on the Oriana to North Cape in Norway. Lynn and I had left Gareth with some teens of a similar age to him while we watched the sun touch the horizon around midnight then start almost magically to rise again.

We went for a few drinks then back to the cabin: expecting to see Gareth safely ensconced there but there was no sign of him.

An hour later and still no sign. It was about 3 am so we decided to go looking for him. We tried the teens disco and although Wayne's World was bodaciously blaring out on a massive telly screen, he wasn't in there.

We searched every nook and cranny of the ship. Twice. There was no-one around except for some cleaners. Back to the cabin. He wasn't there. We were frantic and I felt the panic rising in me to unimaginable levels. We were fearing the worst.

On what must have been our third visit to the disco, Wayne's World was still blasting out. Lynn looked across the room into a long narrow mirror and saw Gaz curled up in a ball on a tiny sofa directly in front of us. How could we have missed him?

We shook him awake, whereupon he lurched out the room and relieved himself of a large number of Harvey Wallbangers into the fjord. We were shaking so much and so relieved to see him, we didn't bother to bollock him for putting us through a nightmare.

That was the worst thing that happened at sea as far as I am
concerned but most of it has been plain sailing and very enjoyable.
Apart from the places you see, it's the people you meet.
Dennis, for example. I'll never forget Dennis.
Dennis had been a handsome fireman with a roguish air and a
twinkle in his eye but when we met him, he was in the final stages of
a wasting disease and it was to be his last cruise. He was on the next
dining table to us with his lovely partner Ingrid and for some reason
he took to me straight away. We spoke for ages even though
he frustratedly had great difficulty in talking and he even held my
hand as we walked round the ship.
We all went to the disco and he forced himself up to dance. God
knows how he managed that.
When it was the last evening of the cruise, he cried as he said
goodbye to me. I was in bits back in the cabin.
Ingrid emailed us a few weeks later to tell us he had passed on and
thanked us for making him happy on the cruise. It was amazing the
bond we had formed in such a short time. I wish I had known him
longer.
We also became friends with an elderly lady from Cumbria who was
a real character and enjoyed a laugh. One night, she confided to me
that every night without fail, she suffered from the same strange
nightmare she'd had since she was a girl.
Her father was a monumental mason working on tombstones and her
recurring dream was that a headstone shattered and flew at her,
causing her to swallow the fragments. She always woke up choking.
I told her I would cure her. I placed my hands on her head in the
middle of the ship's crowded atrium and commanded the nightmare
to go away and never come back.
She thanked me but was very dubious.
Next evening at dinner, she rushed up and hugged me: " *I don't know
what you did but I didn't have the nightmare! It's the first time for
years!*"
It was the same every night of the cruise. No nightmare. We kept in
touch and every time she rang, she reported her amazement that the
nightmare had never returned. She even dubbed me The Miracle
Worker.
The power of suggestion? Probably – but who knows?

Seeing the Pyramids was a highlight - we travelled in an
armed convoy from Port Said with the police and army blocking off
all the side roads. I was feeling a bit like royalty until I looked out of
the window and saw three men wrestling with a gun in the back of a
car which had somehow managed to pull alongside us.

I haven't a clue what was going on but nothing was reported. When
we got there, the place was full of blokes all pestering you with their
tatty statues and the same patter of "*Buy one get one free! Asda
price...*" and slapping their bums like the old advert.

Kinda spoiled the ambience.

Once, we got caught in the worst floods that Athens had experienced
for many years.

It had all started pleasantly enough: we were with out friends Harry
and Doreen and a local taxi driver who showed us the sights. After
visiting the Parthenon, he dropped us off at a restaurant in the Plaka
– the old quarter of the city.

While we were eating, it suddenly went dark and started thundering
and lightning every few seconds. The downpour was like a monsoon.
We came out to cross the road which, without a word of
exaggeration, had turned into a river as the water flowed off the hills.
My mate Harry dropped his camera and it floated off down the road,
never to be seen again. We managed to wade to the taxi and asked
the driver to take us back to the ship.

The whole city was brought to a standstill and gridlocked and we
found ourselves drifting down towards the river where several cars
had been washed away.

The driver, George, listening to the news on the radio turned to
us and said "*we are in beeg trouble now*"

Somehow, he managed to swing his brand new Mercedes round and
go back up the road against the flow of water. Suddenly a manhole
exploded underneath the car and hit it with some force. He carried
on and somehow through his local knowledge managed to get us
back to the ship. Other passengers had not been so lucky and
some had waded miles knee deep in water to return to the ship.

That's what I like about cruising though: something interesting
always happens. We've even been through a hurricane in the Bay of
Biscay and it still hasn't put us off.

One of my favourite ports is Amsterdam and although this story has nothing really to do with cruises, it stands telling as it always makes me laugh when I picture the scene.

A mate of mine who had been to Amsterdam had discovered the delights of the cannabis cake you can get in the cafes over there. When he got home he decided he would make his own. He bought a cake mix from Asda and mixed some cannabis into it.

His wife had gone out with a friend that night for a few drinks so he took the opportunity to bake the cake. He must've put many times more weed in the cake than the recipe called for because as the kitchen heated up, he found himself getting woozy.

It was so hot he stripped off to the waist and then when the cake was done he cut himself a big slice. He felt even woozier and went weak at the knees so he decided it was time to make his way to bed.

Feeling even hotter, he undressed downstairs then completely naked, crawled on his hands and knees up the staircase. He was halfway up when he collapsed and fell asleep.

Suddenly, the front door opened and his wife and her friend were presented with the sight of his big bare arse sticking up in the air on the staircase and his faithful border terrier licking away at it.

Thinking he'd found pleasure in some perverted act, she screamed "You dirty bugger!" which woke him with a start as her friend quickly shot off into the night.

After he'd explained what had happened, she joined him in a piece of cake and they were unable to get out of bed for 24 hours.

I've told that tale on cruises and few times and it always gets a laugh. Well, depending on the company.

GOOD HEALTH!

Good God – I'd forgotten all about you!

I'm glad to say that, apart from breaking my leg twice, I have hardly ever had to trouble the NHS.

I'm a fervent taker of vitamin tablets and put my good health down to my vegetarianism.

This means I tend to avoid doctors wherever possible. Nothing personal – but I'd sooner keep it that way.

However, one ailment that seemed to plague me on and off over a spell of a few years was the dreaded gout.

I know a lot of people think it's funny, due to cartoons of choleric army colonels with their bandage-swathed feet propped on a padded stool but it's one of the most painful afflictions you can get. It has been described as "*like having your big toe squeezed in a vice – then being given one extra turn for luck*".

I first encountered it after doing a show at the Free Trade Hall in Manchester with the Fivepenny Piece group. One of the band members, Eddie Crotty, had a delicatessen and he brought a massive round of farmhouse Lancashire cheese and a big jar of pickles for us to enjoy after the show. He told me to take what was left, so I did and consumed great quantities over the next few days.

It started with a pain in my big toe which gradually got worse and worse like having electric shocks every few seconds in that particular region.

I hadn't a clue what it was and being slightly hypochondriac I thought it was certain to be cancer of the big toe.

It was a build up of uric acid caused by eating all that cheese and pickles which had formed needle sharp crystals in my big toe, setting off the gout.

It reared its ugly head on several more occasions after that – usually again caused by eating too much cheese so now I'm careful not to do so.

I also tend to avoid dentists and once went 36 years without seeing one. This lucky streak ended when I broke a tooth on a piece of gingerbread from Grasmere and had to have it removed.

Aside from the gout, the only other problem I had health wise was a frozen shoulder.

Nobody seems to know what causes this strange phenomenon. It's very debilitating and the lack of mobility in your arm means it's difficult to do everyday tasks.

Once again avoiding doctors, I visited an osteopath who had been recommended to me by a friend.

He tried several different forms of attack on the frozen shoulder – including deep massage; chiropractic and acupuncture.

He practised his art in a large Georgian house and one day as I lay stripped to the waist he shoved about 30 extra long acupuncture needles all down my arm and back. He said he would be back in about 20 minutes but after 90 minutes had passed I started to get a bit worried. And cold.

I heard someone hoovering in the distance then suddenly all was silence. I managed to struggle off the treatment table and wandered all over this massive house looking for the osteopath who seem to have vanished into thin air.

After about half an hour I came to a door marked Private and tapped on it. The osteopath opened it, took one look at me in a dishevelled half naked state and his jaw dropped exclaiming "*Good God – I'd forgotten all about you!*"

He told me it was the worst frozen shoulder he had ever seen and there was nothing he could do to cure it – advising me to go and see a doctor!

Luckily, I'd remembered my Mam's belief in an old Lancashire remedy called knitbone – the wild comfrey plant which was growing wild in our garden. I boiled some leaves up and slapped them on the shoulder. Coincidence or not, the frozen shoulder which had lasted about six months suddenly went away.

The only other equilibrium-botherer I suffer from is tinnitus. Had it for over 35 years and first noticed it when I thought the downstairs telly was making that high pitched noise that they used to make back then when you inadvertently left them switched on. I searched all over the house for the noise before realising it was me! Tinnitus is bloody awful enough to have sadly caused people to top themselves because of it. Mine's bad at times but I'm not going down that route to cure it.

Like I say, I've been lucky enough to be blessed with good health and I'm very thankful although I've had one or two near scrapes...

271

Shortly after Christmas one year, I decided to relax in a bath of Epsom Salts and various essential oils because I had heard it was a good way of detoxing. Lynn told me the water was too hot but I ignored her. After I got out the bath, I was drying myself off but started to feel faint. Next thing I knew, I had blacked out and landed with my throat on the edge of the bath and was so weak I was unable to move. I was slowly choking to death.

I managed to get out a weak cry which was fortunately heard by Lynn who rushed in and thought I'd had a heart attack.

She lifted me off the bath then ran outside and banged on the door of our new next door neighbour - a young lady who fortunately had had general nursing experience and who came charging into the bathroom to find me lying supine and bollock naked on the bathroom floor.

I gave her a weak smile and a "Hi". She must have wondered what the hell was going on but ascertained I was massively overheated and wrapped me in ice cold wet towels until I cooled down. Then, still weak, I crawled along the landing floor on my hands and knees to my bed while Lynn apologised for my arse being on display.

"Don't worry luv. I've seen plenty arse cracks as a nurse" she said before bending over me and muttering" Next time, keep off them fucking hippy oils!"

CUTTING ROOM FLOOR

Sorry about that

One of the worst things that can happen to an actor is to shoot the part then get chopped from the final edit.

This has happened several times to me and it's not bloody nice. It can give you a persecution complex!

I once played a comic character called Stanley Manley in a cop series shot in Manchester. He was a pigeon fancier whose birds were being used to deliver drugs and this involved working with live pigeons and subsequently a dead one that had been shot by some drug dealers.

The pigeon handler informed me the bird hadn't been killed specially for the production but I had my doubts. It was a cracking little cameo that looked to be intrinsic to the storyline but I was dismayed to get a letter from the producer apologising for overrunning and having to excise the part.

Considering you have to audition; learn the lines; rehearse then film the scenes, it comes as a blow to find out your efforts are all in vain.

This also happened on an episode of *"Shameless"* where I spent two long days in Ashton Under Lyne filming the part of a school janitor and only found out the day before it was screened that the role had been cut. The producer sent an apologetic email claiming there had been "a substantial narrative overhaul" which I suppose is producer speak for "tough titty".

In recent years, I have been lucky enough to be offered a number of good character roles but I would love to do a really good film.

If you look up a movie called *"Nature of the Beast"*, you will see my name in the credits but you definitely won't see me in the film.

I played a gun shop owner (filmed the day after the Hungerford shooting massacre btw). You can hear my voice as I'm selling a customer a shotgun but I'm in a darkened spot in the room so you don't actually see me at all!

The same thing happened when I played a backbench MP in the television series *"First Among Equals"* where you could hear me shout rather appropriately *"where is he?"* but not see me.

I still get repeats from that non-appearance even though it was many years ago. Strange business isn't it?

On most jobs I've been treated mainly with respect and it's been a joy to do.

Admittedly, there was one occasion when I had a couple of lines in a Granada series called "The Practice" which was set in a doctor's surgery. One of the main stars turned up and asked what I was playing.

"*Oh, I've only got a small part*" (stop making up your own jokes)
He lifted his head and looked down his nose.

"*I was always told there are no small parts: only small actors*".
I couldn't think of anything suitably witty but I did think of rearranging his parts..

This brings to mind an episode from my early days as an extra in a Granada drama called Chessgame starring the legendary actor Terence Stamp.

There were three of us in the scene: Mr Stamp, me and another extra called Tommy Cocker: a stocky no-nonsense bluff Lancastrian.

Stampy never acknowledged our presence which got up Tommy's nose and he kept standing behind him pulling horrific faces and raising his chunky mitt making out like he was going to cause a fist sized dent in the former 60's sex symbol's skull. I don't know how I got through the scene without corpsing.

Tommy died not long after and his son Mike told me a cracking story about him.

He used to work behind the scenes at a big Civic Hall in Oldham and it was his duty to organise the fall of poppies from a big net in the ceiling after the Last Post had been played as the climax of the local Remembrance Day service in the hall.

He arranged for a co-worker to slowly pull a string which would gently release the poppies to float down on the distinguished gathering below like the annual service in the Albert Hall. Unfortunately,the lad was a bit slow. The Last Post had been sounded. He forgot to pull the string.

There was much shuffling and muttering below as expectant eyes turned upwards. Still nothing.

So Tommy, getting more irate by the second and forgetting he was close to his announcer's microphone bellowed "***DROP THEM FUCKING POPPIES!!!***"– which echoed like thunder round the venue and rather ruined the respectful atmosphere.

This startled the lad so much that he yanked at the string and all the poppies fell out in one huge bunch on the heads of the startled dignitaries.

Tommy, like his son, was a regular in the Rovers' Return. Which brings me nicely to....

FROM FACTORY STREET (EAST) TO CORONATION STREET

They treat you like shit! (Pat Phoenix – aka Elsie Tanner)

There was a peephole a few inches square in a wooden gate on the fringe of Manchester where in the late 1960's my mates and I jostled to have a glance through at the wondrous scene beyond.

"Let me see!"
"No! Let me see! It's my go now".
"Oh OK. But hurry up!"

What excited our adolescent interest? A stripper? A flash sports car? Perhaps lithe and supple young ladies playing netball?
No, it was something far more exciting. It was the spiritual home of Lancashire and a place where magic was made.
It was the original set of Coronation Street.
We'd seen it on the telly and we knew it was codology and in black and white but we were seeing it in colour. It was real and only a short train ride from our home town.
It was all there: The Barlow's house; the Tanner's the Rovers' Return pub; Florrie Lindley's corner shop. Even the blessed cobbles, just like we had back then in my own little Lancashire street.
It was like our little bit of Hollywood and it was thrilling to see.
We would have loved to stroll along that famous thoroughfare but of course we weren't allowed in.
With my face pressed against the gate, never in my wildest dreams could I have envisaged that in years to come I would walk along the famous cobbles many times in various guises and be watched by millions.
I've been extremely lucky enough to play the following:

Delivery man
Eric Priestley, Superstore owner
Gasman
Bert Latham, foxhunter and friend of Jack Duckworth
Insurance Man
Harry Benson, Gazette Photographer
Unnamed photographer

Another unnamed Photographer (again!)
Gerald Unwin, uncle of Shelley Unwin, the Rover's Return Manager.
Nosy neighbour Kung Fu Cliff
History teacher Leslie Rawlins
(and even played former Rovers landlord Jack Walker in a stage part)

How the hell did THAT happen? I'm truly still amazed and immensely proud to have been involved in some small way with one of the world's most revered and long lasting television programmes. I didn't come from an acting family and I never went to drama school but I always had a hankering to be in Corrie and somehow I managed it.

What being in Coronation Street has taught me is if you set your mind on something you really want, you can edge your way towards it - with a little bit of luck and belief.

Let's set the scene.

I'm 13 years old.

There's something new about to start on the telly.

Mam and I are only slightly curious about this new show and as the haunting strains of the theme tune fade, we settle down to watch it not really knowing much about it.

After seeing the rows of two up, two down terraced houses like ours and hearing the familiar Lancashire speech patterns which match ours, we get quite interested at the novelty of it all and Mam shouts to my gran who is upstairs:

"*Mother. Come and watch this new telly programme*".

"*Why? What's it all about?*"

"*People like us*".

She could not have expressed it better.

It was exactly about "*people like us*".

It reflected everything around us in our neighbourhood - from the nosy lace curtain twitchers to the noisy street arguments; from the sparsely stocked corner shop not long after rationing, to the posh kid on the corner who thought he was a cut above the rest. We became instant fans and from then on never missed an episode.

By whatever mysterious process the Universe had in store for me, a little over 20 years later I found myself doing extra work in the Street and I can recall even now the giddy thrill of first treading those famous cobbles which, unlike the ones in our street, hadn't been covered over with tarmac.

I just wish my gran had been alive to see me in it. She would have wondered how the hell I had managed to get inside that little box in the corner of our room. Seriously.

The street we lived in was just like Coronation Street. When I was a kid I knew the names of everybody in all 17 houses on our street and interacted with most of them at one time or another. Even the dogs had surnames – Dinky Knowles, Smokey Smith, Peggy Heathcote, to name but a few.

Peggy's "dad" was Harry Heathcote the jovial local bookie whose face would crumple and cry with laughter each time he told you a funny story.

There was old Ginny Blakemore, a former cotton mill worker and a kindly old soul who used to bring me an ice cream cone when I was ill.

She once dropped the cornet on the pavement and I saw her wipe the dirt off it on her apron before she gave it to me. "*I'd best go back home*", she always joked with my Gran. "*A hundred pounds is soon gone*". Massive amount then, you see.

There was a lovely couple who had a posh educated Ken Barlow type son who once called me and my mate "*common little pigs*" for daring to play in front of his house. I've bumped into him several times in recent years and he's a decent bloke. I remember also wicked Mrs S who used to beat her sister and keep our football if it went over into her backyard.

Then there were two women who lived together and were spoken of in hushed terms but I didn't know much about that sort of thing in those days.

I suppose my Mam had elements of Elsie Tanner in her personality (although not in a brassy sort of way) as she wasn't averse to rowing in the street if she thought some neighbour had acted unfairly towards me or accused me of something I hadn't done.

There was even a lady at the end house who was the spitting image of Minnie Caldwell and just as timid and naive.

She had originally moved there from somewhere called Nob End in Lancashire (It exists – Google it!) and which us kids delighted in making her say on every occasion we met her by asking: "*Where did you say you used to live?*"

"Nob End" came the innocently sweet reply.

Little bastards.

Anyway, back to Corrie.

How was I to know that years later, I would play many different characters in that selfsame programme?

I only know that in those days, I would have had no idea of how a lad like me could get to appear in a show like that. It wasn't something *"people like us"* actually did.

I wouldn't have had a clue how to go about it.

I am still astonished I have been lucky enough to appear in it all those times and can only wonder at the processes that led me to achieve this.

Does the subconscious mind play a part in it or does the Universe really lend a helping hand in those circumstances when you really want something, like some people claim ?

As I say, from that first episode onwards, I became a fan of the Street and remain so.

Seven months after it started I was thrilled to learn some of the cast were coming to my town to make a personal appearance at a summer fair in a youth club only half a mile away.

I went along to see them in a state of high excitement and managed to get the autographs of half a dozen of them including the actors who played Len Fairclough; Minnie Caldwell; Annie Walker and the legendary Elsie Tanner herself.

I never suspected I would have the pleasure many years later of dining with and appearing on a radio chat show with Pat Phoenix who played Elsie and treading the hallowed cobbles that she had trod. I still have those treasured autographs to this day.

When I first got the chance to do extra work in Coronation Street it was a massive thrill -even although at the time I was just part of the street furniture or propping up the bar in the Pub. It was a dream come true nurtured over many years.

It all began in the Rovers' Return…

On my first appearance in the famous pub I was asked by the director if I could play darts. I said yes. I was a fair darter in those days so he handed me three arrows.

"When I shout action! I want you to throw a dart in the bull's-eye. I will be doing a close-up of it and I'm depending on you to do it with one arrow".

He went off to direct and I swallowed hard – my hand unhelpfully shaking a bit as I contemplated the consequences of missing the bull's-eye first time.

On the cue for action, I chucked the dart at the board and missed the bull by three or four inches. I was nervously waiting for the director to shout "*Cut!*" but thankfully he carried on filming the scene.

He later admitted to me he had been having me on!

Shortly after, I was asked to play a guest at Eddie Yeats's wedding and found myself in a minibus heading towards the location with most of the big stars of the day including the aforesaid legendary Pat Phoenix. I could hardly believe it: me sitting in the same vehicle as Elsie Tanner!

She had the reputation of being a firebrand both in and out of character but it was still a shock to me when I heard the words "*they treat you like shit on this programme!*" coming out of her mouth.

I was gobsmacked. How the hell could massive stars like them be treated like shit I wondered but apparently some major deal had been brokered at that time to sell the show abroad and none of the cast had been informed which had somehow riled Pat a bit.

I'm sure it was all resolved in the end but it was a bit of an eye-opener.

Many years later, I did a chat show on Radio Manchester on a panel which also comprised the Chief Constable of Manchester

James Anderton; leading character actor Joe Gladwin and the lovely Pat. We got on like a house on fire and she signed one of my own books: "*Love from one ferocious Lanky to another. Love Pat Phoenix*". Then added "*The only savage Lancastrian just running loose - Pat*".

I was also lucky enough a little later to be invited for lunch with her and her then fiancé the late Tony Booth. There were a couple of reporters in the restaurant and they shouted across to the couple "*when are you going to get married?*" to which Pat teasingly replied "*wouldn't you like to know?*" Sadly, they were later to marry on her deathbed.

Ironically at that meal, Pat was aghast because I was eating blue cheese for afters. She told me there had been a recent story in the newspapers that there was a possibility blue cheese could cause cancer and I should stop eating it which was ironic considering she was a 60 a day smoker which probably led to the lung cancer that finally killed her in 1986. A sad end to a great lady. She was a big star with a big heart.

Gradually, I got more and more extra work in Coronation Street: usually in the Rovers or sometimes as a guest at a wedding or party and was really happy to have my face seen by friends and family in that legendary programme.

The first words I ever spoke out loud in Corrie were "*Mind your backs please girls!*" as I was given a small part as the delivery man to Baldwin's factory. I couldn't have been more pleased if I had been playing the lead in Hamlet.

You can imagine how thrilled my Mam was to see me in the show that we had first watched together all those years before.

Whenever I subsequently appeared on the telly, she was stopped when shopping by people saying " *I saw your David on the telly last night*" and she'd proudly report back to me every time.

My next break came in January 1985, when I was asked to audition for the part of a brewery drayman delivering to the Rovers. After I had read a few lines, the casting director - the delightful Judi Hayfield - asked if I would like to read for a bigger part: that of a superstore owner by the name of Eric Priestley.

Would I?! I could hardly hold the plastic cup of coffee I had been given without spilling it. I read the part and the director, Malcolm

Allsopp said to my relief: *"Well, that worked for me"*. I couldn't believe my ears.

I was given a contract for three episodes at a fee of £180 per episode-less 10% plus VAT agent's fees: not exactly a fortune, but I was just so absolutely proud to have such a proper part in the Street. Before I knew it, a week or so later I was shaking hands with a legend and one of the nicest people in television: William Roache – alias Ken Barlow - who warmly welcomed me to the Street as did several more of the big names including Julie Goodyear - all kindly introducing themselves as though I didn't know who they were.

My scenes involved flogging Ken some modern units to replace his Uncle Albert's ancient sideboard. I recorded a couple of episodes which went very well and was rehearsing a third when a runner came to me and said *"The producer John Temple wants to see you in his office"*.

I thought this is it Dutton: you've made the big time. He's going to offer you a long term contract! With heart aflutter, I went into his office only to be told *" I'm really sorry but due to time constraints, we are going to have to cut your third episode"*.

I left his office totally deflated. Actually though, it proved good experience for the disappointments to come that nearly all actors face in their career.

A lot of actors who get booked to play in Corrie are understandably nervous about fitting in with such an established cast. I can only say in my experience, I have always felt at home there and been made to feel a part of it by the cast and crew alike. Everyone who has been in the programme seems to feel the same.

Production methods have changed so much since my early appearances in Corrie. In those days, it was only two shows a week and we had rehearsal days; technical runthrough days when all the top brass came to watch and the actual filming days themselves.

Now, you more or less run through the lines with the other actors in the green room or some other convenient spot; then a quick rehearsal in the studio before shooting the scene shortly after.

It's a punishing schedule and the regulars have my total admiration for the long hours they work, sometimes deep into the night. How they learn their lines in between the actual shooting is a mystery to me.

Over a cup of tea in the tiny Coronation Street green room kitchen, the late Bill Tarmey, confided he hadn't been able to sleep properly and had work related nightmares when he managed to drop off. Luckily, he found that the Bach rescue remedy recommended by another member of the cast had actually worked in calming him down. It seemed a bit incongruous – Jack Duckworth taking new age medicine.

Walking down the corridor alongside the cast dressing rooms I was disconcerted to hear shouting and bawling emanating from one of the rooms and I thought the members of the cast were having a nasty argument. It transpired that it was Bill and the lovely Liz Dawn rehearsing their parts as the fiery Jack and Vera Duckworth who, as we know had many an on screen row...but never off it.

"We're always shouting" she drawled, with a chuckle.

The two of them had a lovely closeness about them and I remember once when Bill was five minutes late coming back from lunch, Liz was in tears, convinced something had happened to him.

Bill and Liz had been extras in the Rovers before their Jack and Vera days and there was no trace of self importance about them. In fact after doing a stint on the Street, I once bumped into Liz who was doing a promotion for a bank in the Arndale Centre in Manchester and she pointed at me and said to all the fans who had gathered round her *"Hey. Look. He's off the telly!"* as if I was the most important one there. They all knew who she was but hadn't a clue who I was! Lovely woman unaffected by fame.

As fate would have it, I met up with Liz again on a cruise in 2015. She was with her husband Don, a deadpan Yorkshire bloke who was the perfect foil to her sense of humour.

Although, we only meant to briefly say hello, she asked Lynn and me to join them and we stayed chatting together for three hours. Liz, although in poor health and in a wheelchair, was utterly hilarious. Her skin was bruised through years of being on steroids for her lung condition but her eyes still twinkled and she could have you in fits of laughter with a nod, a grimace or a downturn of her mouth. She regaled us with some hilarious stories such as the time she did a curtsy in front of Princess Diana and couldn't get up again so Diana had to bend over and lift her up.

She had met the royal family many times and on one occasion when Prince Charles went round to her dressing room before a show, she was smoking a cigarette and explained to him "*I always have a puff before I put me tights on".* Charles looked bemused and replied "*Why? Does it make them go up quicker?*"

When she met Pope John Paul, she took a treasured battered statuette of St Jude with her which was so old, it had lost its hands. He did a double take at it and looked at her in disbelief.

We dined with them every night and although she had been out of the Street for several years, she was constantly stopped by fans who told her how much they missed her. She always had time to chat and have a photo taken with them.

"*Isn't it nice to have people smiling at you all the time?*" she sighed.

She was full of praise for her old screen partner Bill Tarmey who had died three years previously and she obviously missed him very much.

"*He was a lovely man*" she was fond of saying.

"*He was a Taurus*"

"*Aye*" said her husband Don, dryly: "*So were Hitler*".

I nearly spat my wine over my dinner.

Bill Tarmey **was** a lovely man and, to my mind, a fine comic actor who deserved the success that came to him. I remember talking to him in front of Granada once when I heard a shout of "*There's Jack!*" I turned round and there were about 50 kids hurtling in our direction.

By the time I turned round to Bill, he'd already disappeared!

Liz confided in me it had always been her dream to appear in Emmerdale which amazed me in view of all the years she had spent in Corrie.

I was happy to see she achieved her ambition not long after. We spoke about going on another cruise together but sadly this was not to be as she left us in 2017. She was much loved and missed by all the fans and cast.

A true Corrie legend, she got a well deserved standing ovation at the Soap Awards.

Cheers our kid!

In all my years working on and off in Corrie, I have only met one person I disliked - a one-time regular who treated the extras like dirt, which infuriated me. He had a bullying attitude and made one poor woman stand up so he could sit down, telling her that the extras shouldn't be using the chairs to rest on when there were main members of the cast around. Thankfully, he is no longer in the show.

Although that horrible man was the exception, some walk on artistes seem to think the main actors are sometimes being standoffish with them when in fact, they are probably rehearsing the lines over and over in their heads and working out the tricky camera moves.

In addition to actually acting, you have got to be word perfect; be aware of where the cameras are pointing; take the correct cues; be careful not to step on anyone else's lines; speak at the right level; avoid bumping into furniture and people and sometimes you have to walk to an exact spot marked on the floor by a tiny piece of gaffer tape that you somehow have to spot out of the corner of your eye without the viewers being made aware that you are doing so. Talk about spinning plates!

Screwing up any one of those things could cause expensive filming to be halted and all eyes to turn upon you. It's not like working down a mine but it's a different sort of pressure.

When I see actors doing a long monologue or a lengthy two hander in a soap, I am filled with admiration, knowing all the work and preparation that has had to go into that experience.

It's a relentless schedule. I once did some scenes in Corrie with an actor who was being featured in it very heavily at the time and minutes before we were due to film them, I asked him when he found time to learn all his lines. He replied *"I'm doing it now"*.

His schedule was so packed he only had time to memorise his words minutes before shooting the scenes.

It is embarrassing for everyone when an actor messes up as I recall from the days when I was doing extra work on Corrie and in one scene in the Rovers an actor screwed up about 10 times. It was painful to watch and when he finally got it right, there was an ironic round of applause. Sadly, his brain was going into decline and he had to leave the cast shortly after.

It was also sad to see another actor, the brilliant Bernard Youens who played Street loafer Stan Ogden, in poor shape, having had several strokes. His head was drooping and he couldn't get the words out properly.

Whether you are an extra or playing a main part in Corrie, there are always long periods of time where you are sitting around doing nothing. The difference is that as a featured actor, you get the luxury of a winnebago on location or the green room in the studios. You also get first dibs at the "butty wagon" and are sometimes ferried around in a Mercedes, which is rather nice.

Playing Eric Priestley gave me a taste for what you might term the big time, so I told my then agent I didn't want to do any more extra work, thank you very much. She was quite snotty about it and warned me I might never get any more work in television.

I needed the money and there was more chance of work as a walk on artist but a decision had to be made and I made it. I reasoned that if I continued to do background work, I wasn't going to get much further as an actor so I stuck to my guns and boy I am glad I did.

Each time I do a decent part in the Street, cast and crew sometimes come up and say encouraging words like *"I'm sure you'll be back. It's a great character"*.

It's a privilege to have done all those different parts but up to now, none have had the stickability that the producers and writers have deemed would make a regular character.

I am the Nearly Man of Corrie!

My next part in the Street came four years later in 1990 when I played a gasman who cut off Baldwin's Casuals (not a euphemism). I had an argument with Percy Sugden over it but I did the dirty deed anyway.

That was only a one off, but 15 months later I had a great part as Jack Duckworth's feckless mate Bert Latham who owned a very large black mongrel dog called Boomer which he sold it to Jack as an unlikely Christmas present for Vera.

Unfortunately, the dog terrorised the Duckworths and ate the Christmas turkey. Boomer eventually went missing and was discovered back at Bert's house where it was subsequently revealed Boomer was short for Boomerang. Bert had sold the dog many times in the past but it had always returned to him, as he had trained it to do.

The dog actor was a bit of a strong beast and took some handling especially in a madcap scene we filmed a few weeks later when a drunken Jack, Curly Watts and Bert held a fox hunt on the famous cobbles.

The crafty fox had been snaffling Jack's prize pigeons and Boomer got its scent and chased it all the way into Mavis's garden with me and the lads in hot pursuit. The hunt was abruptly stopped when Mavis bashed me over the head with a rather large frying pan and that was that.

Halfway through that chase I had another argument in the street with Percy Sugden where he had to utter the funny but silly line:" *Oi. You're not from round here. Go and hunt foxes in your own street!*"

The ridiculousness of the line got to me and put a twinkle in my eye causing Bill Waddington, who played Percy, to corpse with laughter, unable to get his words out properly.

When after several attempts, the director berated him slightly, Bill pointed at me in an exasperated manner, exclaiming "*It's not me -it's him!*" like a naughty schoolboy being ticked off by his teacher.

After we shot the scenes, Bill Tarmey was very complimentary and said *"You're bound to be back lad. "*

I was - four years later!

287

Not even as Bert but this time as an unnamed insurance investigator who assessed Kevin and Sally's kitchen after Kevin's dad set fire to it.

Corrie is such a great gig to do and you are always made very welcome and looked after well that it is always with a sense of foreboding when you walk out of the green room after you have finished your stint. Will I be back? Will the powers that be remember me?

Being a native Lancastrian brought up in a terraced house on a cobbled street perhaps that's why I always feel so at home there. I could probably live there if the houses were real.

Working with the Duckworths was always a pleasure because the actors who played them were lovely people. There's also another reason. When I started digging into my family tree, I discovered my Great Great Grandmother was a Duckworth – Betty Duckworth, a silk weaver from Leigh. Yes – I have genuine Duckworth blood coursing through my veins.

I only had to wait slightly less than three years for my next appearance: this time as the devious and slightly pervy Harry Benson, the photographer on the Weatherfield Gazette.

My sidekick was the reporter Duncan Stott ably played by Ian Kershaw who is now a successful playwright. Together we put paid to the church wedding of Roy and Hayley as we chased them all round town in order to do a sensationalist story when we found out that she was transgender.

The is an ironic twist to this story. Ian fell in love with Julie Hesmondhalgh who played Hayley and some years later the two of them got married. They have a fantastic garden party on a slope behind the house in Derbyshire every year to which Lynn and I have been a number of times.

Ian and I reprised the double act when we were sent to cover a protest meeting on the Red Rec where I chained Toyah Battersby to a tree, ostensibly as part of the event but in reality "*to get some pictures for the lads in the dark room*". Dirty Harry!

It's always very poignant to see some of the old Coronation Street favourites deteriorating and in that episode, Brian Mosley who played Alf Roberts looked quite fragile and sadly died not long after.

You would think having established a character with a proper name, that it's one of the occasions when that character might stick. But no. A couple of years later, I was brought in for a couple of episodes as simply "Photographer".

I photographed Jack and Vera receiving a massive cheque for £59,361 from a bookmaker.

Then a few months later, I reappeared to take pics of Curly Watts for his election campaign.

A couple of years elapsed before I blotted my copybook somewhat over an incident involving a really good part which I was supposed to audition for.

I had an advanced script and had been learning it over the course of a few days because I wanted to be word perfect for the audition which involved quite a number of episodes as a potential sugar daddy for the egregious Tracy Barlow. It was a meaty role and I was looking forward to doing it justice.

Because of the importance of the part, I had keyed myself up and had travelled to Manchester for the audition which was to have been the following day but late in the afternoon I received a phone call from my agent informing me the casting session had been cancelled as they had given the part to a well-known actor who turned out to be Bernard Cribbins

I love Bernard but to be honest, I was fuming and I called the very important Corrie casting lady and gave her a piece of my mind. Not the wisest move perhaps but I felt I had to get my frustration off my chest. It felt like I had been strung along and it seemed dismissive and unfair to be treated in that way.

She rejoindered that the matter had been out of her hands and I should be used to such vicissitudes anyway after my long years in the business.

Perhaps she had a point but at least I felt better for expressing my frustration.

I told my agent, Debs, what I had done and she gave me her support. I confidently expected never to be contacted again by the casting lady but to my surprise and her credit, she called me in not long after to audition for the part of Gerald Unwin -the uncle of Shelley, the landlady of the Rovers' Return.

He was a bit of a lad who liked the ladies as well as a smoke and drink and turned up at Shelley's wedding reception.

When I showed up in the Green Room, I was greeted again by Bill Roache who I had met many times before and he extended his hand to shake mine saying "*Dave. Lovely to see you again. What are you playing this time?*" - which seemed to precisely sum up my Coronation Street "career".

The wedding reception scenes were filmed in a function room of a hotel on the outskirts of Manchester and with everybody being crowded in together under the hot lights needed for filming, the atmosphere was so stifling one of the sound engineers actually fainted and we had to stop shooting for a while.

When the wedding was over, so was my part as Gerald.

I sat drumming my fingers for the next eight years until in 2011 I landed the part of a feisty oldish guy called Clifford (no surname) who was a neighbour of Mrs Fishwick, a victim of the notorious serial killer John Stape. Stape pretended to be a delivery man but he was actually returning to the scene of the crime having realised that he had left incriminating evidence near the body of Mrs Fishwick. Clifford (me) broke open the door of the woman's house with a martial arts kick - a yoko geri - earning me the sobriquet Kung Fu Cliff amongst the twitterati.

I hear even the Queen watches Corrie. I wonder if she's chuckled at any of my strange antics on the show such as that same karate episode penned by top playwright Jim Cartwright (now my agent) where, expressing my admiration for the novelist I said "*Oh, I love a good Trollope*"? It's a weird thought.

More years rolled by and I had just about given up hope of ever appearing in the soap again. I'd more or less packed it in when I got a call out of the blue from casting informing me that the director David Kester had asked for me specially to do a funny part as a teacher by the name of Leslie Rawlins who was an English Civil War re-enactor, complete with knee length Cavalier boots. It was one day's work but a great little part.

Is that it? Never say never – but I'm running out of Anno Domini! What more can I say about The Street? It's been great to be a tiny part of it. I can see it outlasting me and most of the people who were alive when it started. Long Live Corrie!

Uncle Gerald and Peter Barlow have a good natter...

I FIND A SISTER

I'm your brother David. I believe you want to speak to me.

Whenever I watched "*Surprise, Surprise!*" in the 1980s, I became very emotional when long lost family members were reunited by Cilla Black.

My Mam did a great job of nurturing, protecting and providing for me but there was always that aching sense of something missing.

I knew my father had a daughter - who was therefore my sister- and I had cousins and probably nephews from his side of the family who I knew nothing about.

In the 1970s, I had travelled to Woolwich in London to seek my dad out as I knew he lived in that area.

It was a half-arsed attempt consisting of me going into a few local pubs and asking people if they knew of a Stanley Grant. Pretty pathetic really.

I subsequently discovered after his death that he had been living about three miles away in Kidbrooke.

I often wonder what his reaction would have been if I had ever found him. I will never know. I fancy his wife wouldn't have been too pleased.

There is no doubt he loved my mother and wanted to be with her. I have a letter sent by him in which he says to her:

"I don't know how to stick it. I suppose eventually I will throw the lot in and come to Lancashire. She knows it's on my mind the whole of the time and taunts me with it.
We hardly ever speak to each other and at times it is almost unbearable.
I wish I had my release from it all: I would be with you quicker than you think. Mabel, it's no use - I love you in spite of what at times you may think to the contrary.
Although you seem to see so much bad in me I'm afraid I can't see any in you".

It's sad that two people who obviously loved each other deeply were kept apart by circumstances.
In the early 80s, I determined to find out more. It didn't have a happy ending though.
I made another trip to London to delve into the records of Somerset House - only to discover my father had died in 1971 of cancer of the oesophagus. A horrible way to die.
Of course I was sad because I knew then we were never destined to meet but I also dreaded telling my Mam.
On hearing my news, she shed a tear but what cut me was she told me she thought she had caught a glimpse of him as an old man walking past the end of our street a couple of times.
As he lived a couple of hundred miles away it was probably wishful thinking on her part and heartbreaking to reflect upon. But it set me thinking. What if it really was him? What if he had travelled all that way on some pretext hoping to catch a last glimpse of Mam or perhaps me? Doesn't bear thinking about really.
To be honest, we didn't talk much more about it after that. I still found it slightly embarrassing to bring the subject up.
A few years later in 1986 I had a phone call out of the blue from my cousin Gwen on my father's side letting me know my sister Joyce wanted to speak to me on the telephone.
This was my own *"Surprise Surprise"*moment.

I was just short of my 40th birthday and discovered there was a quarter of a century in age difference between us. My head was spinning with questions. How would we get on together? Would she have any anger in her because, after all, I was a byproduct of her father's adultery. Would we have anything at all in common apart from an accident of birth?

Feeling nervously excited, I composed myself then dialled the number that Gwen had given me.

Joyce answered in her softly spoken southern accent.

I stammered *"I'm your brother David. I believe you want to speak to me"*.

There was a slight pause…

"Oh. It's you dear. At last…I've been longing to speak to you for years".

My mind was set at rest.

She told me she had wanted to make contact with me but had held back out of respect for her mother. Neither of us had any other brothers or sisters (as far as we knew). I think she too felt something was missing in her life.

That was just the beginning. We spoke regularly on the telephone and made arrangements to meet up at her house in Alcester near Stratford-upon-Avon.

Lynn, Gareth, Mabel and I drove down shortly after but the car – the shitty old Austin Allegro - hit a pothole near Anne Hathaway's cottage, buggering up the suspension and had to be towed to a garage by the breakdown services.

My new nephew Simon came to the rescue by picking us up and taking us to the family home where Joyce and my other nephew Mike were waiting.

I suppose it could have been an embarrassing encounter all round but young Gareth broke the ice with his usual cheeky charm and made us all laugh.

Mam had finally got to meet the young girl in the photograph that she had seen in dad's office all those years before.

Mabel said to Joyce: "*I didn't think you'd want to meet me*" but Joyce was happy to see her, even though she must have had mixed emotions.

We spoke very regularly on the phone over the following years and Joyce filled me in on some stories about our dad.

She said he had been a gambler: as was his father. He had an equable disposition and never lost his temper. I obviously did not inherit those genes.

She later told me that when dad went to Risley, her mum refused to go with him to live up there.

"I'm afraid she didn't like Northerners, dear!" she chuckled, before adding thoughtfully *"No wonder he strayed."*

I knew then that there was no bitterness in her whatsoever.

His wife didn't even want him to go to his own Mam's funeral "up North" but he quite rightly ignored her wishes.

Like my granddad Herbert, Stan had fought in the First World War. He took part in the Battle of St Quentin with the Rifle Brigade and got shot in the leg.

The doctors wanted to amputate his leg but being very strong minded, he told them where to go and subsequently made a miraculous recovery.

Cousin Gwen, a delightful lady, kindly put on a party for my 40th birthday where I met other family members who made me feel very welcome.

Joyce never showed any animosity towards mum – only kindness - as I think she realised what a struggle it had been for her to bring me up without a husband.

Strange to think that they were more or less the same age.

We met up at Gwen's several times and Joyce also came to visit us when we moved to our house near the Lake District.

She was proud that I had written books and was an actor and she told me she never referred to me as her half brother but always her brother.

Through our numerous telephone conversations, she filled me in on family stories and gradually I began to paint a picture in my mind of the man who had fathered me.

Despite his background in the workhouse and children's home he had studied hard to better himself and became an important part of the war effort with his extensive knowledge of munitions.

"He liked a smoke, a drink and a bet" said Joyce.

She also told me a strange spooky story about him. When he left his home down South to work as Superintendent at Risley, the clock on the mantelpiece stopped the moment he left the house. His wife took it to a clock mender who inspected it thoroughly and pronounced it unmendable.

When dad returned home after his long spell up North, he picked up the clock and it started going again. It must have missed him.

She also said that when he was driven up North, he carried an important experimental piece of highly volatile explosive nestled on his lap in the back of the car because he deemed it too dangerous for it to be transported in any other way.

Just think: one pothole and I might never have seen the light of day.

Joyce must have been imbued with some of our father's toughness as one year, she was found on the floor of her home having had a critical stroke and needed urgent surgery performed on her.

The surgeon removed the top of her skull and operated on her brain without administering an anaesthetic (too risky) while she was conscious throughout.

Thankfully, she survived this ordeal and, I'm glad to say, led a reasonably full and active life until her death many years later in August 2014 at the age of 92.

Her last words to me on the telephone were her usual sign-off of "*I'll love you and leave you dear...*"

Somehow, I didn't receive an invite to the funeral.

Joyce; Gareth; me; Lynn and Mabel at our first meeting.

296

LOSING MABEL

Your Mother's got dementia. It's very popular these days.

"*Never look back*" as the saying goes. In some respects, it's good advice as you can't live in the past and you can't anticipate the future. There is only now.
However, if you're writing about your life, you have to look back and there are some aspects that inevitably dredge up sad and unhappy memories.
I wish I hadn't had to write this next chapter. It's a difficult subject to deal with. In fact it's heartbreaking.
Even writing these words is stirring up a cloudy silt of emotions that I hoped had been consigned to the deep within me many years ago. I don't think they ever will be though and like a crack in a dam it doesn't take much to allow those horrible feelings and thoughts flood once more into one's consciousness.
It's hard to chronicle my Mam's gradual decline into dementia. The slow disintegration of someone who gave birth to you, supported and loved you and who you loved in return is one of the hardest things to bear in life and painful to reflect upon.
To begin with, the warning signs were there but we didn't notice them immediately.
Mabel had always enjoyed going out for a drink and a natter in the local club round the corner. It got her out of the house and there were friends in there she had known from her school days.
Suddenly, she stopped going and wouldn't give a reason. Friends tried to persuade her to go out but she didn't seem interested. She started to sound very depressed.
I phoned her every night and during our conversations she began to repeat herself a lot, as I suppose a lot of elderly people do. We drove up to see her every week and took her out for rides which she always enjoyed.
Her complaints about people around her started to grow. She claimed that a particular woman always turned the radio up to maximum volume on her car every time she drove past the house just to annoy her. I took this seriously.

She said she heard some of the neighbours talking about her and criticising her and also claimed that two men had been banging on the back door of the house, trying to break in.

She was prone to accidents. When we took her to her favourite local beauty spot, she was throwing bread to the ducks when she fell in the lake, landing on her back, still clutching her handbag. She scraped her legs and needed several visits to the local infirmary.

She also got knocked down crossing a busy road, causing her minor injuries. She claimed that the man from the chemist's shop who brought her painkillers had sworn at her and abused her, which was hard to take in.

The strangest thing was she started to get very regular bouts of déjà vu, claiming things that had just happened had happened previously when it was obvious they hadn't.

To be honest, these were signs of her impending dementia that we didn't pick up on.

It's very puzzling to look back and to think we missed these signals but perhaps we didn't really want to believe what was happening to her.

Other signs were becoming increasingly difficult to ignore. After our telephone conversations she frequently replaced the receiver upside down and we had to phone a neighbour to go round. She kept a diary in a little notebook but gradually her handwriting became smaller and smaller and eventually as to be almost painfully unreadable.

She sometimes left the key in the door or her handbag or shopping bag hanging on the doorknob outside the house.

We went one day to find a strange woman in the house. She was someone we didn't know who lived nearby and was ostensibly doing errands for Mabel. She smelled of booze and I later discovered she was an alcoholic who seemed to be taking advantage of her, as Mabel was giving her money.

When we cleared the house out later, we found stuff was missing – including Victorian jet jewellery that had belonged to my gran.

Then Mam's behaviour became more alarming.

She told us she had seen big black slugs coming out of the light socket and that famous television entertainers such as Pavarotti had been performing for her in her living room in person: even Ken Dodd, who she disliked intensely. She couldn't grasp the fact that she had only seen them on television.

"Pavarotti was stood right here! I can't get over it. " she exclaimed.
We had her assessed and she was given drugs to help her cope with her condition but it was to no avail.

The situation finally became untenable when it was reported she had been found walking barefoot in a nearby street in the rain.

It brought to mind a memory from my childhood when an old neighbour by the name of Martha Ann was frequently seen walking past our house late at night to the cotton mill where she thought she still worked many years before.

Feeling sorry for her, my Mam used to coax her back to her home. Now she was in the same position -rambling the streets herself.

We lived too far away to look after her and with a youngster in the house, it wouldn't have been fair on him anyway so it was with a heavy heart I phoned the local social services who realised the urgency of her plight and to their credit, arranged for her to go into a local nursing home right away.

I will never forget the day she came down the stairs of number nine inappropriately dressed in many layers of clothes and I led her out of the home she had been born in 77 years before and to which she would never return again. Even now, my heart sinks thinking of that moment.

When she asked where she was going, I had to lie to her and tell her it was a temporary measure *"to get you right"*.

Even though it was for her own good, it made me feel like a traitor. There was guilt at putting her in a home when she had been loyal to and cared for her own aged mother. But there was really no alternative. We lived in a small cottage in a tiny hamlet in the middle of nowhere. Our son was at an important stage of his education and on her last visit to us, she had lost her orientation round the house and nearly fallen down the stairs several times.

It would have been too dangerous.

On the last night she stayed with us, there was a terrible thunderstorm and we watched the display of lightning from our upstairs living room. She had even forgotten she was petrified of lightning and at one time would have hidden under the stairs with her hands over her head.

When we took her to the care home, the manageress took me to one side and muttered: " *Your Mother's got dementia. It's very popular these days"*.

Popular?! I knew what she meant but couldn't help thinking she could have phrased it better.

She also said: " *Don't bother about them. Their lives are almost over. You have to get on with yours now".* – indicating the residents with a sweep of her arm. Well meant I suppose but I felt it was a bit harsh at the time.

Mam's decline was such that she only asked when she was going to go home a couple of times and then gradually forgot about it.

Strangely, she also immediately seemed to forget she was a smoker for she never touched another cigarette nor ever asked for one.

The heartbreaking part was she didn't know who I was and frequently asked me if I had seen Dave Dutton recently. To be unknown to your own mother drags the guts out of you as you look back on all the loving times you had with her and the sacrifices she made for you.

You come away feeling depressed and just want to punch something and scream.

She also started to ask how her mother was and her brother Walter and I just had to lie and said they were both well and would be coming to see her soon.

Mabel seemed to settle in the home and the care assistants loved her Lancashire sense of humour and her catchphrase of "*Ecky peck!*" and they sang all the old songs with her that she knew and loved.

There was an unnerving drama a few months after her admittance.

I was working near London on a commercial and while waiting in a caravan to go on location, I popped out for a newspaper.

There were copies of the Daily Express on the counter of the newsagents and on the front page there was a photograph of a building which looked very familiar.

I couldn't believe my eyes. I'd been there many times. It took a few moments for it to sink in but I recognised the very nursing home my mother was in.

Hurriedly, I bought a copy and as I read it on the way back to the caravan I felt sick to my stomach for the main lead was a claim by a former care assistant that the residents were being ignored and left to their own devices. I was stunned and, naturally, very concerned.

Although I couldn't be sure, I had seen none of this neglect as to me, all the residents seemed happy and well cared for. It was agony enough seeing her in there without having to contemplate anything as bad as that. I don't know how I got through that day, doing that stupid advert.

Just to put you in the picture, I am happy to report that the local authorities did a major investigation and couldn't find anything to substantiate the story, thank God.

That was bad enough but from a family point of view, worse was to happen. Her beloved niece, my cousin Marjorie, had been really distressed to see my Mam in the home when she was first admitted. Inexplicably, she too went mentally downhill astonishingly quickly in a matter of weeks and ended up in the home sitting next to my Mam.

Neither of them recognised the other.

They forgot their previous loving relationship and had fights, frequently having to be separated by the staff and on one occasion dragged each other to the floor in anger.

This is the sheer awfulness of dementia: the fact it takes away who you are without mercy or respect.

If they could have looked into a crystal ball 40 years previously and have witnessed their sad future in it, they would have been horrified to see themselves rolling round on the floor fighting one another in a home.

Marjorie and Mabel in happier times

Of course they also sometimes had great moments of companionship together where they chatted like long lost old friends but still not knowing their real familial relationship.

Our Marj died before Mam. I don't think Mabel even realised she had gone.

Mother's Day was a bad time: you couldn't take flowers because they didn't last two minutes in the hot conditions in the nursing home and chocolates were taboo because of the effect on the old folks' bowels.

Christmas was even worse. You couldn't enjoy the day knowing Mabel's situation. My mother-in-law, Marjorie kindly invited her for Christmas dinner once but it turned into a disaster because of her toilet needs.

She went to hospital a couple of times after a couple of falls. Her treatment there left me distinctly unimpressed.

When we went to visit her in a Bolton hospital, I walked into her ward and found her lying listlessly with an uneaten sandwich on her chest and no-one around.

I complained to the ward sister and she sent round the young nurse who should have fed her in the first place but who only seemed interested in talking about the Take That concert she had been to the night before.

On another occasion in a convalescent hospital, the ward sister complained to me in front of everyone my Mam had been using foul language and it was unacceptable.

I took the stupid woman to one side and said to her furiously:

"You're supposed to be a nurse. Don't you realise that this is what people with dementia do involuntarily? Don't you think my Mam would have been horrified if she could see herself in this condition?"

Before her illness, Mabel hardly ever swore and didn't like me doing so either.

The woman looked slightly shamefaced but I doubt it had much effect on her dealings with the unfortunate patients in her charge. I often wonder if the dangerous material Mam worked with at Risley worked through her system and somehow slowly poisoned her brain.

Inevitably, Mabel gradually faded into her last few weeks but a strange thing happened very shortly before she left us in 2002.

Lynn and I had been paying our usual visit and I spoke to Mam while holding and stroking her hand even though most of the time

302

she was really sleepy. As we were leaving I said *"See you next week Mam"*. She looked up and said *"Okay David"*.

It was the first time in several years that she had called me by the name she had given me when I was born. I was affected greatly by this but it also lifted my spirits hearing my name fall from her lips. It was the last time she called me David and indeed the last time she ever spoke coherently to me because a couple of days later she became very ill and was transferred to a specialist nursing home nearby.

I sat with her a few hours but she wasn't really aware of my presence. It was obvious she wasn't going to last much longer and I held her hand tightly and whispered that soon she would be reunited with her beloved mother, her brothers and sisters who had gone on before her. My father too.

She stirred a little in her bed as if to acknowledge what I had said then as I rose to leave and told her I would see her in the morning, she let out a piercing animal-like howling noise which haunts me to this day.

It seemed to come from the depths of her soul.

I thought she would still be with us the following morning but she died during the night.

I have reproached myself many times for not staying with her and I often wonder if the noise she made meant she was begging me not to leave. If so, the noise is my deserved punishment and it still echoes through my head and brings me tears. I hope she forgives me.

I didn't want to see her lying dead as my experience with my Auntie Phyllis had been distressing. The nursing home told me the doctor could probably sign the death certificate and I wouldn't have to identify the body.

This was the time the authorities were still edgy about the infamous serial killer Dr Harold Shipman. A few hours later, a policeman called on the telephone and said I would have no alternative but to identify her and I remonstrated with him in no uncertain manner resulting in a loud banging on the door at 2am.

He had sent a sergeant and another policeman round to get me out of bed and *"have a word"* with me. The sergeant was quite officious and told me that as he had had to identify his dead grandfather he didn't see why I shouldn't do the same with my mother. I found this

303

unnecessarily intrusive and upsetting and thought it reflected badly upon the police.

The following morning the doctor signed the death certificate and all was made right.

I wrote a eulogy for my Mam but bottled out of reading it at the crematorium for fear of breaking down. It was left to a friend to take over and he made a bit of a botched job of it. I felt I had let her down yet again.

Her friends and former mill workmates came to the service and a few days later we had a small gathering by the family grave in which my great grandfather Sam; my grandfather Herbert and my Auntie Alice lay buried. Surprisingly, there was no tombstone on the grave so I had one made. I stupidly got the year of her birth inscribed wrongly: telling the mason 1922 instead of her actual birth year of 1921.

I console myself with the thought she would have thought it fitting and in keeping with much of her life in which nothing seemed to go right for her.

" *I can't have nowt done proper* " was a favourite complaint. Sorry, Mabel.

There's a reminder of my Mam in the heavens. When I was small, she took me outside one night and pointed out The Plough constellation and how it pointed to the North Star. It must have been something she learned as a Girl Guide.

Nowadays, when I look up into the night sky and see that arrangement, I can't help but think of her and hope she's up there somewhere.

Mabel in her Easter Bonnet in the care home with her beloved grandson Gareth.

THE LAST HURRAH (*SWEARING INVOLVED)

"Stop fannying about and get me booked!"

It's Saturday November 12, 2011.
I'm sitting in a chair in a cold village hall in Barnes. Facing me across a table is the surreal presence of comic genius and pan global superstar Dr. The Rik Mayall (and two lesser known but no less important gentlemen.)
He has a big beaming smile which lights up his face. He shakes my hand and says *"Hi. I'm Rik"* as if I wouldn't know who he was. It's as if I'd met the Queen and she'd said *"Hello. I am the Queen".*
I have no way of knowing that a few months later, this encounter would lead to being crammed with him in a smelly lavatory in deepest Plymouth with me being blackmailed into strangling a well endowed French midget with his own cock in order to donate it to a snowman who didn't have one.
Allow me to explain...
Earlier that month, my then agent Debbie Pine had sent me an intriguing email outlining details of a six part spoken word comedy with an unnamed *"comedy legend"*. The casting breakdown specified *"comedy timing essential and cannot be overawed by lead actor"*.
That was even more intriguing.
The producers told Debbie they were interested in having a look at me for the *"larger role"* and adding *"We think Dave has the potential to be a wonderful disgraced northern comic. It requires him to be showbiz in public but comically withdrawn in the role, drinking with the other lead in a gentleman's club".*
They said that fruity language would be involved and the whole shebang would be set in a mythical, decadent, gentleman's club in which a bored, suicidal, ancient snowman chewed the fat with the great and the good and the ghastly.
Whilst I wondered what drugs these people were on, it sounded a fascinating prospect so I agreed to do the audition and found myself a few days later in Barnes.
I discovered the auditioners would be a Mr Craig Green, and a Mr Dominic Vince (co-writers and producers) and the star of The Young Ones, Bottom and Comedy Strip Presents Rik Mayall who,

they said, would be looking for comic timing and chemistry and they would observe the rest.

No pressure then.

They specified I needed to unleash myself and "*go for it*" as it was an extrovert role that would allow me to truly go wild in the studio!

I arrive in good time at Barnes. A tall figure appears from round the corner of the hall.

It's Craig. He tells me I've arrived five hours early.

I follow him round the side of the village hall and into its musky interior and he introduces me to the two people inside – one of whom is Rik, looking, it has to be said slightly more grizzled than when he played the poncy punk n The Young Ones.

To his right is Dominic: a bespectacled quiet gentleman looking like a defrocked curate. We all shake hands and Craig explains to them that he's squeezing me in because I've turned up earlier than I should.

I'm itching to get started because I've read the bit of the script they sent and it's bloody hilarious. I'm playing a failed Northern club ventriloquist, the sublimely named Bonjour Hellfire, who gets so pissed he drinks five cans of lighter fluid, urinates on his dummy (the late lamented Senor Matador) in front of the fire and incinerates it! I mean, come on!.

Off we go... Or as Rik says "*Let's nail this motherfucker*".

He plays Bonjour's best mate, Elton a devious, knobless immortal Snowman.

I unleash the inner beast and to me it feels right. I'm bloody well enjoying myself and a sly glance up tells me more importantly, the three guys who matter seem to be enjoying it too.

I'm chuckling myself at my lines like "*I never knew my urine was 90 per cent proof!*" but all too soon, it's over. I want more!

So I look up and I say: "*Where's all the really filthy bits? I'd like to do those*".

"*Yes! Let's!*" says a gleeful Rik and Dom finds the *really* mucky bits and I launch straight into it.

The humour flies off the page and Rik and I go for it.

Craig says "*It's wonderful hearing the words we've written actually come alive!*" Dom gets a bit emotional. And that's it: one of the most enjoyable auditions I've ever done.

Several months later… I still haven't heard anything! This is typical torture for a jobbing actor so I send an impudent one-line email to Craig and Dom:

STOP FANNYING ABOUT AND GET ME BOOKED!

A bit impolite but it seems to do the trick as not long after, I get confirmation of the job and six wonderful scripts emailed to me!

A few days later I'm on a train to the recording in Plymouth going through the scripts and laughing like a lunatic at the surreal, bizarre, sheer filthy zaniness of it all.

At Plymouth, I take a taxi to the New Continental Hotel and bump straight into Rik himself: the legend.

"*Dave*!" (the nice man remembers me.) He hugs me. "*Lovely to see you. Thank you for agreeing to do this*". Rik's thanking *me*.

He shows me up to my room which is next to his.

Next day, we rehearse episode number one which has been rewritten an astonishing 15 times by Rik, Craig and Dom.

It's the first time Rik and I have had a chance to work together on the scripts proper and, as in the audition, we seem to have a great rapport which pleases Craig no end.

Soon we are Elton and Bonjour personified and pissing ourselves laughing at the wonderful lines.

It's great to have a chance to see how Rik's comedy mind works and how he questions why he would say a particular phrase or amends a line slightly to suit Elton's character.

I have never seen anyone take such care over a word; a line or a meaning in a script. It's like observing someone carefully and deftly adding the finishing touches to a fine piece of sculpture or, in our instance, a bunch of bawdy badinage.

I throw in a few script alteration suggestions which seem to go down well and now we are really beginning to feel like a team. All too soon, it's time for lunch.

After a lovely Italian meal, we stroll into the crisp afternoon sunshine to make our way back to rehearsals.

As Craig and I lead the way, amicably discussing stuff, we suddenly hear a loud cry of:

"OI!!!! PIGS!!!"

We look at each other in shock. Surely we misheard? It couldn't be….could it?

Then again.

"I SAID OI!!!! PIGS!!!"

We spin round to witness Mayall with his hand cupped to his mouth hollering insults at three nearby burly Plymouth policemen who appear to be busy on a search mission in the locality.

Christ! He's in character!

We lengthen our stride to put as much distance as possible between ourselves and Rik who is palpably dismayed to find his attempts to rile the Plymouth constabulary have singularly failed – much to our relief.

He catches up with us and expresses his disgust at the lack of response from the local constabulary.

"When I shout "Oi Pigs! at the police in London, they always fucking react to me" Rik complains in a really disgruntled manner.

Next morning we pile up at the excellent Deep Blue Sound in Plymouth where we are greeted by Jay and Ben our sound guys and are later joined by Scottish actor Duncan Pow who provides the voices of Ed Mullet the Reporter and the very excitable Fabio. The team is complete.

A quick cuppa and with the usual stirring battlecry from Rik of *"Let's nail this motherfucker!"* we are promptly underway.

We break for lunch where Rik tells us about his terrible Quad bike accident of April, 1998 when he was rushed to hospital with a fractured skull and extensive bleeding on his brain. He was in a coma for several days in a hospital and he reveals that doctors told him that to remove the blood, they would have to take the top of his skull off and scoop it out.

He was advised to put his affairs in order and more or less say his goodbyes to his family as the procedure was not without great risk and could prove fatal.

He reckons the shock of being told this caused the blood clots to somehow vanish of their own accord and the scan on the day he was to have the operation amazingly showed the all-clear!

(It sounds like the similar op my sister Joyce had when doctors removed the top of her skull and performed an operation on her brain while still awake.)

Soon, we are back in the studio doing a scene where poor old Bonjour accidentally downloads animal porn on his computer and gets derided for it in the club, Elton has to quizzically roll his tongue round the words *"Animal fucker? Animal.....fucker?"* which he does with such ingrained comic style, I have to turn away from the microphone and look up to see Duncan biting on his fist..

In between takes, Rik and I enjoy a bit of banter. He takes the piss out of me for my Northern ways and I point out that being brought up in Droitwich makes him neither a Northerner or a Southern Jessie but a mere Halfway Up and Downer. Or something like that.

We discuss our backgrounds and he latches on to the fact I'm illegitimate with the comment: "*Ah, so you're a **proper** actual bastard then, you bastard?*"

It's fascinating to see how Rik plays the different character parts: swapping effortlessly from the silky smooth serpentlike Narrator to the slyly evasive Elton, then from the in-your-face (and knickers) super ego that is Randy Hardy to a belligerent Geordie thug called, inevitably, Bastard.

Then I have a whole chunk where Bonjour gets himself unwittingly into trouble by his ineptness at working T'Internet and finds himself viewing a porn website featuring Cindy from Rochdale and a well hung dog.

Rik has joined the others in the control room while I do my solo piece to the microphone.

When I finish, the door bursts open and Rik runs in beaming.

"*Bloody hell Dave*"

"*Was that alright?*" I enquire.

"*You made my fucking face ache with laughing you bastard!*"

"*We had tears in our eyes*" said Dom.

These are words any actor would be proud to hear – and so I was. And I am genuinely touched when Rik later takes me to one side and remarks:" *You reminded me of me*".

I couldn't ask for better from a professional of his standing and his generosity of spirit makes me warm towards him even more.

When we wrap for the day, we walk back to the hotel and I observe Rik's fearlessness in traffic. He seems to cross the road anywhere except where he should: studiously avoiding Pelican crossings to venture out in the traffic.

I say to him: "*You're thinking 'I'm Rik Fucking Mayall and you can't fucking knock me down'*"

"Too fucking right matey boy" he grins as he strides out to confront yet another set of horn tooting, speeding vehicles.

I surmise he's thinking: *"I've survived a quad crash and been hit on the head a thousand times by a Yorkshireman wielding a huge frying pan, so what's a Fiat Panda gonna do to me?!"*

Next day is our last in the studio. I record my last bits and pieces but I don't really want to leave because I've had such a lovely time but I say my farewells and look forward to seeing everyone again.

Next recordings are a few weeks later.

I arrive at the hotel where Rik is jokingly ordering the hotel staff to carry him downstairs on a throne for breakfast and to have someone always on hand to light his cigarettes for him.

He smoked cigarettes at every opportunity. Whether it be blowing smoke furtively through his bedroom window, standing outside the hotel or taking lots of fag breaks at the studio, he was never very far from a lighted cigarette. He couldn't drink alcohol because of the constant medication he was on – a legacy of his terrible accident. His ancient battered Nokia phone rang an alarm every couple of hours to remind him to take his tablets.

He could eat though – by Christ he could eat. Massive portions disappeared down the old Mayall gullet every time we had lunch or dinner. He was getting quite big and told me he was concerned about losing the very successful Bombardier beer commercial he was starring in because he had started having difficulty fitting into the uniform.

It was a pleasure to share a meal with him though. He quoted speeches from Shakespeare, Godot - even poems from Alice in Wonderland and told us how he and Ade had originally based their madcap slapstick act on the Tom and Jerry cartoons of which they were big fans.

The next day, Rik and I proceed to the studio lavatory to record the hilarious accidental death of Henri LeCoq the midget. We do it in one take and it turns out to be one of the funniest scenes of the show.

Over the next couple of days, we wrap up the series. Rik gleefully shows me excerpts from the second series which is even more outrageous! I'm sad it's all over: I could cheerfully do this every day but, hey, we've nailed the motherfucker! It's been great fun and the show's very funny too.

311

If you want to hear the result, download it from Amazon and the iTunes Store. A broad mind is advisable.

Sadly, though, that second series was never to be made.

Rik said at the time that he wanted Elton to be his last great character and unhappily this proved true.

On June 9, 2014 I was sitting in the living room of my son's home watching Sky News when a banner headline scrolled by announcing Rik had died suddenly at home.

It really was hard to take it in.

I sat there in numb disbelief unable to absorb the awful news. Then I told the rest of my family who were just as shocked. I sent a text to Craig and Dom who had become very close to Rik during the writing process.

It later came to light that he apparently died of a heart attack after a run and I thought back to what he told me about his fear of not being able to get into his Bombardier uniform if he got any bigger. Perhaps he was trying to get his weight down because of that. Who knows?

He died far too early and is mourned and missed by his myriad fans – many of whom I have had the pleasure of meeting at special conventions in his honour in London and Bristol where his comic influence lives on. Thousands of pounds were raised at these events for Headway, the brain injury charity.

He would be chuffed to know that The Last Hurrah has become a bit of a cult and Dom, Craig and I have been invited to speak about Rik and the show on several occasions. We now have myriad friends from his loyal following even as far away as America and the Antipodes, who stick two fingers up Rik style in his memory at the drop of a hat.They will never forget him and neither will I.

I will leave the last word to the writers, Craig and Dom who put a little tribute to me on t'Internet.

I thought twice about putting it on here because it might look a bit big headed but then I thought sod it – it's quite lovely really.

Can everyone say hello to Dave Dutton. He plays Bonjour Hellfire in The Last Hurrah and is the best sidekick Rik had since Ade. He is the nicest man in showbiz, a comedy legend (he has the stories!) and was particularly helpful to the writing team who will love the fucker forever for that fact alone. Rik Mayall thought Dave Dutton was the bollocks and that should be all you need to know. So show him some love would you?

I'm sorry. That made me a bit weepy. Let's move on...

Just the two of us...Dave and Rik aka Bonjour and Elton. A much missed comic genius...

KEEPING GOING!

Anything is possible

I've often played "off Broadway": Manchester to be exact – about 3,334 miles off Broadway! I may never play The Great White Way itself but that's the best part of being an actor. You just never know. (Okay. I admit it's unlikely.)

The second best part is you don't have to retire. You never know what adventure is going to begin with the next phone call. I don't feel much different now than when I was, say, 26 and I'm certain this is because I keep active.

Having said that, I got a bit fed up being sent for castings for parts with little more than one or two lines.

So I more or less packed it in for a couple of years. I thought I'd seen the best of it.

Suddenly, quite out of the blue at the age of 69, I was asked by David Kester - a great director who I had worked previously with - to play a deadpan prison officer in Emmerdale.

I was quite flattered by that! Then shortly afterwards, David booked me in to play a history teacher called Leslie Rawlins in Coronation Street in a very funny scene involving partly dressing as a civil war soldier – complete with an incongruous combination of red cardigan, bow tie and knee length brown boots.

This gave me a renewed enthusiasm so I enrolled with a great agency – Cartwright Higgins in Wigan, run by the brilliant playwright Jim Cartwright and former actress Tracy Higgins.

Then along came BBC's Doctors where I had a great part playing a man with dementia who thought he was Henry the Eighth and who sexually assaulted a visitor because he thought she was his wife, Anne Boleyn.

Heavy stuff but I'd been in enough nursing homes to know the score about that particular condition.

He even made his own crowns and had Greensleeves on repeat...

I do telly stuff when I'm lucky enough to be asked; commercials; stage plays; voiceovers: you name it and I'll have a go at it. I hadn't done stage plays since my schooldays but starting in my 60's I played many different theatre parts including that of a half crab, half robot in a sci fi comedy; a reworked Coronation Street episode; featured in a stage re-enactment of Porridge and even took part in a gruelling but exciting event called One Play One Day where the play is written during the night and you go in to pick up the script at 7-30 am then learn it; rehearse it and perform it twice that evening. Took me two days to fully recover.

The things you bloody do to earn a crust...half man half crab
Grattybar Farloolander. Try saying that with a faceful of tin foil.

I also played the lead in a great little one act comedy called To Be
Frank, written by Sophie Poulston.

TIPS FOR WOULD-BE ACTORS

1. *Learn to treat disappointment as a friend. You'll be hanging*
   around together a lot.
2. *Study people closely. Especially when you're serving them in*
   Starbucks or Pret.
3. *Be nice to people on the way up. (That's if there is a way up.)*
4. *Be nice to people on the way down (That's if you can get any*
   further down)
5. *After auditions, if you think you've got the part, you probably*
   haven't. If you think you haven't got the part, you probably
   haven't.
6. *Go for it anyway. If I can do it, so can you.*

When I'm not acting, I have my great hobby of street photography to keep me happy. I sell my photographs online and one day an American greetings card company emailed and offered £1,200 to use one of my pics on a card. I think that's nearly more than I earned all the time I was with Mr. Dodd!

There is a great book called "*Feel the fear and do it anyway*" which teaches us that by facing up to experiences that at first seem daunting, soon they seem almost commonplace and you wonder why you were scared in the first place. I have done things that I would have never thought I would have been capable of or even had the chance to experience.

Perhaps if I hadn't been thrown in that police cell when I was a kid with the "*short, sharp shock*" it gave me, my life may have turned out differently. I'll never know.

There is a big bonus to getting older. In my experience, I have found that the older you get, the more you gain in confidence. I call it the old boy effect.

When you are younger, you are like the new boy on his first day at school. The big boys look daunting and seem to know a lot more than you do. When you have been in school a few years, you become one of those big boys and gradually become more assured in your behaviour..

Similarly, as you grow older, you will have faced more situations and undergone more life experiences and learned to cope and deal with those different situations, thus building in confidence. I used to find it difficult to talk to people. Now I find it difficult not to!

I hope that the message you will take from the book is anything is possible if you dare to dream and give it a go.

I'm sure my illegitimacy was a big motivating influence on my life. Being set apart at an early age, although I didn't realise it at the time, probably did me a great favour. If I didn't fit in, I wasn't going to be one of the crowd.

Perhaps the performer in me was born at the time I found out I was "different". Perhaps if I'd had a dad in the house I would have gone on to do a regular 9 to 5 job.

I recently saw a good piece of advice which I'd like to pass on, if I may.

It said "*Don't live the same year 75 times and call it a life*".

317

I've done a variety of stuff to stop me getting bored and to keep the mortgage people and utility companies happy. Let's see…

I've been a reporter; television extra; songwriter; dialect poet; front man for a comedy folk group; actor; author; after dinner speaker agency owner; radio presenter;comedy scriptwriter and photographer. I've got a notion that my next step is to be a performance poet. I think you should always have something new to aim at. Stops you getting stale.

All those appearances in Coronation Street, Emmerdale and the like are something I look back on with pride and wonder.

To be honest, I am really grateful for the way my life has turned out. I don't need flash cars or fame. It has been the PEOPLE in my life who have made a difference. My hardworking Mam; my warmhearted Grandma; kind Aunties and Uncles; good teachers; supportive friends and colleagues; my long-suffering, loving and understanding wife Lynn; my kindhearted and funny son Gareth who hasn't been an ounce of trouble; his lovely supportive wife Frances and my adorable granddaughters Sam Daisy and Georgia Florence who have made my happiness complete.

Sam was born near Christmas in 2011 and when Lynn and I went to see her for the first time, she announced her arrival by doing one of the loudest farts I have ever heard. It rattled round the maternity ward and everyone turned and glared at me!

Sam and Granddad- two of a kind…

They took some convincing that the sweet bundle in the cot by the bed was the real culprit.

She has blossomed into a real beauty with a penchant from an early age for wanting to make people laugh just like her dad and me.

My beautiful Sam Daisy. Keeping a close eye on silly granddad, as she used to call me...I'm still silly –it's just that she's stopped calling me that.

She loves acting out scenes and making up and telling stories. Her little sister though has an incredible story of her own...

GEORGIA ON MY MIND

A hell of a story

It's January 2016. There are tears rolling down my cheeks. I'm standing in a critical care unit in a Southampton hospital looking down on a frail, yellow slip of a baby attached to all sorts of wires and drips. I'm wondering what the future holds for her. If she has a future. I'm willing her to live. She's my granddaughter.

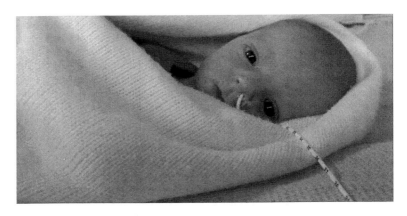

You know how it is. One minute everything is going swimmingly. You've a big smile on your face and the little bluebird of happiness is perched on your shoulder twittering merrily away.
Then suddenly out of nowhere, something happens to wipe the smile off your kipper and the little dickie bird, craps on your shoulder then drops down stone dead.
It's happened to all of us hasn't it? Metaphorically speaking of course. That's how it was in that January. Gareth and Frances had moved to a cosy semi detached house in Perivale near Ealing and were expecting our second grandchild.
Lynn and I had spent a lovely Christmas with them and Sam Daisy and we were looking forward to our new arrival.
Frances had gone over her time and the days seem to drag for all of us but especially her.
Then on the morning of 27 January, I woke to find a text on my phone from Gareth stating the baby had been born; a girl - and he had *"a hell of a story to tell you"*.

320

Indeed it was. It was a story that a few hours later left me in tears and unable to speak.

The baby, who was later named Georgia Florence, decide to arrive in the early hours.. Frances had gone to the bathroom when she suddenly realised the baby was on its way and called out to Gareth for help.

He rushed in and saw her on the floor and the baby ready to make an appearance. With his mobile clamped to his ear as he frantically spoke to the emergency services, he delivered his own daughter as Sam Daisy slept peacefully unaware next door. What a guy.

The ambulance arrived just as he took hold of her and she was rushed off to hospital where there was bad news.

The doctors spotted that our lovely little Georgia had severe complications due to a rare genetic disorder called Cat Eye Syndrome which can appear even without a family history of it.

It gets its name from a hole in the iris which can make the eyes look similar to a cat's. It happens when there's a problem with the 22nd chromosome and between 1 in 50,000 and 1 in 150,000 people in the world have it.

I won't go into the full details but suffice it to say that as Gareth and Frances huddled together in the hospital room awaiting the diagnosis, the nurse asked if they would like to take a picture of the baby as they didn't know what the outcome would be..

Lynn and I didn't know all this of course until later that morning when I managed to talk to Gareth who described what the problems were. They were major and she needed urgent heart surgery if she was to survive.

I choked up. Couldn't speak. Had to pass the phone to Lynn.

The situation was so severe that at one time the doctors talked about sending a helicopter from Southampton to the hospital in Chelsea to take Georgia there for emergency specialist treatment.

As it happened, they sent a team out all the way in an ambulance and rushed her straight to intensive care at Southampton General that very day.

We hurried down to London and Frances's Mam and dad, Jan and David, kindly drove us to Southampton where we spent the next five nights. As you can imagine it was a very emotional time for us all. Georgia was fitted with a stoma as her bowels weren't functioning as they should.

It had also been planned to give her an operation to mend a hole in her heart but the doctors decided she was too small and frail to operate upon. It was carried out successfully some weeks later in a procedure that took the surgeon half an hour just to explain to Gareth what the complicated and skilful surgery involved.

In the first 12 months of her life, she spent time in nine different hospitals and had five major operations.

Mere words seem ineffectual but a massive thanks to Kings College for fixing her liver; Southampton General for the stoma; Royal Brompton for mending her little heart and Chelsea and Westminster for sorting out her plumbing.

She was only allowed home after her first five months in hospital and needed to be fed and medicated through a tube down her nose and throat. The care, skill and attention she was given by the brilliant staff of the NHS was only matched by the love and care given to her by her parents of whom we are so proud.

May I remind you that I was born just before the NHS came into being and cost my family thirty shillings. I can't even begin to consider how much Georgia's ongoing treatment would have cost the family had there been no NHS. We must NEVER lose it or the special people who work within it. It's a jewel in our country's crown.

I must also give special mention to the amazing Ronald Mcdonald House Charity who provide free hotel style accommodation for parents and siblings of poorly children at hospitals all around the country and who really looked after our family at Southampton and King's College Hospital at a critical time.

As a vegetarian, I never thought I would be praising McDonalds but having seen the service they provide at a time of great need I am full of admiration for them.

Sam was delighted when Georgia came home and took to the Big Sister role with relish and lots of loving cuddles.

322

Gareth and Frankie took different shifts to look after Georgia through the night and day and while one slept, the other fed and medicated her every couple of hours.

I honestly don't know how they coped with all this while at the same time caring for a very healthy and boisterous nearly five-year-old who was due to start primary school as well.

It wasn't all straightforward as the baby was in and out of hospital all the time with Frankie sleeping in the bed next to her in different hospitals. On top of this, Gareth was still trying to forge a living as a professional photographer. The strain was enormous.

When Georgia started to eat more solid food and gradually put on weight, we were all relieved. Considering all that she had been through, she bore it bravely and we called her our Beautiful Battler.

The Beautiful Battler

When she first started to smile, it lit up the room and all our hearts. To me, after all she has been through, to see her smile is one of the greatest sights on earth.

When she laughs, my old heart sings.

She continues to make slow but steady progress and may need further operations but she is a very special child.

As Gareth brilliantly puts it "*We have learned so much from her*".

THE OLD BANISTER RAIL

I am walking down the stairs of the house in which I was born.
As I slide my hand down the banister rail, it suddenly strikes me that this is the very piece of wood that my grandma touched when, as a young teenage bride, she first moved excitedly into the house.
The same piece of wood which was touched by her children -my long dead aunties and uncles - as toddlers and, indeed, by me as a young child going " *up the wooden hills to Bedfordshire*".
The same piece of wood touched by my granddad as he made his way downstairs to go and fight in the First World War.
The same piece of wood that was touched by the father who I never knew when he came to stay during the Second World War.
The same piece of wood which was touched by my son and granddaughter on their first journeys up those old steps.
The same piece of wood that my mother slid her hand up as a child and slid her hand down for the last time before her dementia led her to the care home.
I know that I too shall touch it for the last time sometime and when the old house comes to be knocked down it will disappear into history like the rest of us. Just a piece of wood but with much to teach about the continuity and brevity of life.
Thank you for reading about my life. It's time to get back to yours. Have a wonderful one.
Love from The Thirty Bob Kid. Xxx
** **More info on me and my books at www.dave-dutton.co.uk/**
Oh, before I go…..just one more thing….

Please tell that bobby I'm a good boy now!

34766101R00180

Printed in Great Britain
by Amazon